TO MY MIND

TO MY MIND

OR KINBOTES: ESSAYS ON LITERATURE

OMAR SABBAGH

Whisk(e)y Tit

VT & NYC

Many of the essays contained in this volume have been previously published in academic journals, literary magazines, or edited volumes, and the copyright remains with the author.

If you are inspired to use any or all parts of this book in your own project, have a little class and tell us how you wish to use it: miette@whiskeytit.com.

ISBN 978-1-7329596-3-7

For my mother
Maha Faris Sabbagh
Where the reading began

Contents

Preface: An Apology for Criticism (In a
Pompous Vein)   xiii

Part I. A Pedagogical Triptych

1. Water in the Desert   3
2. F(r)ictions from the Critical Imaginary: The   9
   Singular Case of George Steiner
3. In Shy Darkness They Lie: Teaching Poems in   21
   Dubai

Part II. Scholarly Interventions, Or Thereabouts…

4. Love's Knowledge: Realisation Beyond Defence: 35
   Durrell's *Alexandria Quartet* After, and Beyond,
   Ford's *The Good Soldier*
5. Humanism After Humanism: Henry Miller: 57
   Colossus Upon Colossus
6. G.K. Chesterton's London: Traversing   73
   Therapeutic Space
7. The Authority of Soul and The Sole Authority: 103
   Comparing Two Catholic Memoirs: The
   Classical Approach / The Romantic

8. History Free Indirect: Reading Creative Techniques in Lytton Strachey's *Queen Victoria*   119

9. Ratiocination in The Old Pretender: Facets of Rationalism in Henry James's *The Golden Bowl*   139

10. Heavenly Others: Ford, And The Strange 'Impression' of Transcendence   157

11. Animating Places: Reading Fiona Sampson's *Limestone Country* Beneath a Durrellian Lens   175

12. Facets of Exhaustion: The Mystic Antagonism of T.S. Eliot's 'Music'   195

13. Good Neighbours: Reading Love and Loss in Basil Bunting   211

14. Fathering Sons, Or, Re-Hearsing His Race: On Don Paterson   227

15. Translations "About" Ghassan Zaqtan: On the Powers of Laughter   239

Part III. Lasting Occasions…

16. Only Plenitude at the Void: On Christian Wiman   253

17. Mud and Holy Water: A Question of Ends: On Paul Muldoon   259

18. Avant La Lettre: Browning's 'Sludge' and Ford's *The Good Soldier*: A Poetic Reading   265

19. On Fiona Sampson's *In Search of Mary Shelley: The Girl Who Wrote Frankenstein*   277

20. On Svetlana Lavochkina's *Zap*   283

21. Dancing About Rodin: On Patricia McCarthy's *Rodin's Shadow*   289

22. The Headiness, The Heaviness of Womanhood: On Zoe Brigley   297

23. The Virtue of Not Being Able to Totalize: On D. Nurkse's *Voices Over Water*   305

24. The Ways of Empathy: On Fiona Sampson's *The Catch* — 311

25. Macabre Energies: On Svetlana Lavochkina's *Dam Duchess* — 321

26. On Geoffrey Hill — 329

27. Still Points and Turning Worlds: On Fiona Sampson's *Come Down* (Corsair, 2020) — 335

Epilogue: The Charlatan — 345

Acknowledgements — 351

About the Author — 353

About the Publisher — 355

`

Preface: An Apology for Criticism (In a Pompous Vein)

'There is, then, a strange difference between insight and sensation. Unless one is deaf, one cannot avoid hearing. Unless one is blind, one has only to open one's eyes to see. The occurrence and the content of sensation stand in some immediate correlation with outer circumstance. But with insight internal conditions are paramount. Thus, insight depends upon native endowment, and so with fair accuracy one can say that insight is the act that occurs frequently in the intelligent and rarely in the stupid.'[1]
Bernard Lonergan, *Insight*[2]

In the work that follows, a compilation of predominantly previously-published essays on literature, ranging from bona fide scholarly interventions, to reflective articles and review-essays which I deem to be of substantial enough worth, both as themselves and as regarding their objects – I hope to have shown most pressingly a capacity for insight. When speaking of insight, Lonergan sees this phenomenon of rigorous

1. Bernard Lonergan, *Insight: A Study of Human Understanding*, ed. Frederick E. Crowe and Robert M. Doran, Toronto, Buffalo, London, University of Toronto Press, 2008, p. 29.

2. A parallel citation here, globalising onto the more world-historical stage this insight about individual insight. 'This is perhaps the characteristic of his age which separates it most strikingly from our own. It is not so much that we have lost our beliefs as that we have lost the belief in the possibility of having true beliefs.' Robert Skidelsky, John Maynard Keynes 1883-1946: Economist, Philosopher, Statesman, London, Penguin Books, 2005, p. 85.

awareness as the pivot and mediator between the concrete and the abstract. And, with due (and ludic, no doubt) humility, I couldn't agree more. To penetrate individual literary artefacts with one's reading-mind, to unravel and then re-construct their general dynamics so to speak, has been to date my most flourishing gift. And in so far, following Lonergan, as insight is 'a function not of outer circumstances but of inner conditions,' [3] I hold that in coming to know the various works discussed in the book of essays pursuant, among others, I have always been at the same time coming to know myself. [4]

Books have been from a young age not only objects of utmost, bejewelled value to and for me, but, and this is an ambivalent confession, also at the same time, in a manner of speaking, negligible in-themselves; being or turning out to be more like 'stepping-stones' for the growth and development of my overly-burgeoning self and imaginary. As with poets, like T.S. Eliot, say, who are not in a primary way concerned so much with the 'what' of what their poetry says, but more with the musical mood and inkling, the musical inspiration that then trans-spires, I find my own critical persona as poetic, too, and in the same sense. I like, like Eliot, again, to make 'fine distinctions.' It's as if the matter I feed my mind is fed there to allow for certain native compartments of truths to be ratified, again and again – though there wouldn't be said thoughtful compartments if they hadn't (been) developed in the first place by the matter of my readings. Thus, insight, my self-styled most-dominant mode, is a bit like the notion of transcendental truths in Kant.

You see, the trouble many people have or have had with the notion of 'synthetic a priori' truths, is that they do indeed

---

3. Lonergan, op. cit., p. 28.

4. (It would seem, then, that though, as per the Lonergan epigraph, I may well be, thus, 'well-endowed' – yet I seem always to be knowing myself(?))

inhabit a 'no-man's land' between logic and psychology.[5] And
in line with the above I would venture that their domain is that
of *insight*; pivoting between form and content, they evince
the same signal asymmetry. Neither are they logical truths
(2+2=4) which are wholly independent of experience, nor are
they psychological truths (which are based on the empirical
impressions made by experience, and which are wholly
dependent on them) – but rather: truths that would simply
not exist without their empirical spurs, triggers, but which
are none the less logically or conceptually separate from the
latter. The content of the forms so to speak. Time, say, space,
causality: such basic constructs don't mean anything if there
are or were no temporal, spatial, causal objects – or, at least,
some kind of stuff to be made into such. However, time, space,
causality, in this instance, are none the less *not* reducible to the
sum of 'all' the temporal, spatial, causal events or things in all
of human, or at least, reasoning, intelligible history.

All of which is to say, when I write critically, I am being
creative, configurative. The creativity of my analytical bent is
sourced in the asymmetries of the happening of insight. I read
a book, usually a good one, and suddenly, what's (found to
be) true to say of it is both: caused by the empirical content
of the book in question, but also and at the same time, segues
onwards, upwards, into and through my mind, battening,
ratcheting my (sense of) self; *and*, surely, segues, too, towards
and for the next books to be fed into the hermeneutic machine
of which in large part my most intimate self is or has been
forged.

In short: existence, the contingent stuff of reality,

5. For this particular way of formulating the somewhat paradoxical status of
transcendental, synthetic a priori truths, see Theodor W. Adorno, *Kant's Critique
of Pure Reason,* trans. Rodney Livingstone, ed. Rolf Tiedemann, Stanford,
California, Stanford University Press, 2001, p. 22.

whether of self or world (book, in this case), may well precede, chronologically, essence – the parsed significance of any extant datum. But there is an asymmetrical loop-back which figures, interestingly, I hope, in the following sense. *It just does* take an already-meaningful reality, the human mind, essence, to descry *the very precedence* of existence, stuff, data, in the first place. [6] Meaningfulness does indeed (only) *follow* from the data of existence (the critic, me in this case, is derivative on the creative artist and his or her work); but it is the critic, in this (analogising) instance, who puts the primary literary artefact *in that very* prime position. My mind would be nothing without the books that feed it; the books that feed and have fed it, were nothing (to me, as others) until my mind recognised it-self – *as nothing before the books that feed and have fed it.* The bookish life, expressed in my case by critical writing, is not so much a journey: outwards; but neither is it the opposite, a journey, simply, inwards; no. One goes out to go in, and in to go out – all becoming, thus: through, through, and through again.

✳

A final note to append to this brief prefatory note. To say I'm a 'generalist' would be too generous. There are three types, roughly, of critical writing in this book: scholarly interventions, reflective articles, and what I hope are substantial occasional review-articles. My hope is that in the *very few* areas where I might be aptly seen to be intervening in a scholarly manner, that I do indeed deserve that adverb or adjective, 'scholarly.' The reflective articles – *there*, I'm in

6. The basic pattern of this insight here, though made-use-of in an idiosyncratically literary context, is derived in part from some of the thinking in the oeuvre of the contemporary philosopher, Ermanno Bencivenga; see for instance, his *Freedom: A Dialogue*, trans. Author, Indianapolis, Cambridge, Hackett Publishing Company, 1997; or his *The Discipline of Subjectivity: An Essay on Montaigne,* Princeton, New Jersey, Princeton University Press, 1990.

my element, no longer tethered to the requisite, respective scholarly dues deemed, and rightly so, payable. Finally, regarding my 'lasting occasions,' shorter in the main review-pieces. I simply do not review books that don't move or stir me, mentally or otherwise. Which is to say, nearly all my reviews, in this book as elsewhere, are nearly always nearly wholly positive reviews. I see no point in making the effort to write a review unless the book or books in question are not worth the very effort of being noticed and praised for what they do, or have done. Why write a review, entering the world of printed matter, of a book that fails? It simply makes no real sense to do so. If the book has failed then that means, in a manner of speaking, it has made no real telling impact, impression; its modality, at least from my view, which is the view that pertains in this instance, is wholly negative, void; why, then, make, in reviewer-mode, *an even more derivative* impact on the readerly world – about said *impact-less-ness*? It just doesn't add-up, logically-speaking. If it's true to say, as per above, that I like to make 'fine distinctions' – *well*, such nuances are, in my hands at least, always and at the same time, 'nice.'

PART 1

A Pedagogical Triptych

1

Water in the Desert

We are all born in moral stupidity, taking the world as an udder to feed our supreme selves: Dorothea had early begun to emerge from that stupidity, but yet it had been easier to her to imagine how she would devote herself to Mr. Causabon, and become wise and strong in his strength and wisdom, than to conceive with that distinctness that is no longer reflection but feeling ... that he had an equivalent centre of self, whence the lights and shadows fall with a certain difference.
George Eliot, *Middlemarch*

I am often asked by students who espy me from a distance in the library with my nose buried in a book, a pencil in hand readied to scribble marginalia, "what" exactly I am doing. They seem to marvel that someone who has gone through undergraduate then postgraduate study, and who has completed such, would still, well, study. It seems to seem bizarre, if not absurd, to them.

It is a commonplace of course for my generation, a generation with a context before the ubiquity of social media and the onslaught of passive reception of titillating feeds, to complain of the millennials' relative obtuseness.

I complain about the Kindle, still willing to lug 20 kilos of books in my suitcase when travelling for a longish stint. Then they tell me they have invented a new Kindle effect, whereby the 3D-ness of the digital book is made effectual on the screen. But I still complain and grumble. We seem, you see, to be entering a world where what philosophers have called the "brain in the vat" problem is becoming a real possibility. For

3

my generation, one that comes after that problem in ethics from the last quarter of the twentieth century, the problem is epitomized by the *Matrix* trilogy of films. I am also told by a good friend that nowadays people are talking of "Google-glasses", which, once donned, allow one as in some sci-fi movie to negotiate one's whole day of business and recreation with a finger, pinpointing splayed options digitally laid bare before one's eyes. The objection to all this "virtual" being might be that it is precisely the un-controlled, the stuff that happens to us, from outside our horizon, that makes us, or once made us, spurred to be human.

Thus, when my students ask me, or insinuate the question "why literature?", they seem to imply that – unlike engineering or business studies, or even media studies, architecture and visual arts – literature, unless you want to teach the stuff, has no real bankable value; which in effect means no clear career path, no bottom line. This is a phenomenon I have noticed increasingly in Dubai and in the world so aptly epitomized by a certain mercantile ethos resident and dominant in Dubai. When A. J. Ayer wrote his work typifying Viennese positivism – for all its stupidity, from my view – it was still viewed as a strange or not staple view of things. However, in today's world, positivism – and its ethos – is not even named as such: it is the predominant mode of thought. It rules with a diktat, quite unnoticed. Indeed, I am ridiculed, explicitly or implicitly, with vitriol or with a kind of sad tenderness, for thinking myself an "intellectual". Many people seem to think being a self-styled "intellectual"amounts to the banked content of a hundred books say, or a thousand. However, I have always felt, that being a thinking, reading, writing person, an intellectual, is not a matter of verifiable and atomistic knowledge, but actually and emphatically a way of being in the world. Purposely, I do not teach facts in my literature courses; I know my students can Google when Ted

Hughes was born and died, the year Heaney won the T. S. Eliot prize for *District and Circle* or that Louis MacNeice was from an island off the western shore of England, and so on. What I want to teach them is the ability to tell stories. A story has a soul running through it, a thoroughgoing intelligence; it has a cogency and a coherence that is, like a will, beyond any of its addled parts.

I tell them, to start with, that literature, a story, a poem, a drama, and so on, does not just exist. Whether we are writers of it or readers of it, literature not only is something, but at the same time, what it is, is something that takes you somewhere. I generally speak, unfashionably I know, of "authority". I ask them: in common understanding, what does an authority do? Well, it directs you, or if you prefer guides you. It actively takes you somewhere: when you read a poem or a story or what have you, you are not just being fed data, facts – say, what time the hero of the story had lunch. You are fed these bits of information for a reason, or better, a "purpose" (i.e. unlike the latest tweet about some woman called Kardashian, not for pointless titillation, or, on the other side, unending lucre).[1] So if we learn from a skilled author that character "x" had lunch at time "y", it is not just a piece of information that just is. It means something as well. For example, that

---

1. I should note that for all the argument of this article, I do not, wholly at least, exclude myself from being, equally, at times a victim of social media and other virtual paraphernalia. Indeed, in line with this, I would like to quote a passage from early on in Theodor W. Adorno's *Minima Moralia*: "He who stands aloof runs the risk of believing himself better than others and misusing his critique of society as an ideology for his private interest. While he gropingly forms his own life in the frail image of a true existence, he should never forget its frailty, or how little the image is a substitute for true life. Against such awareness, however, pulls the momentum of the bourgeois within him. The detached observer is as much entangled as the active participant; the only advantage of the former is insight into his entanglement, and the infinitesimal freedom that lies in knowledge as such."

informative detail might be included in the story to make you understand how he or she, the character in question, could not have done, for instance, the murder that happened that day at lunch time in a different part of the city. Or maybe, if the said character has lunch repeatedly at the same time and place, for, say, three days, the author might be directing us to understand not just that this character ate three times at the same time and place, but that he or she is an "obsessive kind of character"; or perhaps, that he or she was or is in love with the waitress or waiter; and so on. What is lovely about this scenario, for all my invoking of "authority", is that the possibilities are, if not endless, plural; and that it is "up to us" to decide. Also that "up to us", unlike passive reception of titillating and ultimately pointless or meaningless feeds, literally means our agency, our doing something – which is or might be the hallmark of our freedom.

I speak to them of Kant and Hegel: not quite your prototypical Dubai residents![2] For Kant, the fact/value split is the source of human dignity or worth. The fact that subject and object – the truth of the state of affairs (even in a story, say) and what it means and/or might mean to us – are never for us sublunary beings seamlessly one, is the source of our very humanity. If we were not challenged, daily, to bridge that gap, via the constructions of the Imagination, whether we call it 'Story of a Panic' (E. M. Forster) or the 'Law of Gravity' (Isaac Newton), we would immediately cease being human. For Kant our dignity as the only rational animal known to date is found precisely in the bristle of our lack. It takes an exile to find or hope to find some Ithaca. Just so, I try to offer some kind of slaking in the desert.

Or (a good party-trick to start a class) I ask them: who

---

2. I should of course note here that, while I have read very widely in Kant's and Hegel's systems, I have not done so in German, but only in translation.

here believes there is something existing called "society"? (It works with an equally popular concept: "the unconscious".) Immediately, all my students look at me with ridicule. So I tell them: prove it. Show me with the five senses, verify for me with all the technology we have, based on those senses, where it is? Or, where is the American University in Dubai? (Much like, here, Gilbert Ryle invoking the concept of "Oxford" in his *The Concept of Mind*.) So I tell them it is a metaphor or a concept. But that does not mean their native intuition was wrong. I tell them that when we use language metaphorically like this we are not speaking of thoroughbred fictions; or, if we are, that those fictions are sometimes the realest things. (Indeed, to paraphrase Saul Kripke's *Reference and Existence*, while there is a difference between an actual duck and a toy one, it remains the case that both exist and are real, if with different purports.) Such poetic "leaps of faith"away from the immediately provable, bankable, are an essential part of being human. Hegel called them "speculative concepts", and they signify the soul that percolates and streams, purposively, through the data of existence – due to the godsend of our imaginaries. Because of the fact, in other words, that being human is being meaningful. And to be or become "post-human" – call me an old fogey at a meagre age 35 – is not quite toothsome to my palate.

In short, however much we may have gone "beyond" by way of technology, and geometrically more so, daily, there is something leaden-footed in today's generation of young learners. They reach beyond the skies with all the high-tech paraphernalia at their fingertips, but remain to a certain extent wingless. They build opulent castles here in the desert; but often enough mistake the sweltering mirage for the pools of true, cooling water.

2

F(r)ictions from the Critical Imaginary: The Singular Case of George Steiner

In other words, intention is the link between idiosyncratic view and the communal concern.
Edward W. Said, *Beginnings*

I first read George Steiner standing up by a row of bookshelves in the Borders bookshop in Oxford, while I was an undergraduate residing there. His early compilation of essays, *Language and Silence*, pricked my interest because in it there was a review of Lawrence Durrell's *Alexandria Quartet* and "the baroque novel."

I'd first read Durrell's masterpiece at fifteen or sixteen, a precocious young voracious reader, and, unfortunately for me, I became mildly mono-manic about it, thinking it, in a way damaging to my fiction-reading for many years, the epitome of what good literary work should be. Yes, as a very "French" writer, Durrell is stellar; however, my eyes were occluded by the high purple style. One grows and becomes more sensitized; one widens the scope of one's aesthetic appreciation; one realizes that high style, for all the well-knit plotting, is not *the only* manner of doing things. I'd read, a bit later, someone as central to the British scene as Malcolm Bradbury making fun of Durrell's wooden characters and his overall aestheticism, and I marveled, an innocent still, that

9

he, a great critical mind, should dare cast aspersions on my sometime hero. Indeed, the same once applied to another eminent contemporary critic, James Wood; in an essay he slates George Steiner's use of abstractions and cultural fetishes in the texture of his prose, citing, if I remember correctly, Nabokov in the 1970s also denigrating Steiner. However, taking some of Steiner's critical, or rather, nonfictional work into consideration in this paper, work whose mannered style typi es his far less prolific fiction, I hope to use the great doyen as a case study to answer questions that have plagued me (I: not of course in the same galaxy, let alone league, linguistic or otherwise), about the working relationship between the critical imaginary and the more nominally creative one.

George Steiner has held Professorial Chairs at Geneva and Oxford and Cambridge, and elsewhere. He is not just distinguished, eminent; he is seen by many as one of the last great polymathic intellects, harking from an era when polymathic endeavor was still possible. He is famous for many works, including, say, his *Antigones*, a fascinating study of the history, philosophical, poetic, and otherwise of that archetypal Sophoclean play; his *Real Presences*, honorary lectures, among many honorary lectures in his later career, from the late eighties; his *Grammars of Creation*, slightly later Gifford Lectures; or, far earlier, his short but potent introduction to Heidegger. There are many other works of course, just as distinguished and influential, including his classic autobiography, a main source in this paper, *Errata: An Examined Life*.

The phenomenon of a creative writer, a poet or a novelist, say, writing critically is not just wide-spread, historically as otherwise; it is also almost an unavoidable combination; Virginia Woolf is an instance, or George Orwell. The problematic I want to discuss here, however, is the inverse; that is to say, writers who write in the main in a putatively nonfictional manner, who also, and secondarily from a quantitative perspective, and maybe that alone, write creatively. There are many writers who began as academics and scholars and then shifted, near-wholly, into being creative writers; one thinks of Iris Murdoch, A.S. Byatt, or David Lodge. There are also eminent critics, who write *just as much*, if not more, creative work – and Gabriel Josipovici is a good example here, especially as he evidently possesses a critical and intellectual range to mirror the Steiner discussed in the main in this paper. However, part of the reason I choose Steiner in this working-paper, is not only because I'm familiar with much of his work; not only, to boot, because I teach his fiction, finding it some of the most intelligent fiction I have ever read; but most pressingly: because his fictional output over a lifetime's engagement with literature and the humanities more generally, can be gathered in one chunky volume; indeed, I possess his collected fictional works, and yes, they are one chunky volume. To my mind, this signal asymmetry makes the investigation of the question at issue here, more poignant.

Before I get to the sample fiction, his long short story, "Return No More," first published in book format with two others, equally brilliant, in *Anno Domini*, I want to detail a few of his autobiographical comments in the above-mentioned, *Errata*. My hope is that after I selectively mention some of his self-referential statements, I will be able to see how such autobiographical testimony is lived-out in the consummate execution of his fiction; if not directly, at least indirectly. And then, to end by gathering the insights thus concretely-gained, in order to assess what they reveal in a more global sense about the relationship between critical and creative imaginations. For this problematic has been a knotty feature in and for my own, far less copious, writerly life.

In the first chapter of his (very much "intellectual")

autobiography, Steiner writes: "I have conducted my emotional, intellectual and professional a airs in distrust of theory." He adds,

> The invocation of "theory" in the humanities, in historical and social studies, in the evaluation of literature and the arts, seems to me mendacious. The humanities are susceptible neither to crucial experiments nor to verification.... Our responses to them are narratives of intuition. (*Errata* 5)

That designation, "narrative," is our first clue. On the next page he writes: "The theoreticians in power consider my own work, if they consider it at all, as archaic impressionism. As heraldry" (*Errata* 6). And here's a second clue; for it should be noted that this opening chapter starts like a novel, *in medias res*, with the infinite quiddity of raindrops, merging later into the equally revelatory memoir about receiving as a child a book of heraldry, and the infinite permutations of such colored signs. Radical singularity is the keynote of this opening chapter, and to a certain extent, the whole book.

But to resume: three points here. First: he labels his critical work as not only a "narrative" of "intuition" – but also as eminently "impressionistic," which is another hint at the creative source of his critical work, or perhaps of any. Impressionism, famously, is a term indicating a disparagement of wholly objective "facts," in favor of a perspectival patterning, where scientist becomes artist. Secondly, we have the effect of the content of the chapter on the infinite singularity of things in existence, be they raindrops, leaves, or coats of arms, being mapped onto the formal choices (like choosing to start *in medias res*) made in and of that same opening chapter – which is itself a highly-selective and artistic gambit. Then, in part uniting them, we can say that the very style of the dramatic opening – only later permitting reflection – is both an autobiographical reflection in the representational sense, as well as a reflection of how his imaginary works as a structure of feeling, formally: from detail, and detail, to generality. A little later on, he writes:

> In a perfectly rational and pragmatic sense, a serious act of signification – verbal, imagined, tonal – is inexhaustible to interpretative summation. It cannot be anatomized or held in fixed place. (*Errata* 20)

Meaningful work, then, is beyond précis; it signifies, singularly, only as itself; paraphrasing artistic content is a betrayal. Indeed, echoing some of his argument from *Real Presences*, he writes further on in the same intellectual memoir, his dislike for deconstruction in similar terms. The ineffable seamlessness of music is the epitome of his (alternate) holism.

> All I know is that music is the sine qua non in my existence. It reinsures what I sense to be or, rather, search for in the transcendental. This is to say that it demonstrates to me the reality of presence, of a factual "thereness," which defies analytical or empirical circumscription. (75)

And then: to further insist this Heideggerian note of the wonder at the quiddity of existence, as lived-out to boot in his dramatic, creative recounting of (even) his *intellectual life*, he writes:

> All of us are guests of life. No human being knows the meaning of its creation, except in the most primitive, biological regard. No man or woman

> knows the purpose, if any, the possible significance
> of its "thrownness" into the mystery of existence.
> (54)

And part of this awe-filled wonder at the singularities of
existence is a part, in turn, of his teaching career. He writes
that the pith and point of academic teaching is "To direct
a student's attention towards that which, at rst, exceeds his
grasp, but whose compelling stature and fascination will draw
him after it" (45). The ineffable whole of the literary artefact
is mirrored, thus, in the reaching-towards of the ine able
whole of the budding critical intelligence spurred by such;
like artistic meaning, the process of critical grasping is not
teleologically-closed, but endlessly recursive. And finally, to
link and synergize all I've noted so far, we have him speaking
of the relation of his critical, strictly-speaking intellectual life
with his more nominally-creative works.

> Teaching and the companionship of mutual
> provocation in a seminar, have been my oxygen. I
> cannot imagine my work – even, to a vivid extent,
> my fiction – without them. If I struggle against
> retirement, it is because my students have been
> indispensable. This is good luck. (41)

Taking now as a kind of case study one of Steiner's long short
stories, "Return No More," I hope to show how the features
of his critical life adverted to above can be mapped onto
his creative fictional intelligence, leaving us with a concrete
insight into the problematic at hand. I will start, brie y, with
a small summary of the plot; and only then pick out
features–features, serendipitously, I have myself "taught" –
that evince a critical intelligence permeating through the
(supposedly distinct) imaginative.

"Return No More" is the story of a former Nazi, now disabled, who returns after the war to the French village and the French home in which he had been bivouacked as a conqueror. As part of his Nazi–duty, during that occupation he had the eldest son of the family hanged for sedition on the local ash tree. He returns with the overarching aim of asking for the hand in marriage of the youngest daughter, whom he had fallen in love with during his wartime sojourn. His post-France back-story – which he is just allowed to speak to them, before the younger son's furious murderous anger, and the older ones' angry curiosity – reveals his own (Nazi) suffering. (Indeed, to continue this note of philosophical responsibility, his love for Danielle, is a part of his recognition that, having known all his life only the drums of war, his truest homely experience was while staying with his captives the Terrinoires. And this revelation, as with others, is part of the philosophical maturity of the story's conception, showing as it does how both sides, including the predominant wrongdoers, have suffered.) e overall and problematic theme of the story is to my mind the possibility or not of transcendence, transcendence by love beyond the vicious cycle of an "eye-for-an-eye" and unending reciprocal violence. However, what I want to elicit from this fiction, is the *intelligence* behind its shaping and execution; if you like, to a certain extent at least, the "content of the form"; for this in my view is where we may be able to scent the critical mind melding into a creative one.

The story starts, dramatically, *in medias res*; like his "non-fictional" intellectual memoir, his "examined life." We only learn the name of the limited hero, "Falk," after a good five to six pages. The style is vintage Steiner: rich, evocative, visceral, sensual, mixing with perfectly-judged skill abstractions with concretions, and throughout eminently filmic; and yet this ornate style is never ornamentation; there isn't a single sentence in the work which doesn't take the story, dramatically, forward. Before I get to the three features I want to discuss in the main, features that in my view show how a doyen and distinguished professor of poetics allows his critical expertise to feed into his fiction, I should say that the overwhelming and overarching intelligence of this piece resides, first of all, in its conception. There are, like all great creative writings, subjective tensions to be dramatically resolved in this fiction; those of love, jealousy, hate, curiosity, tenderness, among them. However, the more objective tension, the context of the Second World War and what we know about Nazi evils, not only sets the stage but impacts at every moment, enhances and exacerbates at every moment those very more local, subjective tensions treading the boards. at is the first analytical, as it were: choice and selection.

When Falk enters the drama on the first page, a disabled man carrying a suitcase, the locals heckle him and set their vicious dogs on him to amuse themselves. The dogs are described as "like crazed shadows" in this opening scene (*Anno Domini* 13). Not only does "shadow" foreshadow, as we will see; but there is a contrapuntal effect here. In the last scene, the wedding scene, where Danielle, the younger Terrenoire daughter is now married to Falk, the younger brother, Blaise, hating Falk from the start, draws him into a fatal Bacchanal dance, knowing he can't dance, disabled as he is; and that ending is a re-collecting of the opening. is effect is one of "prolepsis" and/or, depending on which way we are looking, "analepsis." And there are many other examples of this rhythmic shaping, where literal details symbolically map onto later or re-collected details. As throughout, the holism is redolent both formally and quite literally.

Secondly, there is much symbolism in seamless synergy with the literal plot. In his suitcase at the start a Meissen figurine Falk has brought back to France with him is shattered on the ground when the dogs attack him; a symbol thus of how the Second World War showed us the asymmetry between the value(s) of high culture and moral goodness. They played Beethoven and Mozart on the speakers in Auschwitz; the precious Meissen figurine breaks like Falk has been broken, and will be more fatally at the end. It is also, a proleptic symbol, and a part of the "thematic apposition" in the tale. You see, later we learn that the blue pitcher of milk that the young beloved, Danielle, was wont to bring and serve the handsome Nazi officer, was buried by Falk in the barn before leaving France. He had made an oath to himself that if it remained intact till his post-war return, then there was hope, and hope for love. Not only is the "milk" symbolic, for obvious reasons, but the earlier broken gurine, whose shards, in a telling symbolic detail, re ect the a ernoon "light," is mirrored by the intact pitcher. Or take the inhumanity of hanging Jean, the eldest son, on an ash tree. On re-arrival, when the Terrenoires are listening with tight lips to Falk's account of himself, Danielle, destined to marry Falk, brushes past him at a very opportune moment, and before her brother's execution makes an "inhuman" sound (19), reminiscent of the dogs, so to speak. Again in vivid filmic images, seamlessly planted with the literal unravelling of the plot, which in true modernist fashion is *not* chronological, Steiner thematizes the humane, the inhumane, and their respective interpenetrations. And there are many other examples of such telling effects.

But I want to briefly discuss the ending, very dramatic, very intelligent, and eminently ambivalent. Falk and Danielle are at their wedding party. In the ensuing celebrations the reader is made to feel the uncanny, with Danielle, and with Falk. Perhaps her female intuition tells Danielle that an omen bodes; she asks Falk to leave with her. He too, we sense, senses, but decides to stay, to see it out. And then he is driven into a crazed whirling dancing circle; naturally, he falls; and then is trodden and stamped-on to death.

The insight evinced in Falk *staying* betrays immense understanding of the human condition; we are made to feel like guilt seeks out its punishment, which, however counter-intuitive, is true to life. In a similar way, early on in Falk's backstory, the creative intelligence behind the writing is made evident, as throughout, by and in singly-phrased details. He is recounting how returning to his home town, the Americans had bombed a local phosphorous plant; and how the released skin-burning phosphorous was burning the local inhabitants alive. e survivors had jumped into the canal to escape, every so o en bobbing their heads into the air to breathe. The Gestapo, in gas masks, are mercy-killing them, on their desperate requests. Falk asks to help, in order to enter the scene, to find his family. He approaches the canal and sees a young woman, with singed-out amber eyebrows the color of his; she is begging for a bullet; he reaches down to kiss her – then shoots her. The author then has Falk say how he can't be sure, but "he thinks" it was his sister (24). The effect is hellish, harrowing. Not just the unspeakable situation as is; not just having to kill his own sister; but all that, and actually never *knowing* if it *was* his sister or not.

And the ending is similarly a tour de force of authorial intelligence. e last words of the story have Mr Terrenoire standing above the now-killed Falk saying, in two staccato repetitions, that he came back "too soon" (65). And that final dramatic utterance is plosive. The intelligent reader is left in open-ended mystery for all the filmic and concrete determinateness, the "felt life" to use a Jamesian coinage, of the story-telling. It is le for the reader to decide, whether that "too soon" is meant to mean that his ending, and the ending, were or are part of a pre-planned plot to let him marry then kill him; or, whether Mr Terrenoire intends something more purely contingent, as in: it's a shame what happened, but it happened, and it just, in retrospect now, couldn't be helped. is dramatic ambivalence about the truth of the matter is resolutely modernist. Whether love *might have* transcended, in different contingent circumstances, or that it *never could have*, is a problem through the end.

My students often ask me when I teach this story, why I call it an excellent example of psychological realism. The technical or formal features I mention in response aside, they say the whole conception, of a murdering Nazi returning to marry the younger sister of the family he dominated as an unjust conqueror simply isn't realistic. And I reply that it is "realistic" par excellence – for that very reason. Like the autobiographical opening of his *Errata*, which details the quiddities of human existence and experience, this story is so dramatically strange in its whole plot-conception, that it *just must have really happened*, so to speak. What I mean is, the counter-intuitive situation, the fact that the tensions of the drama are extreme, fits no overdetermined or necessitated category of "typical" or at least "stereotypical" experience. The fact that it happened as it did is real in so far as it really, in a manner of speaking, *couldn't have been* expectedly imagined, or made-up. Steiner renders the true nature of historical experience. Any savvy historian will tell you that history is made-up of both, chance, and necessity; reality for the mortal man or woman, being in time, is both singular, and susceptible to induction. And perhaps we are creatively spurred to tell stories, because stories are unique – but also symbolizations of our general experience; or, perhaps better – that singularity *just is* the human condition (its just-ice).

It has been my contention, implicitly here, that all this skill and technique, as merely sampled – evincing real human conditions and real human experience, with all their texture, tensions and radical singularities, is a product of a critical imaginary – one that *understands* in extremis – that is immanently creative at the same time, by the same token. As well as the commonsensical notion that there can't logically be analysis without a prior synthetic whole to break-down, or at least to try to – there is, equally, as many Kantians remind us, no synthesis without its twinned other: analysis.

References

Said, Edward. *Beginnings: Intention and Method*. London: Granta Books, 1985, rpt. 1997.

Steiner, George. "Return No More." *Anno Domini: Three Stories*. New York: Atheneum, 1964: 11–65.

Steiner, George. *Errata: An Examined Life*. London: Weidenfeld and Nicholson, 1997.

3

In Shy Darkness They Lie: Teaching Poems in Dubai

For my students, past and present, at the American University in Dubai

> and alters into someone I have known:
> a passing stranger on the road to grief,
> husband and father; rich man; poor man; thief.
> — John Burnside, 'The Good Neighbour'[1]

> Tact meant not only subordination to ceremonial convention: it was precisely the latter all later humanists unceasingly ironized. Rather, the exercise of tact was as paradoxical as its historical location. It demanded the reconciliation – actually impossible – between the unauthorized claims of convention and the unruly ones of the individual.[2]
> — Theodor W. Adorno, *Minima Moralia*

In one of Jorge Luis Borges' famed middle-period baroque fictions, 'Pierre Menard: Author of the "Quixote"', the Argentinian wizard prefigures in fictive form so much that would become canonical in the fraught annals of post-war literary theory. The central conceit of this fiction is that an author writes *Don Quixote* in the twentieth century, word for word the same as the original – and it is considered, in the metafictional trope of this fiction, a wholly new, "original",

---

1. John Burnside, *The Good Neighbour* (London: Jonathan Cape, 2005), p. 3.

2. Theodor W. Adorno, *Minima Moralia: Reflections from Damaged Life*, translated by E. F. N. Jephcott (London & New York: Verso, 1999), p. 36.

different book. This is because, as Borges would say, following an infamous snippet in Heraclitus, we never step into the same river twice. Which is to say, due to temporal change, all texts "are" or "are read" as wholly different texts – and with the same "objective" content – when they are read in different historical (or otherwise) contexts. Indeed, we owe the very weave-like notion of a "text", in specifically this sense, as compared with a "work", to that late-flowering (and invention of, to a certain extent) "literary theory" in the second half of the previous century. And there is an element of truth, in my view, to much of that work. And there is a (dangerous) element of untruth about it, as well.

Part of the belief, you see, in this notion that every context (radically) changes every text, entails the belief that there simply are no "real" presentations of story, only re-representations. [3] That we are inexorably sundered from the earth of our experience, as soon as it is reflected or reflected upon. It also follows in this school of thought that all reality, therefore, is ultimately, primarily, discursively shaped. While it may be true that skewed conceiving may underpin, thus, material relations of systematically unjust, insinuatingly draconian power, to over-stress this point to the exclusion of the more bare material reality is in my view a dangerous way of going about things; because it seems to suggest that if we had better, more accurate conceiving of whatever reality it might be, on the ground as it were, we would therefore have less systemic injustice and so on. Which I do not believe is so. When a critic of "Orientalism" like the late Professor Edward Said slates the "ism", the fetish of hypostatic takes on historical, political, and cultural realities, he is doing the world good service. But one must not take it too far. Getting the

3. See Edward W. Said, *Orientalism* (New York: Vintage Books, 1994), pp. 272–273.

flu, and making your way, crucially injured, from a bombed-out building in Syria, are the kind of phenomena that remind us that for all the "secularity" of historical and political experience, for all, that is, the idea that history has been and will be made by men and women, not divine fiat – for all that textualist "existentialism", there remains a vital (or pivotal) essentialist truth, a basic reality at the horizon and cusp of all rerepresentational work, which flies in the face, and never gracefully, of all the norms seen to be only, or at least ultimately, discursively shaped. [4] We can only "play", hegemonically coerce, or dye, until, as fortune would have it, we die.[5]

4. Said dilates on (his use of) this concept ("secular") in Edward W. Said, *The World, the Text and the Critic* (Cambridge, MA: Harvard University Press, 1983), pp. 1–30.

5. I would like to note here that, after mentioning Professor Said, the pursuant point is not in any way to imply that that courageous public intellectual somehow elided material realities, quite the contrary of course. The pursuant point only addresses itself to a literary-theoretical position. I also realize of course the obvious point that even if a terror victim, say, of some sort does not shape his or her unfortunate reality, it is mostly true to say that the horrid reality in question is still man-made – but from the other dominative side. That said: my main intention at this point is to temper the sometime-fashionable view that there is no stable centre to human experience – all being (supposedly) contextually overdetermined, all being rigorously susceptible to historicization. The emphasis on the heritage of form in poetry taught from a different culture and time to young Emirati-based students, which forms the beeline of this article, is there to suggest that in such poetic work there is a basic fundament of human truth that transcends, or may (come to) transcend, de-limiting contexts. Indeed, this point, about the (potentially reaching) transcendence of form, might be translated into (the reason) why Kant (one of the serendipitous founders of modernity, and thus, later, of modernism) found it rigorously necessary to posit a "noumenal" realm — even if: one whereof none may speak. Or put otherwise, while all may be necessarily relayed as re-presentation, that "all" (of self and/or world) needs must hang-off or depend upon a more fundamental, or sublime, real – because there simply would be no occasion or ground for re-presentation otherwise. So that when Said

Often, thus, when teaching here in Dubai, I tell my students, in line with some of the aforementioned, that, yes, early twentieth-century experiments with art did lead to the now seemingly impossible feat of being able in a formula, in an abstracted, separated discursive way, to define, totalizing, "art" from "non-art". It is not "objective" anymore; all seems to "depend." In a similar way, late twentieth-century revisionists like R. D. Laing, Michel Foucault, or Gilles Deleuze dispatched the idea of normal psychological health, at times celebrating what is ordinarily viewed as un-health, as somehow more authentic or true to reality.[6] Adding the two, with personal reference, allows me to get across what I see as the truth in this matter. I tell my students that when I was their age, roughly, I had a schizoid period. And while I cannot define, abstractly, for them that this illness was indeed "abnormal", I live the difference, between then and now, performatively as it were. The same applies to art. There is good art, bad, better, worse — if not 100% verifiable as such. Good, better art takes you somewhere, offers and compels a trajectory, mentally, emotionally, and, at the best of times, both at the same time. Bad art is inert, stillborn. I cannot (wholly) define the difference, but like them, I feel and think and judge the experience of any artwork in its performance through me. In short, while one continuously educates a

criticizes the idealistic fetish of the "ism" mentioned, he may well be alerting the world to the idea that reality is truly "beyond", more than, the mind's inexorable re-presenting. In other words, given the two sides of literary and political work in Said's oeuvre – two sides he never wished to be viewed as separate or sundered– Said may well have agreed, perhaps, that existential meaning and essential meaning feed off each other in a perpetual loop-back. So, to close this too-copious endnote: in short, death might be viewed as the locus of the real, the cusp at which we realize; or if you like, death is how we form and/or are formed.

6. I would like to note here that while I have some good reading knowledge of French, I have only read the two French authors mentioned here in English.

sensibility, leading to increasingly compelling ways of understanding art – this true process of discrimination is neither "Objective", nor is it, however, slippery-slope-ish and "anything-goes" "subjective" …

Much of the aforementioned can be seen to work itself out now, in this brief account of how some (mainly) UK poetry goes down, reaches – here in (youthful) Dubai; reaches, though, without historicist context: merely as bone-true literary artefacts which prove poignant and real. By paying special attention to form(s), I hope to offer a way of showing how much poetry that is, at first blush, alien to my students here, is still redolent and powerful in this, their wholly different life-world – spatially, temporally, and also to bridge the two: technologically! The fact that, without biographical or indeed any other contexts, I am able to reach my students, in their own (virtual) context, is a testament, then, to some basic shared reality, which is, in my view: essential.

✳

I want to mention and discuss a few poems here, poems I teach every semester on the universal themes of love and death; also, in tandem, how (in part) I teach poetic forms, like the sonnet or the villanelle. It will be seen, in the main, from these few poems I discuss in some detail that there just is a real and basic truth to some of this verse which, shorn of any context, does still "work" for, and may come to "form", in however small a way, one hopes, a generation replete with digital media, a young data-prone generation, in of all places, Dubai …

When I teach poetry on the theme of death, elegies, two pieces I teach go down very well here; either: in the end, after discussion and elucidation, or, immediately. Take, then, the case of Seamus Heaney's end-poem in his 2006 T. S. Eliot prize-winning *District and Circle*, 'The Blackbird of Glanmore'. Or, what is the best (or at least my favourite) poem in his 1985 (Whitbread Book of the Year, 1986) prize-winning *Elegies* — the sonnet, 'The Kaleidoscope', by Douglas Dunn.

Heaney's masterly poem is at first difficult for this young Emirati-based generation. Its various subtle recursions are alien to them at first blush; the veiled nature of the story-telling done there evinces an obliqueness this generation is not used to. However, it is a perfect example of how I, or one, may teach in a formalist manner. Three features I usually pick up on for them, whether it is a literature course or a creative writing one, are verbal texture (to be expected with a poet like Heaney), the use of syntax and punctuation, line-breaks and line-endings, and the paraphrase-able content, about the cycle of life, which it turns out is less easily grasped than the foregone formalist notes. Yes, the poem comes full circle, from beginning to end, with a repetition –varied though, implicitly – and by how the last verb of the first line is "arrive" and the last of the last line is "leave." This fits with aplomb, but varies also, because, in line with my introductory remarks, although "On the grass when I arrive" and "In the ivy when I leave" are repeated, the places, the contexts of the repetitions render these two "places", "ivy" and "grass", very different in and by and from the end. Indeed, to prove to my students, neophytes, that this is a central concern, I tell them that this formal repetition is mirrored by the "house of life" from which the persona has a "bird's-eye view" of himself: "A shadow on raked gravel" – because it maps onto the earlier "house of death." Which is to say, the ominous blackbird, container of the passed spirit(s), becomes by the end the persona's own container, in that Heaney, supposedly, comes to the recognition of his own impending mortality. By turns, the verbal texture, towards the end of this incantatory poem, of "k" sounds, are onomatopoeic regarding the car-lock "clunking" shut and the "panic" of the blackbird– all this is easily swallowed. To be grasped somewhere between the two notes, I also talk about how syntax and punctuation are content too. After confessing his "love" for the passed (present) "blackbird", the following two lines in the next stanza, are: "I park, pause, take heed./ Breathe. Just breathe and sit … " Why does one "breathe" like that (and after a line-break)? Well, because one is overwhelmed by (the) emotion. But, like the pitting, staccato commas used in the first line here cited, that "Breathe" is also a one-word sentence. The periodic rhythm is at one with the innards of the tale — it lives out, it dramatizes (and my students all know what a "dramatic pause" is) that tale in its formal choices, in that overwhelming feeling is stayed thereby.

Douglas Dunn's sonnet 'The Kaleidoscope' goes down like sugar with my young learners. The turn between octet and sestet, the turn between the warm, subjunctive heurism of "to climb these stairs again" with all its staging of sepia-toned nostalgia, and the "I climb these stairs" which starts the ninth line, and which is a cold wake-up call to the deathly reality, is easily grasped and understood. However, a few features which make this poem, with its kaleidoscopic conceit, are beneficially picked out in my experience. Indeed, her (his passed wife's) "kaleidoscope," creating a hypothetical "symmetry of husbands," is itself a working image relevant to the difference between a "work" and a "text." The "death of the author," however, is replaced by the death of the beloved, and the resultant paradox is the more poignant for that. In that, what is being subliminally suggested perhaps is that the author is she, not he; or, in pivotal, in-forming parallel, that he wishes he had died in her place. The kaleidoscope resulting from the apostrophized beloved's death, not the author's, has a secret: has intimate intent(s). However, two further notes: first, because he is telling a highly concrete and individual tale, Dunn earns his rhythmically used and rhythmically placed use of abstractions like the "grief" in "Grief wrongs us so …" of the penultimate line, or the "hope" or "foresight," say, from earlier. Second, for a poem whose ending runs "I stand, and wait, and cry/For the absurd forgiveness, not knowing why", the use of a frontal rhyme at that ending couplet (along with a rigorous but deft rhyme scheme for the whole sonnet, using half rhyme as much as full) creates a force-field, a paradoxical antagonism, between the euphonic harmony of the formal choice, suggesting grieving now made sense, and the actual sentiment, asking why in, or of, an absurd universe which "wrongs" us in a way we cannot "right."

When I teach a form like the villanelle, Elizabeth Bishop's 'One Art' is at useful deuce with Dylan Thomas' notorious 'Do Not Go Gentle Into that Good Night … ' While I think the former to be the more seasoned and accomplished poem — as may be expected, Thomas often goes down as the more powerful for this young Emirati-based generation. Its hieratic music is more emphatic, of course, and while they nearly always do take to Bishop's villanelle, her paradox at the end, uniting all of us in disaster, and what disaster writes, takes a surprising while to be understood. Whereas, strangely, Thomas' by turns much more abstract and abstractive poem is understood at a pre-reflective level nearly immediately. Bishop's — more the narrative poem — listing in impending order smaller more slight things to larger more abstract ones, and ending in the final unique quatrain on and with the pivotal "you", is not appreciated as much as the well-nigh Psalmic parataxes of Thomas' urgent plea to his father (not that they would put it that way!). Word choice is a useful way of teaching them (the analogous difference between) these poems. While Thomas' more abstractive sensibility is lived out and demonstrated with phrases that have no concrete reference and which are, thus, replaceable, conceivably at least – when Bishop uses anachronistic words like "vaster" and "realms" we know that there is a far more refined, although not necessarily better, sensibility at work. While Bishop's villanelle is deeply serious, there is irony in speaking of "realms" and using a comparative adjective like "vaster" — which is, palpably, out of place, in so far as it is a tad otiose.

Similarly, Fiona Sampson's sonnet, 'Take, Eat', from her 2007 (Carcanet) collection, *Common Prayer*, is quite neatly taught as a metaphysical poem, as paraphrase-able content, formal allusion and conceit, and fittingly for and as a metaphysical poem, via the so-to-speak (transubstantiating) content of the form. I teach my students that this poem, with its titular allusion to the last supper, both speaks of and acts out the difference between, but then the cohering, coalescing of, erotic love and spiritual. At the start "kissing" and "praying" are noted, demotically as not the same. But through the performance, the process of the poem, and through the pivotal turn, which shifts voice and register, they are seen to be the same, or at least homonymous; not only literally, both using the body feature of the "mouth", but figuratively as well, as in the chiasmus of one deifying one's beloved ("Nipple raised to Upper Case") and loving God like an immanent lover ("Capitalised Name"). And the couplet of this sonnet resolves but also resumes the paradoxical coalescing of the main titular trope: of eros and agape being analogies of each other. The darkness in which the lovers at poem's end "lie" (pun) is "shy"; and the lovers "gasp." That last verb is pivotal, in more senses than one. To gasp evokes both: shock and relief.

✳

I recall reading somewhere a letter from Pound to Bridges, in which Pound is excoriatingly critical of the latter for using trite tropes of "flowers" and "sunsets", rather than, presumably, "making it new." But as I get older myself, I find myself agreeing with Bridges' (Georgian) retort: namely, that it was and is still licit to write of flowers and sunsets because it just does remain the case — even in our virtual Emirati or Emirati-based world – that people do indeed still admire and enjoy flowers and sunsets! In other words, for all that modernism – as a precursor and parallel of an existentialist ethos — has taught us: in my view such self-made, self-forged meanings still reside and lie upon a more basic bank of shared essential reality. It may well be the case, in the poetic art as otherwise, that any "new" aesthetic (or experience) only releases its "new" effect if it works from and works up from a basic shared humanity. As T. S. Eliot famously argued, in effect, there just is no wholly true (or truly whole) "originality"; 'Tradition and the Individual Talent' was right on the money for this poet and critic, in so far as "difference" only "makes a difference" when it "differs" from or against some-"thing."[7] Likewise, form, structure, order are not the antonyms of freedom. As many a schizoid adolescent will tell you, or if you like show you, too much childhood license may well preclude integrally free moves in the adult world. No.

7. See T. S. Eliot, 'Tradition and the Individual Talent', in *20th Century Literary Criticism: A Reader*, edited by David Lodge (London and New York: Longman, 1972), pp. 71–72. Indeed, the cooler modernism of the Eliot of this iconic essay is of a similar type to that suggested in the shape of the insight – Hegelian in mode – of the epigraph from Theodor W. Adorno at the head of this article. I would also like to acknowledge here a debt – for this particular way of phrasing the idea of "making a difference" –to Ermanno Bencivenga, *A Theory of Language and Mind* (Berkeley, Los Angeles, London: University of California Press, 1997), p. 89. Indeed, see Edward W. Said, *Beginnings: Intention & Method* (London: Granta Books, 1997), p. xxiii. Here he writes in the two veins of this article: "beginning and beginning-again are historical whereas origins are divine...a beginning is its own method because it has intention" (emphasis added). The very next sentence reads: "In short, beginning is making or producing difference– and here is the great fascination in the subject – difference which is the result of combining the already-familiar with the fertile novelty of human work in language" (original emphases).

Perhaps order, structure, form are the sine qua non for any true and/or truly seasoned "freedom."

PART 2

Scholarly Interventions, Or Thereabouts...

4

Love's Knowledge: Realisation Beyond Defence: Durrell's *Alexandria Quartet* After, and Beyond, Ford's *The Good Soldier*

when something untoward happens, some trauma or damage, whether inflicted by the commissions or omissions of others, or some cosmic force, one makes the initially unwelcome event one's own inner occupation. You work to adopt the most loveless, forlorn, aggressive child as your own, and do not leave her to develop into an even more vengeful monster, who constantly makes you ill in ill-health as in unhappy love. It requires taking in before letting go.

To grow in love-ability is to accept the boundaries of oneself and others, while remaining vulnerable, woundable [. . . .] Acknowledgement of conditionality is the only unconditionality of human love.[1]

I: The Paradox of Being in Time

In *The Alexandria Quartet* Lawrence Durrell attempts to apply relativity theory to the novel form. The first three novels aim to represent the three dimensions of space, with the fourth, the only one to move forward in time, representing the fourth dimension of Time. One of the ways this intention shows up in the novels is the way they illustrate the paradox of being in time.

1. Gillian Rose, *Love's Work*, London: Chatto and Windus, 1995, p. 90-1 and 98.

At the beginning of his *The Logic of Sense*, Deleuze writes of this paradox, illustrating it using the character of Alice in Lewis Carroll's fiction. He takes the incident of Alice shrinking. She shrinks in time, but at any moment during this shrinkage reason is eluded by the antinomian movement, the conjunction and contradiction of opposing senses or directions produced by the fact that it happens in time. At any moment during her shrinking Alice is both smaller than she was and larger than she is going to be. Another version of this paradox is illustrated by Zeno's paradox of the race between Achilles and the tortoise. Because of its comparative slowness the tortoise is given a ten metre head start, say. But once Achilles starts running it turns out, quite rationally, that he will never be able to catch up to the tortoise. For to close the gap he must first close half the gap. To close half the gap he must first close half that. And so on in an infinite regress: the problem is vertiginous. In both instances, motion, movement, embodied action, plain living, defy reason because reason works to create static relations, classifying, whereas life and living are in time and therefore in flow. Reason aims to break down this flow, creating boundaries between one moment and the next, cause and effect, and yet in reality things just feed into each other osmotically, as endlessly dynamic as music. Hence, perhaps, both Bergson's and, before him, Augustine's use of music as a heurism to escape this paradox, to put the only truthful flesh on fluid time.[2]

At one point in *Justine*, Durrell's unreliable narrator, the innocent Darley, calls himself a 'poet of the historic consciousness'. This of course alludes to the central theme of memory and its vagaries in the novel(s) – also a key to

2. See, for instance, Henri Bergson, *Time and Free Will*, trans. F. L. Pogson, London: George Allen and Co, 1913, p. 103-13.

their form. Across the *Quartet*, the narrative builds itself like a patchwork and then palimpsest of scenes, shifting and sliding backwards and forwards in time. At one point Darley says that he will not record his story chronologically, for that would be to render it as history, but rather give it poetic or heraldic form, writing his story as the events became significant for him. For in imagination resides 'reality prime'; only in fiction can one produce the meaning of the pattern and realise character (another recurrent theme in the novel(s)), against the chaos of experience and of living in time, which continues to flow and continues to change the significance of each moment in retrospect, and endlessly. And so these 'sliding panels of the human heart', the *Quartet*, serve to illustrate the relativity of truth, as against the pretensions of any rational history, or any notional 'end of history'. It does this firstly in the sense that at every point in space (for every different person) the story is different; and secondly, because of being in time. It is the very nature of historical research to keep reinterpreting the past, not only as gaps are filled in the historian's knowledge, through new perspectives, new evidence, but also because the relation of the historian's present to the past is continuously changing. And not only this, but also, as expressed in Walter Benjamin's anti-Hegelian 'Theses on the Philosophy of History', because at each moment the counterfactual 'if' suggests that the world could have gone in an infinity of directions (a theme that is eventually developed in *Balthazar*). Thus the (historical) object is illusory. What is left is a heraldic universe, a personal universe. (Indeed, the retreat onto his Greek 'island' to write is the very symbol of this.) (Re)interpretation is all that is left, and becomes one of the central reading directions to emerge from Durrell's novels. In this sense Durrell is a late-romantic, an epigone of the Nietzschean critique of objectivity or transcendence.[3]

II: The Mythoi of Eros and Thanatos: An Objective Pattern

The 'historic consciousness' and 'the Capitol of Memory' also suggest in true modernist fashion a mythological backdrop to the events related in the novel(s). This backdrop is a precursor which acts, in slight contradistinction to the suggestions of radical relativity (above), as (metaphysical) anchor. One thinks, of course, however facilely, of the earlier exemplars of *Ulysses* or *The Waste Land*; or indeed the pivotal role of notions of objectivity in the work of T. E. Hulme or, later, Wyndham Lewis.[4]

Just as Darley reflects on the untimely death of Pursewarden, the main fictional 'artist/writer' character – that the man has been replaced by his writings, his fiction, and has become the mythos that emerges from it, so the novel(s) as a whole have a distinctive mythologizing function. Which is to say, a gambit aimed at stilling time. The backdrop to the fictional Alexandria of *Justine* is the city of Myth, the 'Capitol of Memory'. This suggests a certain changeless stability as opposed to the inveterate process of change and newness already adverted to. The epiphanic or ecstatic rhythm of the writing, the series of 'realisations' reached by the characters

---

3. See, for instance, Friedrich Nietzsche, *The Genealogy of Morals*, trans. Horace B. Samuel, Mineola, New York, Dover Publications, 2003, p. 93.

4. Indeed, Durrell shares his over-determinant opening gambit of the tetralogy (an ominous mythic backdrop), with two preceding colonial novelists, the Conrad of *Nostromo* and the Forster of *A Passage to India*. Indeed, Forster makes mention of Durrell in his 1961 3rd edition of his Alexandria travel guide. In that latter, Forster discusses Alexandria as the city of the 'Soma', meaning, historically, the mausoleum of Alexander. Durrell does so as well, but plays on the term as well, meaning something more generically (psycho)sensual. See E. M. Forster, *Alexandria: A History and a Guide*, Garden City, New York: Anchor Books, 1961, p. xvii and 11, 22. See T. E. Hulme, *Selected Writings*, ed. Patrick McGuinness, Manchester: Carcanet, 1998, p. 68-83 & 180-222. See also, Wyndham Lewis, *Time and Western Man*, ed. Paul Edwards, Santa Rosa: Black Sparrow Press, 1993.

usually after experiences of sex or death are both ciphers of hermeneutic sealing and hermeneutic openness. (Indeed, if one reads these points of 'realisation' closely it will be seen that the imagery surrounding the description is often identical or very similar, which suggests the intentional nature of this epiphanic rhythm.) But there is in fact a tension in the novel(s) between the vertiginous process of discovery, most overtly suggested by the 'Workpoints' at the end of the novel(s), and the concomitant and periodic reaction of stillness and resignation. The tension is a motive equilibrium between Eros and Thanatos deliberately made to regulate the rhythm and pacing of the storytelling. Durrell of course was a strident aficionado of Freud, and not only makes use of him within the tetralogy, but makes use of a passage of his (from a letter to Fliess), as epigraph to the latter. 'I am accustoming myself to the idea of regarding every sexual act as a process in which four persons are involved.' [5]

Assessing the mythic element in *Justine*, George Fraser saw more of the myth of the Quest than of the Foundation.[6] True, there is a sense of endless questioning, of maeutic in these novels, made poignant by the Socratic irony produced by the role of the unreliable narrator, Darley. But this sense of movement and discovery, of Eros is crossed with a spiritual calm, evoked by another repeated rhythm in the writing: mini-narratives invariably followed by passages of reflection, judgment and conclusion – the still reactionary countermovement of death, Thanatos. The prismatic, refracted layering of both plot and character, are set off by an elegiac tone. One reads passages like the following,

5. See Lawrence Durrell, *The Alexandria Quartet*, London: Faber & Faber, 2012 – henceforth AQ; p. 15.

6. See George Fraser, *Lawrence Durrell: A Study*, London: Faber and Faber, 1968), pp. 132-3.

> If she ever knew me at all she must later have
> discovered that for those of us who feel deeply and
> who are at all conscious of the inextricable tangle
> of human thought there is only one response to be
> made – ironic tenderness and silence. (AQ 40)

and despite knowing it to be fiction, relative and potentially
falsified by perspective, in extremis, one can't help sensing the
presence of something transcendent, if via negativa. What it
is in fact is 'acceptance'. Durrell called his *Quartet* from the
beginning of its inception almost twenty years before it was
completed, 'The Book of the Dead'. In his first serious fiction
The Black Book the 'little death' is derided. The writing starts
with bleak perspectives of winter and deadness, and it evokes
the sense of a young man's angst, ennui and melancholy: the
'agon'. And yet in the far more mature work of theQuartet,
although Death again is a central theme, the elegiac tone and
the sweeter rhythms of the prose create a sense of healthy
grieving or mourning, as if something is truly being worked
out and resolved. 'In the midst of winter', again, 'you can
feel the inventions of spring'. Durrell would eventually see
the earlier work, the *Quartet* and his final major work, *The
Avignon Quintet*, as representing three phases in his spiritual
development: the first as the agon, the struggle to be (re)born
as an artist; the second, most popular work as the pathos,
the suffering and the uniting of the artist with his calling,
and the defeat of death; and the third as the 'anagnorisis', the
recognition. [7]

7. Ian MacNiven, *Lawrence Durrell: A Biography*, London: Faber and Faber,
1998, p. 662.

III: Platonic Modernism: A Rum Tallying of Subject and Object

> And, indeed, the symbols themselves seem almost
> to be used in a way similar to the mathematician; as
> when a set of letters may stand for any numbers of a
> certain sort, and you are not curious to know which
> numbers are meant because you are only interested
> in the relations between them. [8]

One of the more recent pieces of myth that lies as
backdrop to Durrell's fictional city is Cavafy's Alexandria. The
opening passages of Justine refer obliquely to Cavafy's 'The
City' (quoted in the appendix of *Justine*) by suggesting in
passage after passage the determination produced by the spirit
of place on its 'exemplars.' Darley writes, for instance, of the
'iron chains of memory', how the city has used him and all the
other characters as its 'flora,' and stresses how he has 'escaped'
onto his Greek island. Indeed, at one point he talks of this
'escape' as a 'remission'. Not only is space then a determinant
of time, but the body itself seems to be given centre stage. In
fact it is really the boundless flow of desire itself that inspirits
the dynamic maeutic of discovery in the novel's epiphanic
movement, and satiation of desire that results in the alternate
passages of conclusion and still reflection. Like the rhythm of
the ocean itself, there is a checkered movement, continuous
between life and death.

One of these pieces of reflection and conclusion reached
early on in Justine suggests that reality is that of the
imagination and that only the artist can give us access to
reality, giving meaning to the pattern as (s)he does. One
revealing pattern which rises almost to a mathematical purity

8. William Empson, *Seven Types of Ambiguity*, London: Penguin Books, 1995,
p. 145.

is that of 'Justine' herself. Directly after we read this short reflection about the artist and reality, we learn that the name of the child on the island with Darley is Justine. Justine the elder was Darley's most central and most fateful love, if not his truest, in the *Quartet*. But the child Justine is Nessim and Melissa's baby. Melissa was Darley's partner and Nessim and Justine are married. An asymmetrical symmetry arises. There is something almost algebraic about the pattern of these relationships; that is, there is something ratiocinative in the vagaries of desire.

At one point, Arnauti, Justine's ex-lover, one of Darley's precursors, also a writer, tells us in his diary that he would like to 'contain' Justine in a book, quite literally. And Darley goes on to fulfill this wish. *Justine* and the whole *Quartet* are not only about the many faces of love, but turn out to be also the very lineaments of the lover's body itself. Darley praises Arnauti for recognizing Alexandria as being the 'City of the Soma'. But the city turns out to be also the body of one's lover. 'When one loves one of its inhabitants, a city becomes a world.' Indeed right at the end of Part II of Justine we find a fabulous metaphorical passage from Pursewarden (the major writer-character) comparing the insides, rhythms and dynamics of the body with the circulation and organism of the city itself. Suggesting ranging desire, as well as numerical identity and determination, the body is where subject and object coalesce, in a kind of dance.

As suggested above, there is a partial identification between Arnauti and Darley. This introduces another almost mathematical or objectivist element to the fiction. In the first chapter of *Ulysses* we learn that Stephen Dedalus has proven that Hamlet was Shakespeare's grandfather, proven it algebraically. And there is something of this algebraic and generational porousness in some of the relationships in the *Quartet*. We get this generational osmosis especially in the relations of the three authors in the novel, Arnauti, Darley and Pursewarden. Sometimes they coexist in time, sometimes they exist genealogically. The paradox is that of fiction or textuality itself. In the writing we have all three as characters in their own right, speaking to us. And yet, both Arnauti and Pursewarden exist chronologically before Darley, both having been earlier lovers of Justine. At one point Darley reading Arnauti's *Moeurs* feels the identification so great that he says he feels like one of its characters, only intensifying the generational primacy of Arnauti.

> Indeed so fascinating did I find his analysis of his subject, and so closely did our relationship echo the relationship he had enjoyed with Justine that at times I too felt like some paper character out of *Moeurs*.

But it is Darley who fathers them in turn, as we only have access to their voices through the prism of his writing. And finally, of course, we have Durrell himself, begetter of all these fictional writers. The author-character relationships both within and without the fiction act as a symbol for the ubiquity of fiction or textuality itself; fact and fiction, object and subject, merge through the very process of writing. The paradox can be best expressed by saying that these are not only written novels we are reading, objects in our hands, but that they are also novels being written *as we read them*. Nabokov produced the same metaphysical *mise-en-abyme* in his *The Real Life of Sebastian Knight*, by also making (the elliptical) writing itself one of the pivotal themes of his (elliptical) novel.

But the osmotic or porous qualities of the relationships in the *Quartet* are not limited to the writer-characters alone. At times it feels like all the characters flow into and out of each other, repeating and adapting each other's statements.

Like Lawrence, Durrell is essentially concerned with oneness, his link to the eastern metaphysics he wanted to conflate with western physics. This idea of a transcendental collectivity, giving the lie to the discrete ego and the individual self, sometimes crops up thematically, but is most apparent in the overall form of the novel. One of the great successes of *Justine* and the whole *Quartet* is how consistent the parallel between some of the themes and the form itself is. To give two thematic examples, we have Clea near the end of Part II talking about the rationing of love, how we each have our own special portion for life, one united portion that is just working itself out in relation to different people throughout our lives. [9]

At the heart of this idea is a collective rather than an individual pattern. And then if we look backwards a little bit, earlier Darley had visited the dying Cohen (Melissa's ex-lover) in hospital, primarily to compare his love for Melissa, as in a mirror, with Cohen's. Just like the idea that comes later of Justine committing adultery with Darley *for* Nessim, Darley, visiting Cohen for Melissa, in her stead, seems to be committing another more narcissistic form of adultery. What strikes one in these examples and throughout *Justine* and the *Quartet* is the way everyone is connected with everyone else, even in death, everyone leaving traces in each other's lives. These themes and happenings are symbolic, that is, a deeper version, of the very plotting in the novels, the espionage that everyone in the end seems to be involved in at some level.

In what is a very impressionistic biography of the great Victorian, Chesterton once wrote of Dickens that we shouldn't consider his literary output as a group of separate novels, but rather as the continuous outpouring of the essence

---

9. Indeed, this Oneness of Love is an ancient Idealist motif, to be found in Plato's *Symposium*.

of Dickensness itself. There is something of this authorial flood in the way Durrell's characters relate to their author. In this respect too Durrell resembles Lawrence quite closely. Not only is there the continuous checkered movement between life and death, as in, especially, Lawrence's *The Rainbow*, but we get the feeling that the very repetition or difference in repetition that is at work in and amongst the characters, is both authors' rabid denial of an outdated realism. It is the modernist and late modernist's emphasis on self-expression-and-discovery through his literary art. And this self-expression of Durrell's, we will now see, is more direct and immediate than that elicited at the last by Ford. Even if Durrell's prose is overtly baroque, it is Ford's use of narrator and yarning voice which renders the more illusionistic effect.

IV: A Reckoning: With, and Against, Ford's The Good Soldier

Undertaken in this evasive mood, confessional writing degenerates into anti-confession. The record of the inner life becomes an unintentional parody of inner life. [10]

Interviewing Durrell in 1959, Kenneth Young reveals that Durrell claimed never to have read Ford's pivotal work.[11] Unlike, say, Alan Judd, some of whose work is self-consciously an epigone of Ford, or, perhaps, Kazuo Ishiguro, Durrell's seeming ignorance of *The Good Soldier* is, if not

10. Christopher Lasch, *The Culture of Narcissism: American Life in an Age of Diminishing Expectations*, New York & London: W.W. Norton and Co., 1991, p. 20.

11. *Lawrence Durrell: Conversations*, ed. Earl G. Ingersoll, Madison, Teaneck: Farleigh Dickinson University Press, & London: Associated University Presses, 1998, p. 49.

suspect, open to question. Below I show some aspects, thematic and formal, in which Durrell is in continuity, uncanny at times, with Ford. I conclude, however, with some reflections regarding the signal difference between the two works, from the (broadly speaking) epistemological perspective, and irrespective of any biographical context. In effect, Dowell is just as much a relativist or subjectivist as Darley; however, it is his (implicit, as I see it) *attempt* at a more stable, objectivist garnering of value from his tale, that fails resolutely. And that failure is *exemplified* by the calculus of his take on love (the major motif of both works) – which, it will be seen, is eminently rum. So . . .

The sexualization of knowledge and language, the unreliability (the shiftiness) of character and/or of memory, are basic facets that unite both novels. Indeed, after in part alluding to these latter features of signifying perspective, but with specific relevance, I will end with the idea of transcendence, the different results in relation to 'recognition'. That latter closure is Durrell's and Darley's, potentially; and Ford's, but *not Dowell's*.

To begin, then, in line to a certain extent with my suggestions regarding Durrell's mathematicity (akin to mythologizing), Dowell, Ford's unreliable narrator, calls his and the main protagonists' relations a 'minuet', a dance of four, however rigid or waylaid. Striking, in this respect, is the epigraph to Durrell's *Justine*, already mentioned. Just above a short passage from De Sade, Freud, as we've seen, suggests that every erotic or psycho-sexual relationship is actually a relationship of four, rather than two – each person having both a feminine and masculine side. Thus, though it is thematized, and glaringly so, in Durrell, one only has to think of the paradoxical gendering in Ford's major work to see the (potential) seed of Durrell's elaboration.

A second (though selective, as ever) correspondence lies

in the simultaneously formal and substantive ideality, if you will, of the two works. As noted with Durrell, the theme of transcending the individual, bordered ego-self is mirrored to a certain extent in the time-shiftiness and the scenic method. These latter two techniques are of course the very underpinnings of Ford's architectonic. However, where it gets suggestive and interesting is to find a passage, like that alluded to in Durrell, in *The Good Soldier*: evoking the same ancient Idealist motif, regarding the Oneness of Love. Dowell is discussing the fleetingness of love affairs for men. And so:

> With each new woman that a man is attracted to there appears to come a broadening of the outlook, or, if you like, an acquiring of new territory. A turn of the eye-brow, a tone of the voice, a queer characteristic gesture—all these things, and it is these things that cause to arise the passion of love—all these things are like so many objects on the horizon of the landscape that tempt a man to walk beyond the horizon, to explore. He wants to get, as it were, behind those eye-brows with the peculiar turn, as if he desired to see the world with the eyes that they overshadow. He wants to hear that voice applying itself to every possible proposition, to every possible topic; he wants to see those characteristic gestures against every possible background. Of the question of the sex-instinct I know very little and I do not think that it counts for very much in a really great passion. It can be aroused by such nothings—by an untied shoelace, by a glance of the eye in passing—that I think it might be left out of the calculation. [. . . .] But the real fierceness of desire, the real heat of a passion long continued and withering up the soul of a man

> is the craving for identity with the woman that
> he loves. He desires to see with the same eyes, to
> touch with the same sense of touch, to hear with
> the same ears, to lose his identity, to be enveloped,
> to be supported. For, whatever may be said of the
> relation of the sexes, there is no man who loves a
> woman that does not desire to come to her for the
> renewal of his courage, for the cutting asunder of
> his difficulties. And that will be the mainspring of
> his desire for her. We are all so afraid, we are all so
> alone, we all so need from the outside the assurance
> of our own worthiness to exist. [12]

The correspondence of motif (and perhaps its tallying with
technique) is quite clear here. However, this correspondence
leads me, via an interlude of Lacanian-inspired analysis, to the
contrast between the effects and the style of mind implicit
in and emergent from the two novels. What is so fascinating
about the above passage is that it is rife with self-contradiction,
symbolically and generically speaking. The first sentence
outlines what Lacan would call masculine structure, which
is capable only of 'phallic *jouissance*': the acquiring of 'new
territory' is equivalent of treating the other as 'object a', that
is to say as a partial object, to be used, to have sex with (just
what Dowell does not intend at this stage of the passage). It is
'phallic *jouissance*' – the phallus, for Lacan, being the signifier
of signification as such, thus indicative of the incompleteness
and elusiveness of satisfaction.[13] The next sentence, however,
clearly describes feminine structure, in so far as Lacan states

12. Ford, *The Good Soldier*, ed. Max Saunders, Oxford: Oxford University Press,
2012, pp. 92-3.

13. See Jacques Lacan, 'The Signification of the Phallus', in *Écrits*, trans. Bruce
Fink, New York and London: W.W. Norton, 2006, pp. 575-84.

that it is usually such singularities that attract feminine structure. And walking 'beyond the horizon' is suggestive of the ineffability, the inarticulacy Lacan reads as feminine structure's capacity for 'Other *jouissance*', which is not positive and existent, like 'phallic *jouissance*', and thus doomed to never-ending slippage and thirst, the physical act of sex in short, but 'exsists' for Lacan.[14] In another context he describes this modality as 'neither being nor nonbeing, but the unrealized'.[15] It is associated by Lacan, as against physical sex, with the concept of 'making love'. Hence perhaps the rather bizarre sentences (being suggested about men) about wanting to be at one with the other. And then Dowell seems to contradict himself by using the singularities, the same quiddities, as leading also to what he terms 'the sex-instinct', meaning the physical act. Finally, he returns to feminine structure by speaking of the desire to 'lose one's identity', to be 'enveloped'. Finishing with that typically Fordian cadence, a dying fall.

Due to what I have construed as the rampant self-contradictions of this passage, at least with the aid of Lacanian insight, Dowell remains evidently guilty of defensiveness, ultimately, the imaginary with its 'identificatory processes'

14. For a detailed rendering of Lacan's views on what he called 'sexuation', 'phallic *jouissance*' and 'other *jouissance*' and the impossibility of a sexual relationship, which is analogous to the impossibility of closure of signification, rendered: 'copula(tion)', see Bruce Fink, *Lacan to the Letter: Reading Écrits Closely*, Minneapolis and London: University of Minnesota Press, 2004. 141-66. The term 'exsists,' as distinct from 'exists' is there to highlight the concept's negativity; which is to say, like the larynx to the (positive or phallic) voice: the absence whose only positivity is as blank ground of the existent or that which is susceptible to indefinite slippage and association.

15. Jacques Lacan, *The Seminar of Jacques Lacan: Book XI: The Four Fundamental Concepts of Psychoanalysis*, trans. Alan Sheridan, New York and London: W.W. Norton, 1998, p. 30.

being a mask over the symbolic as over the real, which may be accessed and activated by the former. The sense of his narcissistic (and abject) identification is the product, not of the sentences referring to 'Other *jouissance*', but rather of his split intentions, *which therefore are none*. And intentionality is the index of agency, which is to say, a hale subjectivity: the possibility as it were of integral action, as opposed to (an unknowing or self-occluded) reaction.

I would like to suggest that there is a basic contrast in the epistemological grounds of the two works, which is shown up especially well by the difference between the two novelists' use of this (just-cited) motif. There is a sense, much-noted, that Dowell ends his 'saddest story' in inchoate meaninglessness, effecting a distinct lack of closure. He has none of T. S. Eliot's 'historic sense' or Durrell's 'historic consciousness',[16] but rather is a 'hollow man' in direct continuity with his 'horror.' Perhaps the distinct lack of election, or discretion between past and present, character and narrator, is the source of his novel-wide pan-ic. In fact, I want to suggest that Dowell ends up being sightless, unlike Ford, by aiming for a static, premodernist, or strictly referential truth – when we know how dialectical truth to reality is, both in general and in Ford's various discussions of 'superimposition', 'vibration', 'haze', 'homo duplex' and so on. In a way, Dowell's (epistemic) gentility is being mocked by Ford; very similar in effect to the latter's critique of Thackeray, as exemplar of an outdated Victorian didacticism and moralism. [17]

16. The idea of a 'historic sense' is also central to Ford's critical and creative itinerary. 'In the domain of History there is no such thing as Time.' See Ford, 'Creative History and the Historic Sense,' in *Critical Essays*, ed. Max Saunders and Richard Stang, New York: New York University Press, pp. 12-13.

17. See Ford Madox Ford, 'On Impressionism' in *Critical Writings of Ford Madox Ford*, ed. Frank McShane, Lincoln: University of Nebraska, 1964; see also

However, Durrell's character seems to be more at one with the manipulations of the artist himself. Perhaps because, unlike Dowell, Darley realises (and realises that he 'realises') that there is a vital distinction between cognitive knowing and that more visceral kind of knowing that is 'realisation'. In the first of the five novels that would make up Durrell's *Avignon Quintet, Monsieur*, we find the following distinction

> "But how to realise?" It was Piers' sad voice now that interrogated the sea-hushed silence and Akkad sighed, though he remained smiling still. He said: "A rather cruel paradox centres about the two notions which we express by the words 'knowing' and 'realising'. You can know something and yet not realise it, not having lived it, as we say, for in our inarticulate way we are aware of the distinction. Realisation is a real sigil conferred upon an experience…[18]

Indeed, in *Clea*, the final instalment of Durrell's *Quartet*, Clea says, '"Yes, but it *hurts* to realise!"' And it is that which I believe distinguishes the two works, in the purview and brief of this chapter. Dowell, simply put, whether an innocent or a wily character, won't let himself be hurt. Mourning, like love, is a process, essentially healthy, which involves recognizing the objectivity of the other, either elsewhere or within oneself, and both/either temporally or spatially. Dowell is far more blind, and blinded, than Darley. Even if Darley, now alone on his island, has lost in passion, both his display of control

Ford Madox Ford, *The English Novel; From the Earliest Days to the Death of Joseph Conrad*, Manchester: Carcanet, 1999, pp. 64-105.

18. Lawrence Durrell, *The Avignon Quintet*, London: Faber and Faber, 2004, p. 141.

over the contents of memory, however elliptical, and the bare
objective datum of the child on the island with him, render
him more humanely fertile than Dowell's aimless echolalia, his
babble, his 'many tongues'. The textual dispersal follows as a
direct consequence (we realise by the end) of a poignantly-
rendered 'authorial' dispersal. Indeed, Dowell's quagmire is
aptly (if serendipitously) voiced by Darley, empathizing, but
sadly, with a type of pathetic failure – a victim of experience
rather than its proprietor – the now-dying Cohen (Melissa's
ex-lover).

> It was as if now that the flesh was dying the whole
> funds of his inner life, so long dammed up behind
> the falsities of a life wrongly lived, burst through
> the dykes and flooded the foreground of his
> consciousness. (AQ 92)

Another novelist who made use of the Idealist motif of the
thoroughgoing Oneness of Love was Graham Greene, in his
The End of The Affair (1951). He was surely influenced by
Ford. After all, he edited some of Ford's work posthumously.
In his introduction to *The Good Soldier* he writes:

> A novelist is not a vegetable absorbing nourishment
> mechanically from soil and air: material is not easily
> or painlessly gained, and one cannot help
> wondering what agonies of frustration and error lay
> behind *The Saddest Story*.[19]

19. Greene, 'Introduction', *The Bodley Head Ford Madox Ford*, I, London: The
Bodley Head Ltd, 1962, pp. 7-12 (p. 12). Indeed, tallying with the central theme
of this essay, the epigraph to Greene's novel, from Leon Bloy, runs: 'Man has
places in his heart which do not yet exist, and into them enters suffering in order
that they may have existence.' I am indebted to Sara Haslam for alerting me to this
significant detail.

However, while Darley shares Durrell's efficient distance to a certain extent, Dowell is more like a peripatetic foil for the mastery of Ford.

As another illustration of this distinction regarding the two differently-deployed narrator-characters, witness the different modes or attitudes implicit in the following two passages of belated recognition, or if you will, 'delayed decoding'.[20]

Darley writes of his affair with Justine:

> When I discovered, for example (what I knew) that she had been repeatedly unfaithful to me, and at times when I had felt myself to be closest to her, I felt nothing sharp in outline: rather a sinking numbness such as one might feel on leaving a friend in hospital, to enter a lift and fall six floors in silence, standing beside a uniformed automaton whose breathing one could hear. (AQ 65)

On reaching a similar retrospective stance on his own affair, Dowell, by turns, evokes and evinces a far more desperate and evidently defensive approach to what should be a more thoroughbred perspective of recognition:

> For, if for me we were four people with the same tastes, with same desires, acting – or, no, not acting – sitting here and there unanimously, isn't that the truth? If for nine years I have possessed a goodly apple that is rotten at the core and discover its rottenness only in nine years and six months less

20. This central term in Conrad criticism was first introduced by Ian Watt in his *Conrad in the Nineteenth Century*, Berkeley and Los Angeles: University of California Press, 1981.

> four days, isn't it true to say that for nine years I
> possessed a goodly apple? (GS13)

Or, as a potential forbear to the last-cited passage from Durrell,
note how Dowell reacts to Florence (his cuckolding wife's)
death. The sentiment is similar. But to have to decide between
a biographical borrowing and a merely objective coalescing
of insight in relation to human loss is perhaps a too exigent
desideratum.

> And I thought nothing; absolutely nothing. I had
> no ideas; I had no strength. I felt no sorrow, no
> desire for action, no inclination to go upstairs and
> fall upon the body of my wife. I just saw the pink
> effulgence, the cane tables, the palms, the globular
> matchholders, the indented ashtrays. (GS 88)

That tangent duly noted, and for all the other circumstantial
(or not) tallying here and there – Dowell remains on the
whole a very different type (and expressive tool) from Darley.
Similar vehicles serve very different tenors.

Thus, relating their respective rationales (or indeed
rationalizations) for narrating their yarns of loss, Darley, again,
is the bolder in rhetoric, Dowell giving off the sense of a more
feeble special pleading. Darley writes, early on: 'I simply make
these notes to record a block of my life which has fallen into
the sea.' There's some striding *hilaritas*, for all the mood of
elegy. Dowell writes:

> You may well ask why I write. And yet my reasons
> are quite many. For is it not unusual in human
> beings who have witnessed the sack of a city or
> the falling to pieces of a people to desire to set
> down what they have witnessed for the benefit of

> unknown heirs or of generations infinitely remote;
> or, if you please, just to get the sight out of their
> heads. (*GS* 12)

The sack of a 'city' is a poignant image, which, of course, is at the operative heart of many of Durrell's allusions and metaphoric burdens. And yet, not so much in the substantive choice of simile, but in the mode in which such hyperbole come across, having been expressed, the 'voice' of Darley is more resolute, more honed, and far less abject than that of Dowell's. While the one is declarative, the other shapes the expression of his loss in a far more passive mood. Darley's sacked city, or indeed self, is evocative of realisation, hale recognition, rather than Dowell's self-occluded and waylaid wondering:

> It was as if the whole city had crashed about my
> ears; I walked about in it aimlessly as survivors must
> walk about the streets of their native city after an
> earthquake, amazed to find how much that had
> been familiar was changed. (*AQ* 77)

One way of putting the distinction (again, in terms of the categories of reflection), is to say that the 'objective' inchoateness of *The Good Soldier* is a result of the subjectively confused and thus pan-icking narrator-character writing, *by hearsay*, of 'The Saddest Story.' Whereas in the later novel(s), the subjective unreliability is due to the objective embracing of a modern(ist) relativity. In other words, because Durrell's narrator, Darley, embraces the illusionism of reality, he allows fate to happen to his characters. In a way, he owns the story in a manner on a par with his creator. After all, Darley is quite unlike the purportedly self-deprecating Dowell, being (within the text or without) *a self-professed writer*. Why else would he be overtly capable of talking of the 'historic consciousness' or 'reality prime' as the product of the imagination?

Darley, then, has (more) 'character' – as well as eliciting character(s) of course. Dowell, as Levenson has noted, represents, or, better, reflects, a kind of writerly, or 'authorial', *dis-integration*.[21]

Unlike Darley's performance on behalf of his near-twin and *impresario*, Dowell's is a product of a structure of feeling more suggestive of what Coleridge called (as opposed to 'imagination') 'fancy'. That Ford was using Dowell's *ethical* gentility as a foil for a storied criticism of moralistic herd-mentality goes without saying. In the end, however, it is this sham, ethical propriety *tied-in with* Dowell's genteel *epistemology* that, because equally outdated, renders him (quite unlike his creator) blind – in a world where we would rather be 'made to see.'[22]

21. See Michael Levenson, *Modernism and the Fate of Individuality: Character and Novelistic Form from Conrad to Woolf*, Cambridge: Cambridge University Press, 2004.

22. This celebrated phrase (adapted here), regarding the desideratum of making the reader 'see' – in both senses, viscerally or imaginatively and epistemologically – derives from Conrad's early literary manifesto, the "Preface" to his *The Nigger of the "Narcissus."* See Joseph Conrad, *The Nigger of the "Narcissus,"* ed. Robert Kimbrough, New York: W. W. Norton, 1979.

5

Humanism After Humanism: Henry Miller: Colossus Upon Colossus

Then Gaudier rose. It was suddenly like a silence intervened during a distressing and ceaseless noise … there, he seemed as if he stood amidst sunlight; as if indeed he floated in a ray of sunlight, like the dove in Early Italian pictures. In a life during which I have known thousands of people; during which I have grown tired and sick of "people" so that I prefer the society of cabbages, goats, and the flowers of the marrow plant; I have never otherwise known what it was to witness an appearance which so completely symbolized – aloofness. It was like the appearance of Apollo at a creditor's meeting. It was supernatural.
—Ford Madox Ford, *No Enemy: A Tale of Reconstruction*. 106

He talked about himself because he himself was the most interesting person he knew. I liked that quality very much – I have a little of it myself….

He could galvanize the dead with his talk. It was a sort of devouring process: when he described a place he ate into it, like a goat attacking a carpet. If he described a person he ate him alive from head to toe. If it were an event he would devour every detail, like an army of white ants descending upon a forest. He was everywhere at once, in his talk. He attacked from above and below, from the front, rear and flanks….

Nobody can explain anything that is unique. One can describe, worship and adore. And that is all I can do with Katsimbalis' talk….
—Henry Miller, *The Colossus of Maroussi*, 28, 20, 32

The very art I practice also runs counter to the idea of a calm farewell to a thinned self. Whatever the writer's aesthetic – from subjective and

57

autobiographical to objective and author-concealing – the self must be
strengthened and defined in order to produce the work. So you could say
that by writing this sentence I am making it just a little harder for myself to
die.
  —Julian Barnes, *Nothing to Be Frightened of*, 88

When most people think of Henry Miller, they think of him
as either a writer of smut and pornography, or as an early
avatar of the sexual revolution in the sixties of the last century,
around which time his most iconic books, such as *Tropic of
Cancer* (1934), were released from their ban in the United
States and elsewhere. Indeed, well before I myself had read any
Miller, I distinctly remember (a great intellectual of eighteen!)
seeing footnote after footnote adverting to Miller in Deleuze
and Guattari's *Anti-Oedipus* – a book, at that unripe age, I
only partially grasped. But the Miller of the "gob of spit"
in the face of form and art, the bare-knuckled, rebel Miller,
is only a small, but operative part of the Miller I want to
discuss. I'm more interested here in the visionary Miller, that
Jeremiah, elegant or inelegant, most consummately revealed
(and revealing) in what I – following in his own train, if
his biographers are to be believed – consider his most
accomplished, moving, and truthful book, *The Colossus of
Maroussi* (1941).

   This latter was written after a rare holiday in Greece, just
before and on the cusp of the outbreak of the Second World
War. The main gambit of these cursory reflections though is
to see how far Miller is able to both express and represent a
kind of humanism in the wake of a dying humanism. Indeed,
one might say that there are two possible ways out of
Nietzsche (whom I see, tritely no doubt, as the most prone
historical icon of the death of a meta-narrative, humanism):
one being the abstract, ratiocinative prose of Beckett, where
the patterns and the recursions, the vertiginous 'technique' are
the keystone of an almost Judaic art; the other, the way of
empathy and concretion, being the highly expressive telltale

mosaics of Miller. This binary distinction, however heuristically useful here, is aptly argued for (without relation to these authors of course) in Wilhelm Worringer's *Abstraction and Empathy*. Worringer sees the first kind of art finding its etiology in pan-ic and anxiety occasioned by the world of time and space, the cosmos – such inquietude leading to the salve or tonic of pattern, as desperate filler; the second, empathic or representational art being a result of being at-one with the surrounding cosmos. It's serendipitous indeed, that regarding the latter, Worringer makes use of ancient Greek art: Miller's *Colossus* book being a work of art about the guilelessness, the open-handed, open-hearted lack of artifice belonging to the mytho-poetic Greece he encountered and the mytho-poetic Greeks he encountered, eponymously captured by Katsimbalis: a man and persona whose rhapsodic monologues mirror Miller's own virtuosity, as he himself notes in the book. Put otherwise, Miller isn't an (or the) "aloof" kind of artist – he is directly engaged and engaging, spilling from the wrists and the jugular. He is at-one with the world, having realized the world is one in essence. Or at least becomes and does so at the time of writing this fabulous book.

> Every individual thing that exists, whether made by God or man, whether fortuitous or planned, stands out like a nut in aureole of light, of time and of space. The shrub is the equal of the donkey; a wall is as valid as a belfry; a melon is as good as a man. Nothing is continued or perpetuated beyond its natural time; there is no iron will wreaking its hideous path of power. [1]

In a very recent (philosophical) study of Miller, *Henry Miller:*

---

1. Miller, *Maroussi, op. cit.,* 146.

The Inhuman Artist, Indrek Männiste has argued that a central part of what Miller espoused as the "inhuman," was his denial of enlightenment or progressivist notions of history and its linear determination upon the present; or, equally, the cowering of that present from some chronological future. Männiste distinguishes between what Miller saw as dying in his time, the "traditional present," and the a-historical or, better, ex-static, "full present," which was to take its place. This latter was elicited by, if not fully instantiated by, the "artist." (Indeed, this mutual immanence or reflexive loop between, or about, destruction and creation is at the heart of much of Nietzsche's thinking and writing.) While I find Männiste's close readings extremely helpful, I propose to show how there is a very strong case to be put forward, which incorporates Männiste's argument, but, if not going thus beyond it, gives it a very different inflection.

One way (exemplified in the *Maroussi* book) in which Miller is "in-human," is that in nearly all his mature work he represents himself as (or as reflecting for us) the worst-off in a so-called progressive modernity (pace Männiste) at which he is at odds. Abyssal poverty for him, reaching ground-zero in the bourgeois (common)sense of material life, is often the sine qua non of his humanism, or that type of humanism I am arguing for. For instance, here he is, echoing the violent rebelliousness of his more famous *Tropic* books, but in a far more controlled and soft-souled, soft-spoken manner:

> Shepherds are crazy folk. So am I. I am done with civilization and its spawn of cultured souls. I gave myself up when I entered the tomb. From now on I am a nomad, a spiritual nobody. [2]

2. *Ibid.*, 93.

I'd like now to link this evident motif in Miller, hallowing the worst-off, with a different part of the same nexus of ideas, namely his relation to narrative. For part of Männiste's discussion of Miller and the "inhuman" has to do with the rejection of narrative, or at least linear narrative.

Männiste argues that part of Miller's (implicit or not) bugbear was Hegelian teleology. And Hegel is the philosopher of (grand) narrative par excellence. However, to (re)invoke Ford – a modernist Männiste doesn't connect Miller with – stories are most compelling and truthful when the protagonist is lost or losing (*in* said grand narrative). In line with some of Männiste's Millerian notions, Ford writes in two places, criticizing modern industrial then technological civilization, as well as (like Miller) rendering the loser, *in extremis*, in that same modern game a spur to that truer (fuller) being which is story, or 'art'.

Science changes its aspect as every new investigator gains sufficient publicity to discredit his predecessors. The stuff of humanity is unchangeable. I do not expect the reader to agree with me in this pronouncement but it would be better for him if he did. The world would be a clearer place then. [3]

> Let your generous sympathies go with the loser – with Pompey as against Caesar; with Anthony as against Octavian; with Romulus Augustulus as against Odoacer; with the Albigenses as against the Catholics; with Charles as against Cromwell; with Napoleon as against the Holy Alliance; with Lee as against Grant; with the Second Empire as against the big battalions; with the South always as against the North – and even with Carpentier as against Dempsey. Always and forever.

3. Ford Madox Ford, *Return to Yesterday*, Manchester: Carcanet, 1999, 139.

For you may be sure that in almost every victory in this category the defeated cause fails because it stands for a higher civilization... [4]

What I want to suggest, after making this unwitting comparison, is that there is a way of connecting the (pace Männiste) discarded traditional present with the so-called full present, which *does not* do away with narrative, but rather takes the claim of narrative at its utmost word. In a sense, one must show allegiance, not to the biographical Hegel, but rather to *the form* of his insight. Not, thus, what both Miller and Ford reject as modernists, "the" univocal grand narrative of modernity, but rather the implicit truth of the latter: namely, that the normative notion of narrative is best served precisely by the polymorphous or infinite multiplying of narratives. In what is an extremely deft reading of Hegel, Ermanno Bencivenga writes towards the end of his *Hegel's Dialectical Logic*, that it is part of Hegel's legacy that we are (after the impact of modernism no doubt) able to:

> Think of the past, of history, as a repertory of diversity, in the specific sense of *projectual* diversity. We must see a lot going on there besides the official line: a multiplicity of false starts, of crushed hopes, of sidelined, forgotten dreams. And we must insist that, for all their being forgotten and sidelined and crushed, those projects are still there, and their presence *in the past* is an indictment of the official line – as much of a substantial incarnation of a normative stance on it as we can get but also, maybe as much of one as we need. We must feel

4. Ford Madox Ford, *Provence: From Minstrels to the Machine*, New York: The Ecco Press, 1979, 182-83.

the cutting corners of the little rocks to which those
(never realized) majestic boulders have been
reduced, and sense that they can still draw blood. [5]

Similarly out-Hegel-ing Hegel, Walter Benjamin's "Theses
on the Philosophy of History" illuminates the same modernist
insight, rigorously playing up the discarded counterfactual
in the infinite interstices of some supposed victor's "positive"
history. He would develop this liberating intellectual move in
his unfinished *Arcades Project,* (in particular, "Convolute N.")

Indeed, in an essay on "Fate and Character," Walter
Benjamin cites Nietzsche. He quotes Nietzsche proposing that
fate *is* character, and then concludes that Nietzsche's thought
means that therefore *there is no (more)* "fate." The idea of the
gods of yore, supposedly, was the principle of stuff *happening
to* one, out of and beyond the neurotic or fixated control of
one's intentionality. Hence in modernist novels, we witness
on the whole the disintegration of character. In vital contrast,
Miller holds fast to this (epic, hopeful) idea of letting the world
affect you. In this sense he is looping back over Nietzschean
shoulders. It is the sine qua non of his most celebrated insight,
that "acceptance" is the key to happiness: his seductive and
rhapsodic humanism – a potent but latent prayer owing just
as much to St. Augustine as Whitman – after the slow eking
away of humanism.

There are two aspects of Nietzsche's revolutionary
thought, at strident and opposed extremes to each other, when
developed in a fertile manner. While with one aspect of his
thinking he does away with (a humanistic) Ratio – whether
we want to call it a discursive, symbolic or transcendental
register – celebrating the (erotic) surface, and being in

5. Ermanno Bencivenga, *Hegel's Dialectical Logic*, Oxford: Oxford University
Press, 2000, 88. Bencivenga's emphases.

Sontag's terms "against interpretation" – with another he offers an implicit caveat and saving clause. By attacking (not so much arguing against) transcendence, reducing all to immanence – a philosopher's thought, say, no longer arrived at in an intelligible and objective way, but part of his temperament, universalizing the ad hominem – he also opened the way to what some might call pan-logism. The latter is in effect the idea that different (to use Kantian terms) "faculties" are no longer clinically bordered off from each other, the empirical from the transcendental say, but are dialecticized, and feed into each other osmotically, polymorphous and perverse. For instance, if it weren't for Nietzsche (and thus Freud) one modernist philosopher, Adorno, exemplary here, wouldn't have been able to have a section or vignette in his *Negative Dialectics* titled, "Idealism as Rage," in which what is in a strict sense an epistemic category is cashed out in (empirical) psycho-sensual clothes; or indeed, nearly every entry in his *Minima Moralia*.

It is this osmosis that typifies Miller's conceit of "Cancer" – the crab being able to move in any direction at once, rather than bound by binaries of forward and backward, or strictly left and right. (Not to mention the nominal parallel of the, metaphorical or not, use of astrological "constellations.") To invoke Ford again, witness this slaying of chronological or linear sensibility. He is discussing technical discoveries and insights shared with his sometime early modernist collaborator, Conrad:

> We agreed that the general effect of a novel must be the general effect that life makes on mankind. A novel must therefore not be a narration, a report. Life does not say to you: In 1914 my next-door neighbour, Mr. Slack, erected a greenhouse and painted it with the Cox's green aluminium paint. If

you think about the matter you will remember, in
various unordered pictures, how one day Mr. Slack
appeared in his garden and contemplated the wall
of his house. You will then try to remember the
year of that occurrence and you will fix it as August
1914, because having had the foresight to hear the
municipal stock of the City of Liege you were able
to afford a first-class season ticket for the first time
in your life. You will remember Mr. Slack – then
much thinner because it was before he found out
where to buy that cheap Burgundy of which he has
since drunk an inordinate quantity, though whisky
you think would be much better for him! Mr. Slack
again came into his garden, this time with a pale,
weaselly-faced fellow, who touched his cap from
time to time. Mr. Slack will point to his house wall
several times at different points, the weaselly fellow
touching his cap at each pointing. Some days after,
coming back from business, you will have observed
against Mr. Slack's wall …. At this point you will
remember that you were then the manager of the
fresh-fish branch of Messrs. Catlin and Clovis in
Fenchurch Street …. What a change since then!
Millicent had not yet put her hair up …. You will
remember how Millicent's hair looked, rather pale
and burnished in plaits. You will remember how it
now looks, henna'd; and you will see in one corner
of your mind's eye a little picture of Mr. Mills the
vicar talking – oh, very kindly – to Millicent after
she has come back from Brighton …. But perhaps
you had better not risk that. You remember some
of the things said by means of which Millicent
has made you cringe – and her expression! ….
Cox's Aluminium Paint! …. You remember the

half-empty tin that Mr. Slack showed you – he
had a most undignified cold – with the name in
a horseshoe over a blue circle that contained a red
lion asleep in front of a red-gold sun ....

And, if this is how the building of your
neighbour's greenhouse comes back to you, just
imagine how it will be with your love affairs that
are so much more complicated. [6]

Of another, though less central, colossus, George Seferiades,
Miller writes with admiration: "He had a way of looking
forwards and backwards, of making the object of his
contemplation revolve and show forth its multiple aspects."[7]

At first blush one might think of Foucault's "webs" of
infinite and radical asymmetry, the zero-sum world of
differential powers, in the first volume of his *History of
Sexuality* – another version of a polymorphous rejection of
enlightenment or progress or humanism. Indeed (to revert to
my opening), Foucault wrote an Introduction to that very
Deleuze and Guattari work. But it is my intention here,
however briefly, to elicit the way in which there remains a
humanistic hopefulness in Miller's vision, especially instanced
by this illuminating work of illuminations, *The Colossus of
Maroussi.*

In this work as elsewhere, Miller often thinks of man, at
his normative best, in his essence, in "angelic" terms. And from
Aquinas we know, or are piqued to be informed, that angels,
unlike men, are each and every one of them a species unto
themselves. Miller's vision, implicit throughout his work, is
equivalent to the "utopia" or the "messianic" regulative ideal

6. Ford Madox Ford, *Joseph Conrad: A Personal Remembrance*, New York: The
Ecco Press, 1989, 193-94.

7. Miller, *Maroussi, op. cit.,* 47.

often invoked by Adorno or his mentor, Benjamin: namely, a *society* of *absolute individuals* – a paradox and contradiction in terms for our finite minds. Furthermore, in this work, Miller forever intimates, as another topical motif, the central moral of Adorno and Horkheimer's *Dialectic of Enlightenment*. He signally links outward or civilizational repression (a witless and soulless technological expansion) with inward repression – of our sensual and dependent natures. He evinces the by turns Foucauldean dialectic of an instrumental reason targeted to free the subject, which (up-)ends up by subject-ifying him.

That said, for Miller the whole man is the man who becomes a god by realizing that the gods are beyond his (strictly speaking) ego-tistical control or, more tellingly, "organization." Those discarded dregs of society, as he often portrays himself, are thus icons and indices of the essence of humanity. Indeed, towards the end of this Greece book, he laments and concludes that it wasn't men who humanized the gods, but the gods who humanized men. In one sense, for all his vitriol against inhibitive religious organization, Miller is highly re-ligious: he believes that suffering, wound-ability, the privation incumbent on love, is a transcendental spur – quite unlike so-called "post-structuralists." Indeed, I have always felt it a potent paradox that such post-modern thinking holds in common with a pre-modern religious ethos the idea that man is not his own regulator pulling himself up from his own bootstraps. Whether we call it God, or "*nom de père*," both say that there was a world before us and there will be a world after us. And yet, Miller's soliciting of epiphany and "realization" in order to grow (transcend) as artist and (thus) as man is far less over-determinant (and emptying, or (quite literally) soul-destroying) than the "post-structuralist" rut. He may seem deterministic here, below, but his godly determinism is a source of liberation, manumission, not of the chains of a radically imperfect, zero-sum world. Transcendence: in a word, the "solution."

> At its best thought is but speculation, a pastime such as the machine enjoys when it sparks. God has thought everything out in advance. We have nothing to solve: it has all been solved for us. We have but to melt, to dissolve, to swim in the solution. We are soluble fish and the world is an aquarium.[8]

Another way of expressing this humanism or hopefulness, if *via negativa*, is to invoke perhaps one of Miller's most central writerly techniques, in this magnificent book as elsewhere: the litany. Umberto Eco writes in his (recent) *Confessions of a Young Novelist* that the centrality of lists, in medieval gothic as in his own work, is not only to list an empirical plethora, but also, and more significantly, to rhythmically indicate and point to the infinite or to infinitude. Which is another way of making the writerly soul – in essence, for Miller or his eponymous hero, a monologist – a-kin to a god. Each point of a web-like rambling monologue is the (mythic or timeless) center; or, to put it in Ford Madox Ford or Conrad's terms, "life does not narrate." The element of true, live *quidditas,* of rubble and contingency is registered in his tale-telling. It is forever more story than plot. We learn in Miller of a thousand ways in which, to paraphrase Forster on *Aspects of the Novel,* the "king married the queen," but very rarely of the totalizing motivation or rationalization that would render event and annal of event infertile and defunct, obsolete. He is what Benjamin would call a "storyteller." (The first aphorism

---

8. *Ibid.,* 162-3.

in Nietzsche's *The Gay Science* praises a life for life's sake, rather than one servile to a "because….")

What I'm trying to intimate is that when Nietzschean perspectivism is *embraced*, when the writer recognizes the inadequacy of language and understanding to the world, artifact of the hermeneutic circle or what Kermode called in a different setting, the "genesis of secrecy" – he approaches a new kind of transcendence: where the (un-honed) expressive echolalia, however noisome and unmanning, becomes sublimated into the life – something Miller hints at towards the end of his ecstatic experiences and ecstatic renderings of his (de-ontic) day of rest in Greece. If Miller means anything, he means that kind of "real assent" opposed to "notional assent" (Newman) which allies the suffering artist with (all) the wretched of the earth; all those: radically at the mercy of the gods.

> I give this record of my journey not as a contribution to human knowledge, because my knowledge is small and of little account, but as a contribution to human experience. Errors of one sort and another there undoubtedly are in this account but the truth is that something happened to me and *that* I have given as truthfully as I know how. [9]

And this: despite his very un-Sartrean and a-political anarchism. His politicization of civilizational failures is as I say more epic than quotidian. He admits to rarely reading newspapers: he talks of the contemporary civilizational failures from the perspective of millennia beyond. And so on….

Miller's life and art are different, parallel vessels towards

9. *Ibid.,* 237-8.

sublimating egotism, *but not by self-effacement*; rather by an electrically-charged self-expression that runs into silence at the last, when each atom or morsel of self is spent in (onto) the world, and the page. A deep-bellied kenosis, then. In Adorno's terms, he uses "the subject to critique the subject." However much he may have rejected purposiveness, his diatribe against such is very much purposive. And his aesthetics is one of salutary exhaustion, rather than scenic delicacy and tiptoeing precision. The latter is perhaps the more "artful"; but the former's artifacts only exist or go rendered into type *in order for* them to be transcended, like a ladder kicked away after the climb, like Zarathustra's mountain, Christ's Golgotha – from wherefore unto commending….

Perhaps the temporal (and narratological) paradox is named best by Nietzsche's slogan and/or injunction to: "become what you are."

Works Cited

Adorno, Theodor. W. *Minima Moralia.* Trans. E.F.N. Jephcott. London: Verso, 1999.

Adorno, Theodor. *Negative Dialectics.* Trans E .B. Ashton. London: Routledge, 2003.

Adorno, Theodor W., and Max Horkheimer. *The Dialectic of Enlightenment.*Trans. John Cumming. New York: Continuum, 1998.

Barnes, Julian. *Nothing to be Frightened of.* London: Jonathan Cape, 2008.

Bencivenga, E rmanno. *Hegel's Dialectical L ogic* Oxford: Oxford UP, 2000.

Benjamin, Walter. *The Arcades Project.* Trans. Howard Eiland & Kevin McLaughlin. E d. Rolf Tiedemann. Cambridge,: Belknap Press, 2002.

Benjamin, Walter. *Illuminations.* Trans. Harry Zohn. Ed. Hannah Arendt. London: Pimlico, 1999.

Benjamin, Walter. *One Way Street.* E d. Amit Chaudhuri. London: Penguin, 2009.

Deleuze, Gilles & Felix Guattari. *Anti-Oedipus: Capitalism and Schizophrenia.* Trans. Robert Hurley, Mark Seem, and Helen R. Lane. London: Continuum, 2004.

E co, Umberto. *Confessions of a Young Novelist.* Cambridge, Massachusetts & London, England: Harvard UP, 2011.

Ferguson, Robert. *Henry Miller: A Life.* London: Hutchison, 1991.

Ford, Madox Ford. *Joseph Conrad: A Personal Remembrance.* New York: Ecco Press, 1989.

Ford, Madox Ford. *Provence: From Minstrels to the Machine.* New York: Ecco Press, 1979.

Ford, Madox Ford. *Return to Yesterday.* Manchester: Carcanet, 1999.

Ford, Madox Ford. *No Enemy: A Tale of Reconstruction.*

Manchester: Carcanet, 2002.

Forster, E.M. *Aspects of the Novel*. London: Penguin, 2005.

Foucault, Michel, *Discipline and Punish,* trans. Alan Sheridan, London: Penguin Books, 1991.

Foucault, Michel. *History of Sexuality*. Vol. 1. Trans. Robert Hurley, London: Penguin, 1998.

Gilson, Etienne. *The Christian Philosophy of St. Thomas Aquinas*. Trans. L.K. Snook, Notre Dame: U of Notre Dame P, 2006.

Kermode, Frank. *The Genesis of Secrecy: On the Interpretation of Narrative*. Cambridge: Harvard UP, 1979.

Männiste, Indrek. *Henry Miller: The Inhuman Artist: A Philosophical Inquiry.* London: Bloomsbury, 2014.

Miller, Henry. *The Colossus of Maroussi*. New York: New Directions, 1958.

Miller, Henry. *Tropic of Cancer*. London: Harper Collins, 1993.

Newman, John Henry. *An Essay in Aid of a Grammar of Assent*. Ed. Ian Ker. Oxford: Oxford UP, 1988.

Nietzsche, Friedrich. *The Gay Science*. Trans. Walter Kaufmann, New York: Vintage Books, 1974.

Nietzsche, Friedrich. *The Genealogy of Morals.* Trans. Horace B. Samuel, Mineola, New York: Dover Publications, 2003.

Nietzsche, Friedrich. *Thus Spake Zarathustra.* Trans. R.J. Holingdale, London: Penguin Books, 1969.

Sontag, Susan. *Against Interpretation and Other Essays.* London: Penguin, 2009.

Worringer, Wilhelm. *Abstraction and Empathy: A Contribution to the Psychology of Style.* Trans. Michael Bullock, Chicago: Elephant Paperbacks, 1997.

6

G.K. Chesterton's London: Traversing Therapeutic Space

Christ is contingency....
There is a sense in which love's truth is proved by its end, by what it
becomes in us, and what we, by virtue of love, become.[1]

Romance is the structural core of all fiction: being directly descended from
folktale, it brings us closer than any other aspect of literature to the sense of
fiction, considered as a whole, as the epic of the creature man's vision of his
own life as a quest.[2]

The major aim of this paper is to show that G. K.
Chesterton's adolescent identity or life crisis provides the most
essential clue for a revealing reading direction throughout
his *oeuvre*. And secondly, to show that both Chesterton's
autobiographical experience, and his views, which grew out of
the former, can be seen to be expressed and worked-through
in his portrayals of London. Thus, though his two "London"
novels—indeed his two most well-known novels—*The
Napoleon of Notting Hill* and *The Man Who Was Thursday*,
provide the central purposes of this paper, I will be alluding
to much of his *oeuvre*, not necessarily all London-related. I
begin with a basic description of his mental crisis, as it comes

1. Christian. Wiman, *My Bright Abyss: Meditation of a Modern Believer* (Farrar,
Straus and Giroux: New York, 2013), pp. 16, 19.

2. Northrop Frye, *The Secular Scripture: A Study of the Structure of Romance*
(Harvard University Press: Cambridge [MA], 1976), p. 15.

down to us from Chesterton's own work and that of his biographers. This will lead me, progressively, into the meat of my thesis—regarding the pivotal importance for all Chesterton's views of his adolescent experience, *and* the (perhaps) *more contingent use* of "London" as a heuristic space to work-through both: biographical life experience, and incumbent biographical philosophic itinerary.

At the opening of the fourth chapter of his *Autobiography*, titled, "How to be a Lunatic," Chesterton talks of "the darkest and most difficult part" of his "task; the period of youth which is full of doubts and morbidities and temptations; and which, though in my case mainly subjective, has left in my mind for ever a certitude upon the objective solidity of sin."[3] He talks of sadistic fantasies, "the worst and wildest disproportions and distortions of more normal passion." And how, although he had never committed even the "mildest crime," how "quickly" he "could imagine the maddest" one.[4] One further quotation from this chapter will enable us to enter into the beginnings of making sense of this experience, and its relation to his intellectual life. He writes, "At a very early age I had thought my way back to thought itself. It is a very dreadful thing to do; for it may lead to thinking that there is nothing but thought." And significant, as we will see, not only to the operative problem of solipsism and its cognates, but for these in relation to the two adventure stories already mentioned, he continues, "At this time I did not clearly distinguish between dreaming and waking." [5]

The period in question was Chesterton's time at the Slade School of art. Dudley Barker, the one biographer who uses the archived personal notebooks of Chesterton the most, talks of

3. G. K. Chesterton, *Autobiography* (Fisher Press: Sevenoaks [UK], 2000), p. 77.

4. G. K. Chesterton, *Autobiography* (Fisher Press: Sevenoaks [UK], 2000), p. 89.

5. G. K. Chesterton, *Autobiography* (Fisher Press: Sevenoaks [UK], 2000), p. 88.

this period of two to three years, detailing Chesterton's evident sense of overwhelming guilt due to his fantasies of sexual violence.[6] Chesterton's notebooks of the time are replete with images of devils, witches and demons.[7] Unlike Barker (the one biographer to my knowledge who suggests potential latent homosexuality), Coren discounts such a view, seeing the crisis in more common-sense terms as a result of the sudden loss of a schoolboy structure and atmosphere, and the sudden loss of access to friends.[8] Dale, another biographer, would seem to be in agreement (implicitly) with the latter, when she argues that Chesterton's Catholic views were the result of slow, progressive use of his intelligence, rather than a reaction to adolescent trauma[9] I, myself, take the view, unlike the latter two biographers, that Chesterton's crisis is the most telling factor in understanding the major tenor of his work, London-related or not.

Before entering onto Chesterton's views of lunacy or madness, it is apposite to say, in deepening the view just mentioned, that the idea of his having thought himself back to "thought itself," is of the utmost significance in understanding his views, his style, his method, and his stories or fables. What I want to suggest is that Chesterton's rationalism was both source of his crisis, and in a different mode source of all his success and brilliance. Puritanical repression of his bodily nature might be seen, in retrospect, as the source of his breakdown; and yet, his signal ability, in fiction and non-

6. Dudley Barker, G. K. *Chesterton: A Biography* (Constable: London, 1973), pp. 48-51.

7. Dudley Barker, G. K. *Chesterton: A Biography* (Constable: London, 1973), p. 56.

8. Michael Coren, *Gilbert: The Man Who Was G. K. Chesterton* (Regent College Publishing: Vancouver, 2001), pp. 42-44.

9. Alzina Stone Dale, *The Outline of Sanity: A Biography of G. K. Chesterton* (William B. Eerdmans:: Grand Rapids [MI], 1982), pp. 34-35.

fiction, and throughout his *oeuvre*, was to find revealing patterns in which to couch empirical data—be it a biographical fact in the life of Dickens or, say, his own life-story at the beginning of *Orthodoxy*, in which he explains his odyssey and homecoming to Christian orthodoxy in terms of a whimsical, but telltale, analogy: of a man travelling the world only to find that after all his endeavours, the farthest reach is to land at home.

It is of the essence to Chesterton's life and thought that he happened all his life to "have loved edges; and the boundary line that brings one thing sharply against another." All his life, he "loved frames and limits" and maintained, "that the largest wilderness looks larger seen through a window."[10] Part of what Marshall McLuhan called Chesterton's "metaphysical intuition of being,"[11] or what Hilaire Belloc (longtime friend and fellow-traveller) distinguished as "the heart of his style," "lucidity," "produced by a complete rejection of ambiguity," and a "complete exactitude of definition,"[12] entailed his apperception of "intrinsic" and "ultimate things," so that grasping one minor feature of his thinking, one might derive the whole.[13] Or, take Chesterton himself, who writes, in his biography of Saint Francis, that Francis "sees more of the things themselves when he sees more of their origin; for their origin is a part of them and indeed the most important part of them."[14] That he would repeat a cognate idea, to give only one instance, in another biography, of William Blake, suggests

10. G. K. Chesterton, *Autobiography* (Fisher Press: Sevenoaks [UK], 2000), p. 33.

11. Hugh Kenner, *Paradox in Chesterton* (Sheed & Ward: London, 1948), pp. xi-xii.

12. Hilaire Belloc, *On the Place Of Gilbert Chesterton in English Letters* (Sheed and Ward: London, 1940), p. 34.

13. Hugh Kenner, *Paradox in Chesterton* (Sheed & Ward: London, 1948), p. 8.

14. G. K. Chesterton, *St Francis of Assisi* (House of Stratus: London, 2001), p. 39.

how autobiographical these insights into others really were. He writes:

> The brilliant man seems more lumbering and elaborate than anyone else, because he has something to say about everything. The very quickness of his mind makes the slowness of his narrative. …Every fact or phrase that occurs in the immediate question carries back his mind to the ages and the initial power. Because he is original he is always going back to origins.[15]

This basic hyper-ratiocinative feature is at the root of all his thinking, and was not only the vehicle for late adolescent disease, but also the route towards roots and integration or individuation. Indeed, the solution to his crisis, as lived, came through reading Whitman, and his unrivalled yea-saying and cosmic optimism;[16] through realising, that is, the basic fact of *metaphysics*: that anything was better than nothing[17]

As Quentin Lauer has argued, Chesterton was "intuitively rational,"[18] which is why at the beginning of his spiritual autobiography Chesterton prefaces the ideas of the book as the development of certain "mental pictures."[19]

In the second chapter of this book, titled, "The Maniac," Chesterton, no doubt drawing on the experience already

15. G. K. Chesterton, *William Blake* (Cosmo: New York, 2005), pp. 126-129.

16. Alzina Stone Dale, *The Outline of Sanity: A Biography of G. K. Chesterton* (William B. Eerdmans: Grand Rapids [MI], 1982), p. 35; M. Coren, *Gilbert: The Man Who Was G. K. Chesterton* (Regent College Publishing: Vancouver, 2001), p. 56.

17. G. K. Chesterton, *Autobiography* (Fisher Press: Sevenoaks [UK], 2000), p. 90.

18. Quentin Lauer, *G. K. Chesterton: Philosopher without Portfolio* (Fordham University Press: New York, 1991), p. 10.

19. G. K. Chesterton, *Orthodoxy* (Dover Publications: New York, 2004), p. 1.

described, discusses in an idiosyncratic manner, the source of lunacy, morbidity, or what the Edwardians called "monomania." In particular he makes the point that insanity is not due to too much imagination; rather it is the product of "reason." [20] Mirroring both what we have seen to be his malady and his boon, he writes, opposing two of his key words, "poet" and "logician":

> To accept everything is an exercise, to understand everything is a strain. The poet only desires exaltation and expansion, a world to stretch himself in. The poet only asks to get his head in the heavens. It is the logician who seeks to get the heavens in his head. And it is his head that splits. [21]

The madman for Chesterton is that person, not bereft of reason, but possessing reason, and reason alone. [22]

In adolescence he had thought himself back to thought itself—so here in this chapter he talks about the dichotomous thinking of the maniac, and his solipsism, which entails a mind not being able to think itself out of itself. [23] And significantly, the next chapter is titled, "The Suicide of Thought." Chesterton's various deployments of these ideas to do with mania, lunacy, and (as it happens) their *locus classicus* in adolescent experience are apparent elsewhere in his *oeuvre*, peppering his insights over many fields of enquiry and exposition. In his first commissioned biography, *Robert Browning*, he immediately instantiates a point to be developed later, namely that, as Lauer put it, his efforts at understanding

20. G. K. Chesterton, *Orthodoxy* (Dover Publications: New York, 2004), p. 9.

21. G. K. Chesterton, *Orthodoxy* (Dover Publications: New York, 2004), p. 10.

22. G. K. Chesterton, *Orthodoxy* (Dover Publications: New York, 2004), p. 11.

23. G. K. Chesterton, *Orthodoxy* (Dover Publications: New York, 2004), pp. 11-15.

the other were efforts of "self-understanding."[24] He writes
that, contra some conventional views of Browning's
intellectuality, Browning was primarily a "poet" and not what
"the French call an intellectual."[25] Discussing *Pauline*,
Chesterton extemporises:

> It is the utterance of that bitter and heartrending
> period of youth which comes before we realise the
> one grand and logical basis of all optimism—the
> doctrine of original sin. The boy at this stage being
> an ignorant and human idealist, regards all his faults
> as frightful secret malformations, and it is only later
> that he becomes conscious of that large and
> beautiful and benignant explanation that the heart
> of man is deceitful above all things and desperately
> wicked[26]

It was Chesterton's view that Christianity de-linked the crime
from the criminal. In another of his biographies, *Charles
Dickens*, we find by way of yet another example, the
following:

> For completeness and comfort are almost the
> definitions of insanity. The lunatic is a man who
> lives in a small world but thinks it is a large one: he
> is a man who lives in a tenth of the truth, and thinks
> it is the whole. The madman cannot conceive any
> cosmos outside a certain tale or conspiracy or
> vision....Hence the more clearly we see the world

24. Quentin Lauer, *G. K. Chesterton: Philosopher without Portfolio* (Fordham
University Press: New York, 1991), p. 8.

25. G. K. Chesterton, Robert Browning (House of Stratus: London, 2001),
pp. 14-15,23.

26. G. K. Chesterton, *Robert Browning* (House of Stratus: London, 2001), p. 12.

divided…the more certain we may be that we are slowly and quietly going mad. The more plain and satisfying our state appears, the more we may know that we are living in an unreal world. For the real world is not satisfying….For there is but an inch of difference between the cushioned chamber and the padded cell.[27]

In the same way, when writing, say, of Blake, Chesterton diagnoses madness in his subject, if any there were, in the contraction of his mind. Blake is not mad for having visions, or taking supernatural reality as a given: he is only mad when he is unable to accept, Job-like, the inevitable "mess" which needs must be context for a reasoning mind; when, as Chesterton articulates it, Blake acted like a "logician."[28]

And yet Chesterton's views on madness and reason can be illuminated from a wider perspective. Indeed, the sorts of ideas and arguments made use of below, not only elaborate Chesterton's insight, but elaborate them in a way which hooks immediately into the storied element of Chesterton's vision.

When Chesterton writes, approvingly, of Browning, that he was clever enough to understand his poetry, but *not* clever enough to understand himself or his own character, [29] we are alerted, in negative, to Chesterton's critique of the "suicide of thought," or, otherwise put, self-consciousness. Equally, unlike some mad adolescent "idealist," Browning never loved "humanity," but rather (particular) "men."[30] For Chesterton, "Rationalism can live upon air and signs and numbers. But

27. G. K. Chesterton, *Charles Dickens* (House of Stratus: London, 2001), p. 66.
28. G. K. Chesterton, *William Blake* (Cosmo: New York, 2005), p. 79-84.
29. G. K. Chesterton, *Robert Browning* (House of Stratus: London, 2001), p.1.
30. G. K. Chesterton, *Robert Browning* (House of Stratus: London, 2001), p. 109.

sentiment must have reality; emotion demands real fields, the real widows' homes, the real corpse, and the real woman."[31]

Thus, another key word for Chesterton, almost a synonym for him for (his special take on) lunacy, is "Puritanism." The problem with Puritanism was that it was too extreme as a theory, unbalanced and disproportionate, making no distinction between worst and moderately bad. [32]

The other point, implicit in Chesterton's critique of Puritanism, is that, in its attempt to purge human worship of all ritual and sensuality, leading to a purely spiritual relationship with God, it mimics the modern "Titanist" (Michael Mason's term)[33] attempt at complete domination over matter. In his *George Bernard Shaw* Chesterton writes:

> I should roughly define the first spirit in Puritanism thus. It was a refusal to contemplate God or goodness with anything lighter or milder than the most fierce concentration of the intellect. A Puritan meant originally a man whose mind had no holidays. To use his own favourite phrase, he would let no living thing come between him and his God; an attitude which involved eternal torture for him and cruel contempt for all living things. It was better to worship in a barn than in a cathedral for the specific and specified reason that the cathedral was beautiful. Physical beauty was a false and sensual symbol coming in between the intellect and the object of its intellectual worship. The human brain ought to be at every instant a consuming fire

31. G. K. Chesterton, *Robert Browning* (House of Stratus: London, 2001), p. 28.

32. G. K. Chesterton, *Robert Louis Stevenson* (House of Stratus: London, 2000), p. 21. 1959).

33. Michael Mason, *The Centre Of Hilarity: A Play Upon Ideas About Laughter and the Absurd* (Sheed & Ward: London, 1948.)

which burns through all conventional images until
they were as transparent as glass.[34]

He goes on to compare the psychological attitudes of
Catholicism and Puritanism. He says that due to this extreme
detachment of Puritanism, it cannot allow for any
inconsistency; it is purely calculative and consistent—a point
meant to illuminate an aspect of Shaw's intellect. Alternatively,
the Catholic can accept inconsistency.[35] This is in fact
Chesterton's primary objection to Shaw. A theme runs
throughout his critical biography of Shaw, which criticises
Shaw for looking at the inner and central experience of human
beings, their emotional and imaginative engagement with the
world, their motivations, from "the outside." As an
"unromantic writer…[Shaw] cannot imagine the motives of
human life from the inside." And yet for Chesterton, "the
mental attitude of romance…is the only key to real human
conduct":[36]

> The world has kept sentimentalities simply because
> they are the most practical things in the world.
> They alone make men do things. The world does
> not encourage a quite rational lover, simply because
> a perfectly rational lover would never get married.
> The world does not encourage a perfectly rational
> army, because a perfectly rational army would run
> away.[37]

34. G. K. Chesterton, *George Bernard Shaw* (House of Stratus: London, 2000),
p.11.

35. G. K. Chesterton, *George Bernard Shaw* (House of Stratus: London, 2000),
pp. 12-13.

36. G. K. Chesterton, *George Bernard Shaw* (House of Stratus: London, 2000),
pp. 45, 78.

The world here stands for human nature. Thus it is the lyrical, imaginative things that are most natural: the things on the inside that make man such a strange creature from the perspective of the naturalist observing him from the outside. Even "The logician…must have sentiment and romance in his existence; in every man's life, indeed, which can be called a life at all, sentiment is the most living thing." [38]The inside, motive, is the most living thing. All this as a critique of what Chesterton saw as Shaw's puritanical and unhealthy form of detachment—what, later, T.S. Eliot would call in his essay on the Metaphysical poets, "the dissociation of sensibility."[39]

Catholic Christianity, the centre for Chesterton, was implicitly dramatic and wild and thrilling, not only because it happened to capture the singular and strange nature of reality itself, instead of diluting that reality in flaccid abstractions, but because it forced man into a position where his thinking and his acting were always a question of life and death.

> All Christianity concentrates on the man at the crossroads. The vast and shallow philosophies, the huge syntheses of humbug, all talk about ages and evolution and ultimate developments. The true philosophy is concerned with the instant. Will a man take this road or that? That is the only thing to think about, if you enjoy thinking. The aeons are easy enough to think about, anyone can think about them. The instant is really awful: and it is because our religion has intensely felt the instant that it has in literature dealt with much battle and in

37. G. K. Chesterton, *George Bernard Shaw* (House of Stratus: London, 2000), p. 43.

38. G. K. Chesterton, *George Bernard Shaw* (House of Stratus: London, 2000), p. 33.

39. T.S. Eliot, *Selected Essays* (Faber & Faber: London, 1999), p. 288.

> theology dealt much with hell. It is full of danger,
> like a boy's book: it is an immortal crisis.[40]

This sense of imminent crisis (rupture in and as the heart of reality, the heart of matter) is implicit, for Chesterton, once one recognises responsibility to absolute moral Goodness (God), and realises the awfulness of free will and choice: "Decision is the whole business here; a door must be shut forever. Every remedy is a desperate remedy."[41]

Some connections now with more contemporary thinkers may be a way to hook the formal problem at issue, the self-defeating nature of hyper-rationality, with the various other kinds of "monomaniac" abstractions which are thematised and storied in Chesterton's two London novels.Bernard Williams's notion of the importance and significance of "moral luck," as against Enlightenment ethical theories which try to necessitate value in a taut and univocal manner, is useful here.[42]

The crux for Williams's critique, to be brief, is in a manner posed against the kind of contracted rationality which Chesterton complains of. In a sense, highly relevant to my discussion of novels, Williams's highlighting the priority of first order, "thick" concepts, as against formalist "thin" concepts captures Chesterton's "communitarianism" (to use an anachronistic term). Examples of thick concepts might be, say, "courageous," or "honest." "Thin" concepts are those such as "right." What differentiates the two, and specifies Williams's Chesterton-like critique of contracted reason, is the fact that the first kind of concept makes sense only in a lived context, a shared "moral space," to use a term of Charles Taylor's.[43]

---

40. G. K. Chesterton, *Orthodoxy* (Dover Publications: New York, 2004), p. 129.

41. G. K. Chesterton, *Orthodoxy* (Dover Publications: New York, 2004), p. 14.

42. Bernard Williams, *Moral Luck: Philosophical Papers 1973-1980* (Cambridge University Press: Cambridge, 1999), pp. 1-39.

Thin concepts, by contrast, are products of abstraction, and are less primitive, essentially derivative. In one sense the Catholic insistence that man is a wedding of spirit and matter is indicative of a thick, or non-reductive, conception of human being. Whereas the whittling of such concepts into more abstract residues is, like a form of monomania, a result of a puritanical infinite regress, where the subject has nothing "objective" against which to gauge his individuation, his growth or development as a human being. Indeed, one of Williams's best and most well-known books is titled *Ethics and the Limits of Philosophy*; the "limits" being of the essence.[44]

Another philosopher of ethics also provides insight to the problem under discussion, speaking as we are now, globally. In her *The Sources of Normativity*, picking out the rub of self-consciousness, Christine Korsgaard writes of the origin of reflexivity in a way which is illuminating of Chesterton's own account, "The morally good human being comes to feel guilty about *having* natural impulses and *being* an animal. Eventually this leads to extreme self-hatred, which in turn produces a revolt against the world of nature, and a hatred of life itself, and finally ends in complete nihilistic collapse,"[45] which indeed happened to Chesterton. So perhaps the answer, as with Chesterton, is that: "Just as reflective distance gave us control over our animal nature, so maybe reflective distance from our self-control could give us control over it."[46]

Or, as Adam Phillips puts it in a recent work, perhaps

43. Charles Taylor, Sources Of The Self (Harvard University Press: Cambridge [MA], 1989).

44. Bernard Williams, *Ethics and the Limits of Philosophy* (Fontana Press: London, 1993).

45. Christine M. Korsgaard, *The Sources of Normativity* (Cambridge University Press: Cambridge, 1996), p. 159.

46. Christine M. Korsgaard, *The Sources of Normativity* (Cambridge University Press: Cambridge, 1996), p. 160.

"We need, in other words, to know something about what we do not get, and about the importance of not getting it."[47]

In his (groundbreaking) work on Kant's life and thought, Ernst Cassirer refers to one of Kant's sayings, that "he who as a man yearns for the time of his childhood must himself have remained a child."[48]

Perhaps we might see Kant, as arch-rationalist, having such a sentiment because childhood modes of understanding do not (at least not necessarily) involve abstraction, so much as a kind of animist or magical way of making sense. In contrast, it is significant to his style or his method, as well as his fables (not to mention his life-experience), that Chesterton valued the child-like in the world. *The Man Who Was Thursday* is subtitled, "*A Nightmare.*" Similarly, though not a "dream," *The Napoleon of Notting Hill* is essentially mytho-poetic, fabulous, rather than realistic. At either a structural level or a generic one, both London novels invoke fantasy and by way of fantasy childhood. And both are serial adventures.

Before all this I should of course state my central thesis: which is that, much like C.P. Cavafy's iconic poem "The City," Chesterton's London is a space to be traversed in fable, which signifies most centrally the quest of the self towards integration and individuation. In Cavafy's poem, the city is a metaphor for the self. And just as in the poem the persona realises that no ship exists to take one from the city, we realise in the process of the poem's revealing conceit, that there is, ultimately, no escape from one's own self. The way in which this realisation is relevant to Chesterton is as follows: namely, a recognition of dependency, or if you like, creature-liness, is

47. Adam Phillips, *Missing Out: In Praise of The Unlived Life* (Hamish Hamilton: London, 2012), p. 33.

48. Ernst Cassirer, *Kant's Life and Thought*, translated by James Haden (Yale University Press: New Haven, 1981), p. 15.

vital to becoming a more independent and humane person. It is more rational to accept that not all is reducible by reason. If one cannot escape (abstract or separate from) oneself, then what is suggested is a "thick" rather than "thin" conception of normative selfhood. Similarly, the eminently structuralist features in Chesterton's novels—dichotomies, inversions, *doppelgängers*, and so on—are there to show up a mono-manic sensibility, filled and fuelled with recursions and poetic conceits of self-consciousness, *as well as* the necessity of such an *agon*, as it were, for the incumbent *anagnorisis*. Privation is a way towards plenitude; darkness is put into relief by light.

One feature of both London novels is that, like Dickens's Gospel-invoking tale of *Two Cities*, light and darkness are made use of, both within the fables and as metaphors for blindness and in-sight. For instance, "The Battle of The Lamps" chapter in *The Napoleon of Notting Hill*, and the fact that the Head of Police in *The Man Who Was Thursday* recruits all the detectives, including the hero, Syme, in darkness. In the first, the loss of light in the middle of London, leads the more utilitarian-thinking side into recursive blindness and in-fighting, all to suggest that abstract logic, such as utilitarian standardising of all value, needs must lose. And in the second, the darkness, again part of the story's inner workings, is also a metaphor for the darkness of the self to itself, until the requisite, incumbent revelation or disclosure.

Childhood is foregrounded in Chesterton's first (London) novel. Not only is there an element of Lear-like or Carroll-like nonsense to much of the dialogue—a feature to be analysed presently—but one of the central and most revealing parts of the story links the childhood fantasies of chivalry of the "fanatic" Adam Wayne with both his development and the development (or operative regression) of London's boroughs into atomised pseudo-mediaeval city states. When in the middle of the action he takes the chemist, as one example, for a "necromancer," his animistic or Quixotic way of reading reality is highlighted as part of the overall executive conceit of the novel, which is a pendulum between fanaticism and tomfoolery, between value and cynicism.[49]

Which latter, cloven or not, are like two versions of rationality.

Here are some examples of childlike playfulness from *The Napoleon of Noting Hill*:

> "I keep having my hair cut, but it keeps on growing again."[50]
>
> "I have never visited Parson's Green, or seen either the Green or the Parson...."[51]
>
> "So Mr. Buck and me we put our 'eads together... ." "'Your heads together!' I can see it! Cannot you do it now? Oh, do do it now!"[52]

What is going on here at a microscopic or micro-logical level is the whole purport of the novel. When in non-sense mode the joker, Auberon Quin, takes metaphorical speech literally, he is taking it like a child, animistically, which is in fact, to Chesterton's glory, the opposite of a schizophrenic, according to Freud, who treats "concrete things as if they were abstract."[53]

49. G. K. Chesterton, *The Napoleon of Notting Hill* (House of Stratus: London, 2001), pp. 82-83.

50. G. K. Chesterton, *The Napoleon of Notting Hill* (House of Stratus: London, 2001), p. 12.

51. G. K. Chesterton, *The Napoleon of Notting Hill* (House of Stratus: London, 2001), p. 48.

52. G. K. Chesterton, *The Napoleon of Notting Hill* (House of Stratus: London, 2001), p. 56.

This anti-abstract element of childhood mentality is redolent throughout the novel, as is its opposite. In the opening, as one telling instance, Auberon Quin sees two acquaintances wearing tailcoats from behind, and takes them for "dragons" walking backwards[54]

The so-called fanatic, Adam Wayne, takes on the banner of Notting Hill's city state, due to a local loyalty: it is Notting Hill where he was a child and fell in love and played boys' games,[55] which is to say his motivational set is "thick" in Williams's sense, and this, as against puritanical universalism, is in his favour. Not only does the opening to the tale satirise the men of science, like Wells, who, in true nineteenth-century manner, predict the future according to projections from current tendencies, but these "adults" are compared unfavourably to children's games like "Keep tomorrow dark." Another version of this opposition comes in the two consecutive chapters, "The Council of the Provosts" and "Enter a Lunatic." The one side thinks in abstract, utilitarian manner, regarding a building project which needs to make use of a certain "Pump Street" in Notting Hill. The businessmen, the adults, are willing to offer huge sums, inordinate sums, to the Provost of Notting Hill, Adam Wayne. But this quixotic young man refuses all sums for the *quidditas* of a street. Chesterton once wrote, "If everything is trying to be green, some things will be greener than others; but there is an immortal and indestructible equality between green and red."[56]

53. Sigmund Freud, The Unconscious, translated by Graham Frankland (Penguin: London, 2005), p. 85.

54. G. K. Chesterton, *The Napoleon of Notting Hill* (House of Stratus: London, 2001), p. 11.

55. G. K. Chesterton, *The Napoleon of Notting Hill* (House of Stratus: London, 2001), p. 67.

56. G. K. Chesterton, *Charles Dickens* (House of Stratus: London, 2001), p. 109.

Some of the characters, the inveterate "adults" as it were talk as "we moderns" and of "civilisation."[57]

Indeed the major conceit of this fictional world, eighty years in the future, is that the sovereign is picked by lot, arbitrarily. This is efficient because it is assumed that all are the same, in brilliance or in idiocy.[58] It is precisely this inter-substitutable manoeuvre between concrete persons, which, traditionally, has been the first argument against utilitarian reasoning.[59] Furthermore, near the opening of the action, the soon-to-be-King, Auberon Quin, claims, like the sometime Chesterton as we have seen, to have been "emptied of all pleasures but folly";[60] and this folly, like Chesterton's solipsism in adolescence, is articulated by one of the "adult" characters, attempting to grasp Quin's slippery nature, as follows: "He has gone round the mental world, so to speak, and found the place where the East and the West are one, and extreme idiocy is as good as sense. But I cannot explain these psychological games."[61] This, as opposed to Adam Wayne, for whom the only "just" wars and the only "humane" wars were and are "religious" ones.[62]

In line with the communitarian spirit, in which values

---

57. G. K. Chesterton, *The Napoleon of Notting Hill* (House of Stratus: London, 2001), pp. 20-21.

58. G. K. Chesterton, *The Napoleon of Notting Hill* (House of Stratus: London, 2001), p. 23.

59. Bernard Williams, *Moral Luck: Philosophical Papers 1973-1980* (Cambridge University Press: Cambridge, 1999), pp. 1-5.

60. G. K. Chesterton, *The Napoleon of Notting Hill* (House of Stratus: London, 2001), p. 29.

61. G. K. Chesterton, *The Napoleon of Notting Hill* (House of Stratus: London, 2001), pp. 13-14.

62. G. K. Chesterton, *The Napoleon of Notting Hill* (House of Stratus: London, 2001), p. 69.

like freedom are not self-justifying, but only so for what they allow for, at the end of the tale, when one city-state, Notting Hill, has become an empire, Wayne acknowledges that he had fought not to replace one form of abstract universality for a different one; rather he had fought against all other particulars for the right of those particulars to be each, and differently, particular.[63] And this is synchronous with the doctrine of analogy, by way of which Oneness regulates plurality. To join my earlier note, regarding the use of light and dark, with this latter point, it is clear from most observers' witness that Chesterton's very style and method, hooking the "unseen" onto the "seen"[64] is an enactment or, better, "embodiment"[65] of this weighted relativity. As Williams argues in relation to relativism: one must have a unifying criterion in the first place to understand difference between two life-worlds, and it is perfectly possible (as here) to understand that others have their own reasons, and to understand those reasons and how they bind those others, without oneself being bound by them.[66] Furthermore, this continuous repartee between unity and plurality shows up in Chesterton's very style and voice. An instance of Chesterton's analogising method:

> Dickens had all his life the faults of the little boy who is kept up too late at night. The boy in such a case exhibits a psychological paradox; he is a little too irritable because he is a little too happy. Dickens

63. G. K. Chesterton, *The Napoleon of Notting Hill* (House of Stratus: London, 2001), p. 167.

64. Hilaire Belloc, *On The Place Of Gilbert Chesterton in English Letters* (Sheed & Ward: London, 1940), pp. 39-41.

65. Roger Scruton: *Sexual Desire: A Philosophical Investigation* (Continuum: London, 1986).

66. Bernard Williams, *Moral Luck: Philosophical Papers 1973-1980* (Cambridge University Press: Cambridge, 1999), p. 142.

was always a child in society, he was splendidly sociable, and yet suddenly quarrelsome. In all the practical relations of his life he was what the child is in the last hours of an evening party, genuinely delighted, genuinely delightful, genuinely affectionate and happy, and yet in some strange way fundamentally exasperated and dangerously close to tears.[67]

This is a perfect example of the way Chesterton, like his creation Father Brown, is able to turn sight into in-sight; like Father Brown, whose knowledge of sin from the confessional equips him resolutely, Chesterton was able to account for the other, whether in the past or present, in an internalist way: not only did he value sentiment *tout court*, but he is able to manumit sentiment in and through his reader. And yet for all his integrity, he was often accused of sophistry,[68] or it was judged that his thought was ruined by his paradoxical manner of expression or voice.[69] However, following Kenner's outstanding book, I see Chesterton's manner as the incarnation of his insight. To paraphrase Kenner, who in turn is paraphrasing the doctrine of analogy: the grass exists, and the grass exists grossly. [70] One way of putting it, is that just as "London" is the regulative space for all these developments, so the very personhood of Chesterton was a unity which

67. G. K. Chesterton, *Charles Dickens* (House of Stratus: London, 2001), pp. 12-13.

68. G. K. Chesterton, *Orthodoxy* (Dover Publications: New York, 2004), p. 3.

69. See William James, *The Correspondence of William James*, vol. 3, edited by Ignas K. Skrupskelis and Elizabeth M. Berkeley (University Press of Virginia: Charlottesville, 1994), p. 329; William James, *The Correspondence of William James*, vol. 2, edited by Ignas K. Skrupskelis and Elizabeth M. Berkeley (University Press of Virginia: Charlottesville, 1993), p. 225.

70. Hugh Kenner, *Paradox in Chesterton* (Sheed & Ward: London, 1948), p. 30.

permitted such appreciation of others. And the verse "Dedication" to Hilaire Belloc in *The Napoleon of Notting Hill* opens with as it were the obverse of Cavafy's conceit, "For every tiny town or place/God made the stars especially." It is the obverse or perhaps a more emphatic version of "The City." Every town or place is like a reflector of God. Every point in animate space is the centre of the world, God's (the divine spark) Word, Logos or Ratio, allowing for, or indeed, rendering this. Where with Cavafy one is stayed in the inexorable rut of the same self, a bit like the dithering Hamlet, here, like a development or what Hegel would call a "determinate negation," the self is redeemed, made (infinitely) special, a quiddity. However much biographically separate from Cavafy, Chesterton needs the rut (hence the mad arithmetic of his novels) in order to show the redress offered. Indeed, perhaps it is significant that in his *magnum opus*, *The Alexandria Quartet*, Lawrence Durrell makes use of the mythos of the old poet of the city (Cavafy), but nearly always at moments of crisis, be it to do with sex or death.

As London in this fiction is atomised into particulars which relate to each other, so Chesterton was a traipsing detective throughout his writing career, unveiling in charismatic fashion the moral psychology of his different subjects and of his self—often both at the same time. Though at a biographical level, and in a particular sense, Chesterton derided "Impressionism," he was himself in a different way one of the most effective of impressionists. Before this is addressed, it should be recognised that the very idea of traversal, traversing the town, is associated in Chesterton's work with inversions and dichotomies, the essence of a rationalistic mentality or structure of feeling.

Take for instance the doubled and doubling inversions, eminently redolent of the cerebral, which the reader will have come to understand by the end of chapter three. Gregory, the "real" anarchist, has been advised by the head of the anarchist Supreme Council ("Sunday") that the best disguise for his anarchism is to dress exactly like an anarchist. He, a sincere anarchist, aims, in the opening action, to join that very Supreme Council, who, it will turn out, are not anarchists, but are pretending to be anarchists in order to fight the intellectual disease of anarchism. Gregory, for all that, is not voted onto the council. On the other side, from the opening action, we have Syme who is a police officer (though formerly "poet") not pretending to be anything but a lawful member of society who, it turns out, now pretending to be anarchist, is voted onto the anarchist council, intending to subvert their activities. As the story evolves, each suspected anarchist is disclosed or unveiled as a fellow police detective. And to top it all, "Sunday" (of whom at one point, after many revelations, it is thought that, as head anarchist, he had purposely kept all police enemies on the council, near at hand)—that very Sunday is discovered to be the head of Police. I do not intend to do the arithmetic. What I do intend to do is to show how this structuralist structure, in its near mathematicity, is both an effect of Chesterton's rationalism, and an allegory for how to *overcome* both the panic and its hyper-rational "reaction formation."

To begin, then, with generic features.

Unlike more, on the face of things, technically astute literary artists, both novels involve highly contrived coincidences. This in my view is part of the point. Like a logician or a mathematician, the modalities, as it were, of Chesterton's fictions, are *de dictu*, rather than *de re*. What this means is that Chesterton is not trying to have a realistic plot but rather, like a game of chess, introducing counters which have sense only within the constructed system of the author. When Chesterton called *The Man Who Was Thursday* "a very melodramatic sort of moonshine,"[71] it was because of this very "parabolic" or contrived effect. In my view, the root of melodrama is the absence of real drama or real dramatic tension. But more than that, as a parable, so to speak, it has everlasting value. A metaphor, as Scruton argues, is not important for what it stands for[72] but rather for the experience it generates. However, an allegory, metaphor's more rationalistic parent, is important in so far as it offers not just one-to-one significance, but, like all analogical thinking, one-to-many. In Wilhelm Worringer's terms, Chesterton, while seemingly empathic in viewpoint, was in these contrived fables using space to redeem or redress that kind of Pan-ic and "dread of space" which was the psychological root of an abstractive sensibility.[73]

However, these aspects of (manic) duplicity and inversion, when taken as content rather than telltale architectonic, also reveal something about Chesterton's view of Christianity. So for example, "Sunday" may evoke what Burke distinguished from the beautiful as the "sublime," a product of fear. And yet he is also, by the end, a product of love—which corresponds to the beautiful.[74]

But in so far as this novel is a "nightmare" it inverts the world, turns the world upside down for intelligent reasons.[75] Indeed, Ian Ker has ventured the proposition that Chesterton was most himself as an avatar of Dickensian grotesquerie;

71. G. K. Chesterton, *The Man Who Was Thursday: A Nightmare* (Penguin Books: London, 1986), p. 185.

72. Roger Scruton, *Beauty* (Oxford University Press: Oxford, 2009), pp. 1-2.

73. Wilhelm Worringer, *Abstraction and Empathy: A Contribution to the Psychology of Style*, translated by Michael Bullock (Elephant Paperbacks: Chicago, 1997), pp. 4-23.

74. Roger Scruton, *Beauty* (Oxford University Press: Oxford, 2009), pp. 72-73.

75. G. K. Chesterton, *St Francis of Assisi* (House of Stratus: London, 2001), p. 36;G. K. Chesterton, *Orthodoxy* (Dover Publications: New York, 2004), pp. 74-116.

and thus concludes that Chesterton's Dickens book is like the master-trope of his work.[76]

And yet, Chesterton called his sprawling London adventure "a nightmare" because he didn't intend the Janus-faced "Sunday" to represent "the Deity." Rather, as articulated by some of the characters towards the end, Sunday is part of a fable which configures Chesterton's period of panic and being at the mercies of the pipes of pan; which we might see as the return of the repressed, his bodily nature rebelling against an overly puritanical mould. This in turn makes the traversed story a kind of working-through or transference for that original experience. The structure of Christianity was paradoxical in the same manner. It is the immanent marriage of, as one of the titles of Chesterton biographies has it, "wisdom and innocence."[77]

Or, in a different context entirely, what Gillian Rose dubs, the "sacred circle": "This is the historical event: the *Ereignis* of the *histor*, the judgment in which all judge and all are judged... ."[78]

These two London allegories are adventure stories, or parables. They are in the tradition of Don Quixote, and serialistic. However, the sort of psychological change, the sudden "happening" as against the "vast machinery of modern life" with its "wanderings" and "enlightenments"[79] is more transformative than that generic feature might suggest. It is

---

76. Ian Ker, *The Catholic Revival in English Literature: 1845-1961* (Gracewing: Leominster [UK], 2003), pp. 84-85.

77. Joseph Pearce, *Wisdom and Innocence: A Life of G. K. Chesterton* (Ignatius Press: San Francisco, 1996).

78. Gillian Rose, *Dialectic of Nihilism: Post-Structuralism and Law* (Blackwell: New York & Oxford, 1984), p. 67.

79. G. K. Chesterton, *The Napoleon of Notting Hill* (House of Stratus: London, 2001), pp. 155, 95, 82.

embodied, as Slavoj Zizek notes, in the notion of adventure (a-venir). [80]

What I am suggesting is tantamount to the difference which Edward Said makes in his first study of Conrad, between "growth" and "evolution."[81] Another way of suggesting how Chesterton, to quote James on Conrad, "gloried in a gap,"[82] is to consider, as analogue as ever, Jurgen Moltmann's problematisation of evolutionary linearity. He argues that in the process of moving from smaller parts to larger more complex parts, the problem is that the achieved end-product (at whatever stage) is qualitatively *more* than the sum of the part or parts that preceded in the linear tale being told.[83] This problem of the necessary intransitivity for integral experience, that election or as earlier "decision" is crucial, is equivalent to the very question of "normativity," or the impossibility of deriving an "ought" from an "is." And what I am suggesting is that this principle, like the Christian notion of "development," is akin in a different context, to allowing for contingency; or at least, what an Edwardian would call "the missing link" is the reason why no account of meaningful reality can be wholly totalised in human concepts or understanding; that reason is more rational when it accepts, as it were, the inexorability of authority. This is because essential to the Christian notion of "development" is organicity: which is to say, the growth and progression of dogma or doctrine through the ages is not unilinear, but rather conditioned from

80. Slavoj Zizek, *Less Than Nothing: Hegel and the Shadow of Dialectical Materialism* (Verso: London, 2012), p. 264.

81. Edward W. Said, *Joseph Conrad and the Fiction of Autobiography* (Columbia University Press: New York, 2008), p. 27.

82. Henry James, *The Future of the Novel*, edited by Leon Edel (Vintage Books: New York, 1956), p. 281.

83. Jurgen Moltmann, *Ethics of Hope*, translated by Margaret Kohl (Fortress Press: Minneapolis, 2012), p. 125.

the end, in both senses. And the end, however regulative, is inaccessible to human reason. Another way of putting it is that the supersensible conditions, regulates, and directs the sensible world. It takes the eccentric exception to reveal the significance of central meanings in our lives. Something not quite reducible by reason has to be accepted for a more commonsense use of that very reason.

Chesterton makes his gambit for the rationality of authority in the first chapter of his *Autobiography*, "Hearsay Evidence." Here he makes use of the fact that he cannot empirically verify his own birth. That he must take it on trust. Indeed, this idea of the impregnable nature of ultimate, primitive reality, the metaphysical mystery at the heart of our physical reality, is directly associated with (as per above) poetry, or the romantic things in life. In that, much like with one of Chesterton's most avid readers and epigones, Jorge Luis Borges, the evocative word in a poem is viewed as irreducible to synonym or definition.[84] If it has its right place in the poem, then it is "thick" with the quiddity of reality. That said, though, Chesterton did indeed deploy a recurrent critique of what he called "Impressionism," evident in his world from late nineteenth-century aestheticism.

The "gleam of hope" which Chesterton said was intended to emerge from his London "nightmare" is akin with his reason, both ethically and logically, for disparaging "Impressionism." The latter, like "poetry," "lunacy," "secrecy," puritanism" and so on, is also one of his key words. One example will suffice, though it recurs throughout his *oeuvre*. That "modern tendency" called "Impressionism"…is skepticism.

---

84. Jorge Luis Borges, *This Craft of Verse* (Harvard University Press: Cambridge [MA], 2002).

It means believing one's immediate impressions at the expense of one's more permanent and positive generalisations. It puts what one notices above what one knows. It means the monstrous heresy that seeing is believing. A white cow at one particular instant of the evening light may be gold on one side and violet on the other. Impressionism is to say that she really is a gold and violet cow. The whole point of Impressionism is to say that there is no white cow at all[85]

It seems that Chesterton refuted this argument in the manner of Kant's doctrine of "apperception" or, nearer his time, the argument of Frege. This latter was to say, if all I had were sense-impressions ("ideas"), it would follow that I myself am one too. But if I myself am one, then there is no purchase on any of the others. Therefore with the realisation of the subject or the self, comes the idea of objectivity.[86]

Or, consider Louis A. Sass's view on this issue, writing on the "paradoxes of delusion" and taking as his ground for study Wittgenstein and his obsession with the category error of solipsism, as well as the Schreber of Freud's notorious study. In the spirit of the Chesterton we have encountered so far, Sass writes, "In Wittgenstein's view, the futile questioning characteristic of philosophers tends to arise from some hitch in, or withdrawal from, the normal context and flow of existence." "The real discovery... is the one that makes me capable of stopping doing philosophy when I want to—the one that gives philosophy peace, so that it is no longer tormented by questions which bring *itself* in question."[87]

85. G. K. Chesterton, *William Blake* (Cosmo: New York, 2005), pp. 137-138.

86. Gottlob Frege, "The Thought: A Logical Enquiry" in *Philosophical Logic*, edited by P.F. Strawson (Oxford University Press: Oxford, 1967), pp. 17-38.

But then as Levenson has argued the doctrine of Impressionism involved both elements of self-effacement, and elements of self-expression.[88] As I have already suggested, where Chesterton was skeptical of Paterian aestheticism, he most definitely can be dubbed an impressionist if by that we mean a persona which is charismatic, works by hyperbole, and "makes an impression." Indeed, for Ford Madox Ford, this charismatic element was an integral part of what he meant by impressionism.[89] To add to this, as already noted, Chesterton, to his bane and to his boon, read himself everywhere. His Browning is him; his Dickens is him; and so on. But what's interesting, in briefly comparing Chesterton to Conrad, say, or to Ford, is that, as one instance, *The Napoleon of Notting Hill*, for all its purposive artificiality and crudeness, is a harangue against "standardisation," if in a more populist mode. So that in some ways John Carey is wrong to make a hard-and-fast dichotomy between someone like Chesterton, or his own hero, Bennett, and the more so-called high-brow modernists. [90] This is not of course to call Chesterton by any means a "modernist." Rather to unsettle the overdetermined nature of that appellation, and all the suggestions of elitism that come in its train, or in its wake.

T.S. Eliot once wryly wrote, "We are not all so completely immersed in ignorance, prejudice and heresy as

87. Louis A. Sass, *Paradoxes of Delusion: Wittgenstein, Shreber, and the Schizophrenic Mind* (Cornell University Press: Ithaca & London, 1994), p. 108.

88. Michael Levenson, *A Genealogy of Modernism: A Study of English Literary Doctrine 1908-1922* (Cambridge University Press: Cambridge, 1986), p. 115.

89. Ford Madox Ford, "On Impressionism" in *Critical Writings of Ford Madox Ford*, ed. Frank MacShane (University of Nebraska Press: Lincoln, 1964), p. 36; *The March of Literature: From Confucius' Day to our Own* (Dalkey Archive Press: New York, 1998), p. 4-5.

90. J. Carey: *The Intellectuals and the Masses: Pride and Prejudice among the Literary Intelligentsia: 1880-1939* (Faber & Faber: London & Boston, 1992).

Mr. Chesterton assumes. He seems always to assume that what his reader has previously believed is exactly the opposite of what Mr. Chesterton knows to be true." For all the teasing, though, Eliot is not saying he disagrees with Chesterton. Indeed eighteen months later he would write in a letter to Chesterton of his sympathy in political and social outlook, as well as his delight in Chesterton's Dickens book.[91]

And as with Ford and Eliot, one might also make a thin connection with Conrad. For surely one way of thinking of Chesterton's fabulous adventures—which offer London as an open space for therapeutic working-through of various secretive lunacies—is, under the rubric again of Cavafy, to think of Chesterton's Syme or his Wayne as (optimistic) negatives of Conrad's "Kurtz" or "Lord Jim." Indeed, the whole notion of "solidarity," which was at the centre of Conrad's outlook, has its thoroughgoing root in the tradition of Christian social doctrine.

If we take Pippin's view (cognate with the late twentieth-century Bernard Williams) that Modernism in the arts was a reaction and backlash to the Enlightenment ideal of an absolutely self-determining, selfregulating self,[92] then there is more in common between that very modernist ethos and a pre-Cartesian world. Otherwise put, both religion, or the need for roots, and, say—as a prime exemplum of modernist constructivism and textuality—psychoanalysis, are effective only as part of a protean mission to convince us that something came before us and something after; that we are not gods pulling ourselves up from our own (too cerebral) bootstraps.

---

91. Joseph Pearce, *Wisdom and Innocence: A Life of G. K. Chesterton* (Ignatius Press: San Francisco, 1996), p. 357.

92. Robert B. Pippin, *Modernism as a Philosophical Problem: On the Dissatisfactions of European High Culture* (Blackwell: Oxford, 1999), pp. 1-15.

In effect, it is the sanity of "Father Brown," as against the mad crime of "Gabriel Gale."[93]

93. G. K. Chesterton, *The Poet and the Lunatics: Episodes in the Life of Gabriel Gale* (House of Stratus: London, 2001), pp. 69-91.

7

The Authority of Soul and The Sole Authority: Comparing Two Catholic Memoirs: The Classical Approach / The Romantic

When man passes from physical fear to dread and awe, he makes a sheer jump, and apprehends something which could never be given, as danger is, by the physical facts and logical deductions from them. (Lewis 9)

I. On Hilaire Belloc's The Path to Rome

Near the beginning of *The Path to Rome*, Hilaire Belloc prepares his readers for the journey to be taken with an autobiographical reflection which we will see, with a little literary critical teasing, to be, in a manner, the underlying motif of the whole book (part tra– velogue, part intimate diary, part spiritual reflection). He seems to date the experience and the expression of this work to a watershed moment in his life, a site for sea-change:

> … it is the moment (not the year or the month, mind you, not even the hour, but the very second) when a man is grown up. When he sees things as they are (that is, backwards) and feels solidly himself. Do I make myself clear? No matter, it is the Shock of Maturity, and that must suffice for you. (Belloc 20)

As will be shown, what this signifies is in essence the central parabolic purport of this work: namely a physical journey which becomes sacrament, a metaphysical journey. What Belloc is intimating is that a quantity of life is reached where or when mere quantity results in a deep qualitative shift. This note is not only an intimate record, but, having been an experience, becomes transfigured into a philosophical reflection:

> ... But perhaps ... you don't believe in Catastrophes, or Climaxes, or Definitions? Eh? Tell me, do you believe in the peak of the Matterhorn, and have you doubts on the points of needles? Can the sun be said truly to rise or set, and is there any exact meaning in the phrase, 'Done to a turn' as applied to omelets? You know there is; and so also must you believe in Categories, and you must admit differences of kind as well as of degree, and you must accept definition and believe in all your fathers did, that were wiser men than you, as is easily proved if you will but imagine yourself for but one moment introduced into the presence of your ancestors, and ask yourself which would be the fool. (20)

This eminently conservative (and quite Chestertonian) sentiment allows entry for the Ratio or Word. Which is to say, the faith put in common reason (or in quotidian language), is made into a cipher, for faith in the more global purpose of existence. Indeed, at one point, this sacramental principle (the physical into the metaphysical) is invoked when Belloc, wishing, writes, 'Could this book be infinite, as my voyage was infi- nite' (118). 'You who have never taken a straight line and held it, nor seen strange men and remote places, you do not know what it is to have to go round the common way' (217). And that 'straight path' is both a physical description of the empirical journey, and, clearly, holds a more figurative sense. And it is only by walking (which is the major manner of travel for Belloc in this voyage) a 'straight path'—unlike travelling by bicycle or railway or by car, which latter routes 'avoid climbing save when they are forced to it'— that 'anyone can pass from ridge to ridge and have this full picture of the way he has been' (71). Again, that 'straight way' is both a topographical gambit and a spiritual one. Indeed, the 'value of this book'—after being 'astonished by a thousand accidents, and always' finding, 'things twenty-fold as great as I supposed they would be, and far more curious'—is the 'straight light of adventure' (98). And to repeat, that coming-to is both physical and metaphysical. This sacramental in-sight is expressed in many different ways, presently to be elicited from the text.

As a kind of mid-wife to that text, reconstructing this major tenor via strategic sampling, what I want to suggest throughout the pursuant discussion is that the principle which authorises the transfiguration at stake is that of soul, and animation. In different ways physical nature speaks with animistic personality in Belloc's hands. And this soul is both his own, that of the tempestuous paths and natural topography, as well as of the antique Europe of the Faith—whose animating nub is or was, of course, Rome. Just as Belloc makes (playful) use of 'omens' (250) in his recounted journey, so that very journey has its own sacramental telos. 'My pilgrimage is to Rome, my business is with lonely places, hills, and the recollection of the spirit' (252).

Witness the following two passages, like two horns of a dilemma. Their opposition, pitted against each other here, is both exemplary of the anthropomorphic personification redolent throughout the recounted journey, as well as holding between them a kind of Odyssey and homecoming so typical of that romance mythos which is Catholic Christianity.

> Then a little wind passed over the vast forests of Lorraine. It seemed to wake an indefinite sly life proper to this seclusion, a life to which I was strange, and which thought me an invader. Yet I heard nothing. There were no adders in the long grass, nor any frogs in that dry square of land, nor crickets on the high part of the hill; but I knew that little creatures in league with every nocturnal influence, enemies of the sun, occupied the air and the land about me; nor will I deny that I felt a rebel, knowing well that men were made to work in happy dawns and to sleep in the night, and everything in that short and sacred darkness multiplied my attentiveness and my illusion. (35)

> Had not the trees been so much greater and more enduring than my own presence, and had they not overwhelmed me by their regard, I should have felt afraid. As it was I pushed upward through their immovable host in some such catching of the breath as men have when they walk at night straining for a sound, and I felt myself to be continually in hidden companion- ship. (87)

Whether for good or ill, the places of his journeying and rest are infused throughout with personality. 'The great clouds stood up in heaven, separate, like persons; and no wind blew; but everything was full of evening. I worshipped them so far as it is permitted to worship inanimate things' (279). '[V]ery soon I fell asleep, still thinking of the shapes of the clouds, and of the power of God' (280). Much like the illustrative manner of his long- time friend and co-religionist, G. K. Chesterton, at times Belloc evinces both irony and at the same time, a deeply parabolic imagination. Which is to say, there is a soul in the things he observes: a kind of plastic infinity within (the) finite things.

> Never ridicule windows. It is out of windows that many fall to their death. By windows love often enters. Through a window went the bolt that killed King Richard. King William's father spied Arlette from a window … . When a mob would rule England, it breaks windows; and when a patriot would save her, he taxes them. Out of windows, we walk on to lawns in summer and meet men and women, and in winter windows are drums for the splendid music of storms that makes us feel so masterly round our fires. The windows of the great cathedrals are all their meaning. But for windows we would have to go outdoors to see day- light. After the sun, which they serve, I know nothing so beneficent as windows. Fie upon the ungrateful man that has no window-god in his house, and thinks himself too great a philo- sopher to bow down to windows! May he live in a place without windows for a while to teach him the value of windows. As for me, I will keep the high worship of windows till I come to the windowless grave. Talk to me of windows! (123)

The potent blend of irony and serious sentiment is like a parallel to the suggested paganism redolent in the work—in service of something beyond such. Indeed, catholic in both senses, colloquial and specific, Belloc writes of all his known pleasures as having come 'from an intimate union between my body and my very human mind, which last receives, confirms, revives and can summon up again what my body has experienced' (108). This re-collecting as it were of the spirit is, again, a metaphor for the seam of mind and body, which is the soul or the personality.[1] 'It is a great rule to examine every new thing, and to suck honey out of every flower' (99). And yet,

> So little are we, we men; so much are we immersed in our muddy and immediate interests that we think, by numbers and recitals, to comprehend distance or time, or any of our limiting infinities. Here were these magnificent creatures of God, I mean the Alps, which now for the first time I saw from the height of the Jura … . [They] could strike one motionless with the awe of supernatural things. Up there in the sky, to which only clouds belong and birds and the last trembling colors of pure light, they stood fast and hard; not moving as do things of the sky…. They occupied the sky with a sublime invasion: and the things proper to the sky were

---

1. A philosophical parallel and illustration: 'Suppose a magician is hired to perform the old trick of making the emperor and peasant become each other. He gets the emperor and peasant in one room, with the emperor on his throne and the peasant in one corner, and then casts the spell. What will count as success? Clearly not that after the smoke has cleared the old emperor should be in the corner and the old peasant on the throne. That would be a rather boring trick. The requirement is presumably that the emperor's body, with the peasant's personality, should be on the throne, and the peasant's body with the emperor's personality, in the corner. What does this mean? In particular what has happened to the voices? The voice presumably ought to count as a bodily function; yet how could the peasant's gruff blasphemies be uttered in the emperor's cultivated tones, or the emperor's witticisms in the peasant's growl? A similar point holds for the features; the emperor's body might include the sort of face that just could not express the peasant's morose suspiciousness, the peasant's a face no expression of which could be taken for one of fastidious arrogance … ' (Williams 11–12).

forgotten by me in their presence as I gazed. (158–9)

A melee, then, of propriety and impropriety. Indeed, later, having arrived in Italy, Belloc speaks of the Italian Lakes as possessing 'the beauty of a special creation; the expression of some mind'. His 'enchanted experience' was one in which 'the single sense of sight had almost touched the boundary of music' (234–5). Which is to say, the strictly-speaking spatiotemporal: *to that beyond such.* 'The mountains', by turns, 'from their heights reveal to us two truths. They suddenly make us feel our insignificance, and at the same time they free the immortal Mind … ' (200).

> These, the great Alps, seen thus, link one in some
> way to one's immortality … . Let me put it thus:
> that from the height of Wiessenstein I saw, as it
> were, my religion. I mean, humility, the fear of
> death, the terror of height and of distance, the glory
> of God, the infinite potentiality of reception
> whence springs that divine thirst of the soul …
> (159)

II. On Ronald Knox's A Spiritual Aeneid

' … there is no such bully as a logical mind … ' (Knox 174)

Though Ronald Knox mentions Hilaire Belloc's *The Path to Rome* with significant admiration in his autobiographical record of the process of his conversion from Anglicanism to Roman Catholicism (192), his spiritual account is very different, both formally and substantively. As he himself writes, his story is told in a 'dispassionate' manner (210). Unlike the emotive animism (heuristic no doubt) of Belloc's memoir, Knox, in the main (there are exceptions, as we'll see) is resolutely staid.

The main crux of his journey is the problem of 'authority'. And it is a ratiocinative or categorical question for him. For both as author and as character he always eschewed 'spiritual experience' as a ratification of the faith (175), and was highly wary of the decep- tive part that 'emotion' might play in one's spiritual life (176). In the (penultimate—more on this conceit later) 'Epilogue', he writes how he 'turned away from the emotional as far as possible, and devoted', himself 'singly to the resignation of my will to God's Will' (214). In tandem with this authorial approach, is his diagnosis (in hindsight) of the signal difference of the sacramental wing of the Anglicanism of his time, with Roman Catholicism.

> The fact is, on the one side, that we all believed in (Roman) Catholicism as a system which worked, which held ordinary men and attracted the poor where Anglicanism did not; we all agreed that the Roman system—the preaching of Penance and attendance at Mass as obligatory, the preference for short and businesslike services, the attempt to stimulate devotion by means of the rosary, benediction, etc.—was the right way of going about things: our only difference between ourselves was how much it could be done prudently, and how much of it an intelligent theory of Anglicanism could carry. (Knox 81–2)

For unlike his view of Catholic teaching (to which he eventually subscribes), Anglicanism for Knox was not categorical dogma, but 'a living body of people to whom I had a message', (86). Knox's mission in this early work is to stress how worthy the thirty-nine articles were of renewal via return to the Roman via itself. In effect, the extant problem was that unlike the (hale) automatic authorisation of the Roman Catholic who,

> does not stop twice to ask whether he is being loyal to the Pope, or the Church, or the tra- ditions of the Church, or to his Bishop … owing to the paucity and the ambiguity of its title-deeds, and the widely different points of views adopted by its dignitaries, the Church of England allows of no such comfortable conclusions … (113)

Unless you are 'temperamentally Anglican' (113). And as we have seen, Knox both as stylist and as believer is suspicious of the temperamental factor. '[I]t is true that there is a sense in which Catholicism can be taught, and ordinary Anglicanism cannot' (18). The latter, for Knox, is 'not a system of religion nor a body of truth, but a feeling, a tradition … . you do not learn it, you grow into it; you do not forget it, you grow out of it' (18).

Having said that Knox's main crux is an intellectual acceptance of legitimising authority, more than any subjective spiritual or emotional experience or inclination, and that his manner of writing mirrors this ascetic approach, it should be noted that there are some passages which are (again, much like G. K. Chesterton, who was Knox's 'earliest master and model' [149]) more engagingly pictorial. What is admirable is that due to their rarity, they stand out with more force within the otherwise restrained weave of the writing. Two instances, then, towards the end of the recounted spiritual journey:

> Picture the schoolboy, who after terms of surreptitious smoking, when the necessity of pre- caution and the consciousness of being a

'sportsman' were elements in his pleasure as real as the fragrance of the tobacco itself, presented by an aunt, on going up to university, with a new pipe and tobacco-pouch. Something of the same blasé appreciation makes itself felt in the mind of the modern Anglican extremist when he is invited to admire Catholic services; he has not merely done all this before, he has done it defiantly, deliberately, with the joy of the contest to encourage him. (203)

It was as if I had been a man homeless, and needing shelter, who first of all had taken refuge under a shed at the back to an empty house. Then he had found an outhouse unlocked, and felt more cheerfulness and comfort there. Then he had tried a door in the building itself, and, by some art, found a secret spring which let you in at the back door; nightly thenceforward he had visited this back part of the house, more roomy than anything he had yet experienced, and giving, through a little crack, a view into the wide spaces of the house itself beyond. Then, one night, he had tried the spring, and the door had refused to open. The button could still be pushed, but it was followed by no sound of broken hinges. Baffled, and unable now to content himself with shed or outhouse, he had wondered round and round the house, looking enviously at its frowning fastnesses. And then he had tried the front door, and found that it had been open all the time. (214–5)

Much like John Stuart Mill (in his *Autobiography*), towards the end of his memoir Knox records a period of radical disenchantment, where having believed that 'to hold no briefs was to be less than a man', now he found himself, 'briefless: I did not know what cause I wanted to win; I could argue on most points dispassionately; I did not know what to convert people to' (189–90). This kind of *acedia* is quite commonly found in the annals of young spiritual journeys; it happened to Newman and, equally notorious, though in a different context, Carlyle.

It seemed to Knox that there was something of the circular in anything but the legitimate authority of the Roman faith. Knox, then, deftly reasoning yet again:

> If you ask 'Who are the Orthodox?' you will be told 'the people who hold the Orthodox Faith.' If you ask them how it is the Orthodox Faith they say 'Because it is held by the Orthodox Church.' And the Nestorians will say exactly the same of themselves—and who is to choose between them? … But if you ask a Catholic 'What is the Catholic Faith?' and are told it is that held by the Catholic Church; if you persevere, and ask what is the Catholic Church, you are no longer met with an irritatingly circular definition, 'The Church which holds the Catholic Faith;' you are told it is the Church which is in communion with the Bishop in Rome. (194–5).

On a personal level, rather than the equally elaborated discursive level, Knox feels that without that authoritative justification, his own roles as a priest (consecrating the Host and so on) are null and void (173–4). Elsewhere, more discursive as I say, he says that though his extreme sacramentalist Anglicanism was diametrically opposed to the recent latitudinarian trends, he never advocated the removal of Modernist clergymen from their benefices; and not because he was against such disciplinary action on principle, but because: 'there was no machinery which could justifiably persecute either the Modernists or ourselves' (157). Analogously, and significantly, again, down to cool reasoning, he argues that when he looked back at heresies like Arianism, and asked how it came about being a heresy: he realised that it was just a (contingent, we assume) effect of what he calls 'hard-swearing.' (The same epiphany had occurred to Newman in the 1830s.) Not himself having the authority (as yet), he argues himself into seeing that what 'became' 'heresy' had nothing intrinsically heretical about it, just a minority status rendered anathema by major fiat (194).[2] This is one of many examples (more below) of how Ronald Knox uses the authority of his *nous* as it were to show the gaping need of an absolutely necessary authority outside that same labile (but soul-destroying) tool. 'I believed that the authority of an infallible Church was necessary to the confident preaching of any Christian doctrine' (138).

Indeed, summarizing the satirical *reductio ad absurdam* of his tract 'Reunion All Round', his anti-modernist credentials are relayed with wit. It is also a fine example of how intellect shorn of something before or beyond it, can tie itself up in logical muddles.

> If (as the British public seemed to think) it was the
> duty of all Christian bodies to unite for worship,

---

2. This reflection had me thinking of an analogous reflection, from the realm of psychoanalysis. Just as both sides (during his time of rationalistic doubt), of heresy and orthodoxy, seem con- tingently placed in respect to each other—in one of his essays, prominent psychoanalyst, Adam Phillips, writes of how it is not just, for instance, the narcissistic personality who appeals in the session (as more generally) for (unhealthy) 'narcissistic supply'; but that the very analyst diag- nosing such narcissism is, via the diagnosis, aiming for his own narcissistic supply. Qui bono? (Phillips 200–25).

sinking their differences on each side, why should the movement be confined to Christians. What about the Jews, from whom we were only separated by the Council of Jerusalem? And if the Jews, why not the Mohammedans? We could always split the difference between monogamy and tetragamy by having two wives all round … . I went boldly forward to the case of atheists, and suggested we might join with them in common definition of the Divine Nature, which should assert it to be such as to invoke Existence and Non-Existence simultaneously… (146–7)

This (to use an anachronistic term) 'communitarianism', is an argument against what might be called 'Carlylism', whereby the important thing is merely to have faith in some- thing outside and above oneself, *but irrespective* of 'what' that depository of faith should be. Indeed, the particularity of Christianity, and especially in its more authoritative or cat-egorical form (Roman for Knox), is an effect of its radically conventional authority. The fact that Christianity's mythoi make use of paradoxical patterns, makes it that much more authoritative (for some). Knox accepted the 'paradoxes' of his religion

as, if anything, a test of its genuineness; not on any barren principle of credo quia absurdam, but on the ground that the kind of doctrine which shows less signs of having been tampered with by rationalism is likely to represent the least contaminated tradition about the deposit of the faith … (107)

In a similar vein, C. S. Lewis writes:

> If any message from the core of reality were ever
> to reach us, we should expect to find in it just that
> unexpectedness, that willful, dramatic afractuosity,
> which we find in the Christian Faith. It has the
> master touch—the rough, male taste of reality, not
> made by us, or, indeed, for us, but hitting us in the
> face. (15)

The master touch: indeed.

To return to Belloc: at both beginning and end of his
work, he renders a very Sterne-like conceit, dithering about
both: beginning and ending. Similarly, Knox has an 'Epilogue'
before the final chapter, which is titled 'Prologue'. And this is
because 'it is never too late to have a Prologue while you are
in his service Who says: "*Ecce nova facio omnia*"' (225).

But more importantly for the notion of sacramental
transfiguration—the play in both works, highlighting,
recursively, the notions of beginning or of ending—is the idea
that a Calvary narrative is like (and literally) a 're-volutionary'
narrative. Which is to say: it is a 'life-story' beyond a 'lifetime'[3]; primarily because it involves going abroad (in order) to
return home.

> For an Aeneid involves not merely coming home,
> but coming home to a place you have never been
> in before—one that combines in itself all that you
> valued in the old home, with added promises of a
> future that is new. (Knox 1)

> What is it, do you think, that causes the return?
> I think it is the problem of living; for every day,
> every experience of evil, demands a solution. That
> solution is provided by the memory of the great

3. I'm indebted for this formulation to Herbert McCabe's *Law, Love, Language*.

scheme which at last we remember. Our childhood
pierces through again … . But I will not attempt to
explain, for I have not the power … (Belloc 142) [4]

Only the tussle with rootless, rationalistic doubt, or with
sublime or rugged natural topographies (however figuratively
depicted), permits in both cases discussed the incumbent
experience to become one's own. One must as it were die to
live; to live, if you like, with any authority.

References

Belloc, Hilaire. *The Path to Rome*. London: Nelson and Sons,
1902.

Chesterton, G. K. *Orthodoxy*. Mineola, NY: Dover, 2004.

Knox, Ronald C. *A Spiritual Aeneid*. London: Burns,
1958.

Lewis, C. S. *The Problem of Pain*. London: Harper, 2002.

McCabe, Herbert. *Law, Love, Language*. New York, NY:
Continuum, 2003.

Phillips, Adam. *Promises, Promises: Essays on Literature and
Psychoanalysis*. London: Faber, 2000.

Williams, Bernard. *Problems of the Self*. Cambridge:
Cambridge UP, 1999.

4. See, as a telling parallel, G. K. Chesterton, *Orthodoxy*: 'the main problem of
this book … How we can contrive to be at once astonished at the world and at
home in it … ' (2). Or: 'I did, like all other solemn little boys, try to be in advance
of the age. Like them I tried to be some ten minutes in advance of the truth. And I
found that I was eighteen hundred years behind it' (4).

8

History Free Indirect: Reading Creative Techniques in Lytton Strachey's *Queen Victoria*

'Life being all inclusion and confusion, and art being all discrimination and selection, the latter, in search of the hard latent *value* with which alone it is concerned, sniffs round the mass as instinctively and unerringly as a dog suspicious of some buried bone.'
Henry James, Preface to *The Spoils of Poynton* (52; original emphasis)

'In the domain of History there is no such thing as Time.'
Ford Madox Ford, 'Creative History and the Historic Sense' (12–13)

Introduction

When Ford Madox Ford, one of the most redolent icons of British modernism, speaks of creative history as having no such thing as 'Time', he is articulating a common modernist rebellion against chronology. Indeed, after Joseph Conrad's death, Ford not only articulates this animus against chronological narration, as not true to life and consciousness, but also actually mimetically instantiates his point in a well-known passage making use of a certain 'Mr. Slack' (*Joseph Conrad: A Personal Remembrance* 193–4). In Lytton Strachey's *Queen Victoria* (1921), a work now smoothly included in the annals of the 'new biography', not only, as throughout Strachey's work, is it the case that the prose is not quite modernist or experimental, but also that the tale is told, broadly speaking, chronologically. However, this to my mind only enhances his very modernist argument: debunking, but with tenderness, Victorianism and its biographical hagiographical methods, as if to mimic the mode of romance were to show up its limitations against the real like an immanent critique, using the weapons of the foe against it. The implicit assumption in this paper echoes Max Saunders' claim that 'life-writing is central to modernism' (456).

Indeed, Strachey's *Queen Victoria* is dedicated to his close friend, literary colleague and modernist icon, Virginia Woolf.[1] And though, at the time, Woolf declared the Strachey work under consideration here 'flimsy', later in the late 1930s she was to propose that Strachey had done for Victoria what Boswell had done for Johnson (Holroyd 496). To cite Saunders again, 'The idea of great historical sweep was something that was increasingly to preoccupy Woolf, culminating in the historical pageant of Between the Acts' (458).[2] And that hint at dramatising history will be a significant part of the purport of this paper. Strachey, as we will see, not only dramatises the historical record, but also makes precocious use of near-filmic effects. Strachey, as Michael Holroyd notes, revolutionised the art of biography by 'the use of the genres of fiction' (495). He moved between the representational mode of biography, where real individuals become idealised and typed, and the kind of 'imaginary portraiture', which, Saunders writes, begins, by contrast, 'with a type or idealization, and particularizes it by casting it in biographical form' (462).

1. Regarding Woolf's literary relation with Strachey, specifically to do with her two novels parodying and re-inventing the biographical form, *Orlando* and *Flush*, see Saunders (456–8). In this context, see also Marcus on *Orlando* and/as biography (116–21) and on features of *Orlando* that Saunders (above) also discusses (117–18).

2. For some contemporary commentary on Woolf in this respect, see Lee (28–44).

This hypostatic approach, a way of parsing or framing the particular individual subject in question as a 'type', which then becomes part of a typological imaginary, was practiced by Walter Pater well before Strachey. It was of the essence, so to speak, of his (Pater's) aesthetic criticism, to both make use of and embody gestures (after rendered 'types') of connoisseurship. For Pater, artistic works were not discursive artefacts, and were 'untranslatable', thus, into any other medium than that in which they successfully breathed human vitality and pleasure (131). In so far as each work or each artist offers 'an order of impressions distinct in kind' (131), in Pater's idealised portraits, the excitement he found in his subject and his subject matter was always of a kind, so to speak, which he could not 'get elsewhere' (51).[3] As Denis Donoghue has written, 'Pater was interested in history for the images it offered and the feelings it inspired, but in the end the only history he cared about was that of someone's mind […]'. Or, later, connecting the 'renaissance' studies to Pater's Imaginary Portraits, 'The chapters on Renaissance artists […]' were, 'of certain great types of being, with just enough veridical matter to keep them in their frames' (126, 197–8). Thus, it would seem that Strachey's idiosyncratic approach to imaginary portraiture, for all its modernist animus against Victorian rigorist moralism, had Victorian forebears. That said, Pater is and has often been seen as one of the most potent precursors of what is broadly conceived of as 'modernism' (see McGrath).

If Strachey here presents us with the equivalent of a 'romantic novel' (Holroyd 490), its status as romance dovetails nonetheless with more modernist paraphernalia. Strachey is an 'artist', as Woolf dubbed the 'new biographer' in her seminal essay 'The New Biography' (Marcus 92), reflecting in impressionist manner the truth as he sees it, both of himself

3. See, as another example, Pater (61).

and, at the same time, what that self detects in the past of his subject matter. As a romancer, he is offering access to the truth, or perhaps only a truth, via eminently skewed (or selective) representation – imaginary representation. And again, he would seem to have a Victorian forebear in Pater in this endeavour. Here, Pater both speaks of Botticelli, and of himself as well, mirroring the Botticelli he describes – thus preceding Strachey in the manner of impressionist biography, whereby biographical subject and biographer's self mutually inform each other:

> But the genius of which Botticelli is the type usurps the data before it as the exponent of ideas, moods, visions of its own; in this interest it plays fast and loose with those data, rejecting some and isolating others, and always combining them anew. (Pater 53–4)

It has been noted, tartly, that Pater 'should not have called his book Studies in the History of the Renaissance. His sense of the Renaissance wasn't historical' (Donoghue 126).

And yet, the impressionist method seems quite apt for a history of a self, a biography. While in one sense Strachey follows Nietzsche's injunction for history to be 'monumental' (*Untimely Meditations* 70), pragmatically affecting at a meta-historical level as he did the future course of biographical discourse; in another sense, Strachey's biographical techniques are there to romanticise and rivet a reader away from the hammer of any pragmatic impact.[4] In short, his representation of the contents of a certain 'fate' has also proven to be fated. Unlike with Victorian modes of biography, Strachey is

---

4. See Nietzsche's 'On the Uses and Disadvantages of History for Life' (59–60, 64, 70, 76). In these exemplary places, Nietzsche overtly praises a historiography that aims for a dramatic pragmatic impact.

certainly not trying, overtly at least, to moralise to a public, or make some kind of quasi-political statement.[5] But there is morality in style, technique; by entertaining his readership, perhaps he teaches them by the bye, by the wayside; his techniques are put to use, then, to render history impressionist, and also live; and liveness is a kind of truth, and one we all share. His contemporary, and a prolific impressionistic biographer, G. K. Chesterton, was also intent on romance, believing that motive and the romantic conception of things were after all the most humanly real.[6]

However, it is not so much what Strachey says about his subject that is of the utmost significance in this paper. Rather, it is what he says and is able to say, above all that, via the techniques he uses, to construct sense from and through his subject. The first of these has to do with his predominant use of free indirect style and its cognates, in relation to his tell-tale use of characterisation; the second discusses the well-known use of psychological and indeed psychoanalytical insight; the third speaks to how he is able via a rhythmic use of different focalisations to link and (implicitly) dovetail and at times fully meld objective history with subjective history. To follow this, I discuss his choric use of stage-like beginnings and endings; finally, picking out more objective features of his manner and method, I aim to show how he uses meta-historical tropes, literary critical insight at a time before such literary critical techniques as 'implied reader analysis' were firmly established, as well his near-filmic effects here and there.

5. See in this respect, though not strictly speaking directly related to biography, Collini's *Public Moralists* (on John Stuart Mill, for example, 121, 130–4, 151) and *English Pasts* (for example, 119–43 and on Mill again 122, 132).

6. See, as only two small instances, Chesterton's 'William Morris and his School' (22) and *George Bernard Shaw* (45).

History Free Indirect, And So On...

While from the opening of *Queen Victoria* Strachey makes use of dramatic dialogue, it is – as we are assured by footnotes – well sourced. That said, his predominant mode of characterisation makes use of an often speculative free indirect style, making his tale as much an impressionist one as one based in the historical records. Much like E. M. Forster's near-contemporary (1927) dictum regarding the 'novel', Strachey moves with a dramatic 'rhythm' between being inside the frame and outside it (Forster 167). In other words, Strachey moves deftly between the medias res of a historical character in the drama of his or her present and the more stable historian's point of view. And here again, Pater appears as a telling precursor. Indeed, speaking of 'rhythm', Pater's notorious comment about all arts aspiring to the 'condition of music' is a very apt notion in this context (135). The aestheticist desideratum for an ineffable seamlessness of form and content also plays out in Pater in a way that speaks to the Strachey discussed so far and below, in so far as Pater's impressionism seems to wish to unite the quiddity of his individual, idealised or better, ideal types, with that of the historical period in question. Writing of Pico Della Mirandola, Pater explains, then:

> He had sought knowledge, and passed from system to system, and hazarded much; but because he believed there was a spirit of order and beauty in knowledge, which would come down and unite what men's ignorance had divided, and renew what time had made dim. (49)

In this hale description of a humanism uniting by the redress of (the philosophic) art the men of the artist's time, Pater seems, too, to be speaking of his own impressionist humanism. Pater is 'uniting' the 'type' in question with the type of redemption he offers, or offered, to his times. The unificatory process is thus happening on, at the very least, three interlocked levels: the individual artefacts of an artist's art and their unification into a type, effected by Pater; the historical artist with the historical time, via the now-parsed significance of his art; and the conjunction of the two, via the now-forged unity of Pater and all his readers.[7] And to repeat, this impressionistic method of reading the universal through the individual and vice versa was carried into, not only Strachey's works, but those of contemporaries, too, such as G. K. Chesterton. For instance, Chesterton wrote in his biography of Saint Francis (1923), of how the Saint's unique mysticism was both rooted in and emblematic of the period and ethos of the contemporaneous 'troubadours' (34–42); that, among other

7. A paradox of such kinds of aestheticism, whether intended to be so or not, in writers such as Pater, Wilde, James, Strachey, or Chesterton, is that in so far as they evince impressionism in the texture of their texts, they unite subjectivism and, in a different way, objectivism. For the impressionist there is no (to use Hegelese) 'substance', or at least none until and as an effect of 'essence'; there is no 'factual' datum (worth its name), rather only what that datum (first might) mean to a sensitised subject. And in so far as this holds as a generalisation, then in a way impressionism and humanism conjoin, strangely, in the (implicit) attitudes of such writerly figures. The hypostatic method, typological, evinces both abstractive unitive processes and the most concretely individual tastes. The figure of Christ, chief romance, chief romancer, in a way, was similarly both judge and judged. Regarding the Christian paradigm as the source of the structure of romance, see Frye's *The Secular Scripture*. More pressingly, see in this respect Nietzsche's *Twilight of The Idols and The Anti-Christ* (for example, 158, 163, 184). Among other things, here – in a work in which Nietzsche (eponymous modernist) accuses Platonic essentialism of cowardice in the face of reality (118) – while Nietzsche is scurrilously critical of Christianity as an institutional religion, he does indeed praise the man 'Christ' himself, for much the same reason or animus ratcheted behind his own Zarathustra (163). Christ, implicitly for Nietzsche, was his own master, the god of himself; he was both subject (individual biographical man) and object ('Christian-ity'), seamlessly, musically almost, at one.

impressionistic historical tropes, regarding St Francis, or indeed, within many of Chesterton's numerous impressionistic biographies.[8]

Whether it is getting 'in' a character, such as early on in *Queen Victoria*, his very Dickensian portrayal of George III (8); or, alternately, the scenic use of selective details to insinuate (idealised) character, Strachey's narrative is indeed proto-novelistic.[9] There are many examples peppered throughout with a canny rhythm, of both direct diegetic characterisation, as well as a prolific use of free indirect style. The first can be sampled here, regarding Lord Palmerston, in a chapter titled after the great statesman:

> But Palmerston, busy with his plans, his ambitions, and the management of a great department, brushed all such considerations to one side; it was his favourite method of action. He lived by instinct – by a quick eye and a strong hand, a dexterous management of every crisis as it arose, a half-unconscious sense of the vital elements in a situation. He was very bold; and nothing gave him

8. It should be noted here that biographically Chesterton overtly derided and opposed 'impressionism' throughout his oeuvre. That said, he most definitely can be viewed as an impressionistic biographer. See, for instance, Sabbagh. Moreover, in the context of this essay, it should be noted that Chesterton himself has an early, short article, titled, 'Queen Victoria'. Indeed, one of Chesterton's most well-known works was and is *The Victorian Age in Literature* (1913). For useful commentary on this, see Ker (328–41).

9. See also Strachey regarding 'King William': 'A bursting, bubbling old gentleman, with quarter-deck gestures, round rolling eyes, and a head like a pineapple, his sudden elevation to the throne after fifty-six years of utter insignificance had almost sent him crazy. His natural exuberance completely got the better of him; he rushed about doing preposterous things in an extraordinary manner, spreading amusement and terror in every direction; and talking all the time' (38).

more exhilaration than to steer the ship of state in
a high wind, on a rough sea, with every stitch of
canvas on her that she could carry. (152)

Or, again with the emphasis on diegesis, here Strachey
contrasts Gladstone with Disraeli, the former's 'very antithesis':

It was not his habit to harangue and exhort and
expatiate in official conscientiousness; he liked to
scatter flowers along the path of business, to
compress a weighty argument into a happy phrase,
to insinuate what was in his mind with an air of
friendship and confidential courtesy. He was
nothing if not personal [...]. (253)

Or, near the close of the work, again, a summation in diegetic
mode:

in the impact of a personality, it is something
deeper, something fundamental and common to all
its qualities, that really tells. In Victoria, it is easy to
discern the nature of this underlying element: it was
a peculiar sincerity. Her truthfulness, her single-
mindedness, the vividness of her emotions and her
unrestrained expression of them, were the varied
forms which this central characteristic assumed. It
was her sincerity which gave her at once her
impressiveness, her charm, and her absurdity. (304)

Contrasting with this more traditional historian's viewpoint,
however, throughout the work characters are also mimetically
inhabited. Having purchased 'Balmoral House' in 1848,
Victoria's free indirect style runs: 'Now she could be really
happy every summer; now she could be simple and at her
ease; now she could be romantic every evening, doting upon

Albert, without a single distraction, all day long' (192). Or then, when it was time to leave and turn homewards: 'She could hardly bear it; she sat disconsolate in her room and watched the snow falling. The last day! Oh! If only she could be snowed up!' (196). Indeed, at one point this inhabiting of personality, a predominant mode in the book, extends itself by personification to the nation, to the public. In her widowhood now, having retreated from the public, and carrying the cross of her idolatry of her passed husband, the Prince Consort, Albert, Victoria

> did not understand that the picture of an embodied perfection is distasteful to the majority of mankind [....] The cause of this is not so much an envy of the perfect being as a suspicion that he must be inhuman; and thus it happened that the public, when it saw displayed for its admiration a figure resembling the sugary hero of a moral story-book rather than a fellow man of flesh and blood, turned away with a shrug, a smile, and a flippant ejaculation. (233)

Throughout the work Strachey acts like a psychologist; he even dubs himself one directly at one point (275). As Holroyd writes, part of Strachey's originality lay in the 'psychosexual insights' entailed by his 'sexual temperament' (490). In both felicity and doom, then, note two instances of speculative historical psychology; the first, happily speaking of Disraeli, and the second, unhappily of the Prince Consort. Both are reflections of Strachey – where that genitive is both, self-reflexive and not so:

> In women's hearts he had always read as in an open book. His whole career turned upon those curious

entities; and the more curious they were, the more intimately at home with them he seemed to be. (Strachey 252).

In fact, in two places nearby, the psychologically insightful portrayal of Disraeli not only seems to reflect Strachey's own self-awareness, but also simultaneously names the way in which that very detecting self portrays selves in the configurations of his artistic biographical endeavours. Thus much like the effecting of the representation of the eponymous queen herself, using the same forms of imaginative dexterity, Disraeli here sees into Victoria like the puppeteer Strachey sees into them both:

> He realized everything – the indirect complexities of circumstance and character, the pride of place mingled so inextricably with personal arrogance, the superabundant emotionalism, the ingenuousness of outlook, the solid, the laborious respectability, shot through so incongruously by temperamental cravings for the coloured and the strange, the singular intellectual limitations, and the mysteriously essential female element impregnating every particle of the whole. (252)[10]

And that last choice of present participle is telling. Like Strachey, 'impregnating' his tale with such layered insight, Disraeli, too, seems to be both inside and outside the frame, '[a]ctor and spectator both' (260). And those 'two characters' blended so intimately that they 'formed an inseparable unity, and it was impossible to say that one of them was less genuine than the other' (260). Indeed, in a relatively recent and copious

10. See Strachey's two descriptions of Victoria's temperamental craving for the exotic, one regarding Lord Melbourne (198) and the other Disraeli (257).

study of 'Auto/biographical discourses', Laura Marcus starts her chapter on Strachey (and Woolf) and the 'new biography', by indicating that at this time in the modern history of biographical discourse the biographer was considered to have a well-nigh '"transferential" relation- ship to the biographical subject' (90–1). It is no wonder, then, given that Strachey saw Victoria as a 'martyr to anal eroticism' (Holroyd 490), that he would spend lengthy passages towards the end of this work describing Victoria's obsessive collecting and collections as psychological fetishes to shore up a deep fear of mortality and the passing of things (Strachey 292).But, otherwise, he seems also to inhabit the insight he deals towards Prince Albert. In this passage, there is a dominant Jamesian theme (from 'The Beast in the Jungle', say, or the central scene of his *The Ambassadors*)[11] of an uncanny living on the verge of live experience, but never making it real, detailed again with reflexive intents:

> For in spite of everything he had never reached to happiness. His work, for which at last he came to crave with an almost morbid appetite, was a solace and not a cure; the dragon of his dissatisfaction devoured with dark relish that ever-growing tribute of laborious days and nights; but it was hungry still. The causes of his melancholy were hidden, mysterious, unanalyzable perhaps – too

11. In these two works by Henry James, the thematic concern has to do with the main (male) characters, who find themselves, at the end of their (un)signifying lives, having lost out on the opportunity to have really effectually lived their lives, precisely because of the paradox that they had been always on tenterhooks, awaiting the nebulous opportunity to do so. See, for example, a famous passage in James's *The Ambassadors* where the main character 'Strether' advises his (central) younger companion, in the wake of now-realized lost opportunity, to grab life, the chance to experience, as it were, by the horns (131–4).

deeply rooted in the innermost recesses of his temperament for the eye of reason to apprehend. There were contradictions in his nature, which… made him an inexplicable enigma: he was severe and gentle; he was modest and scornful; he longed for affection and he was cold. (208)

That mildly enervated image of a 'dragon' tells us much about Strachey's involvement or investment in such a portrayal. Like Strachey, Albert, to continue, was 'lonely, not merely with the loneliness of exile but with the loneliness of conscious and unrecognized superiority' (208).[12] And then, once the Prince Consort is long-dead, Strachey discusses how Victoria not only allowed John Brown, her closest Highland servant, to boss her about, but that she verily 'enjoyed it' (272). Again, in psychologist mode, Strachey extemporises:

The eccentricity appeared to be extraordinary; but, after all, it is no uncommon thing for an autocratic dowager to allow some trusted indispensable servant to adopt towards her an attitude of authority which is jealously forbidden to relatives or friends: the power of a dependant still remains, by a psychological sleight-of-hand, one's own power, even when it is exercised over oneself. (272)

And this psychological insight may work as a metaphor for that quid pro quo between subjectivism and objectivism that has already been noted as a feature of Strachey's narrative rhythm. One of the most apparent techniques observable here is the dovetailing and signal linking of characterological histories with a more universal, quasi-objective rendering of accounts. Speaking of the covert influence of Victoria's former

12. Also, Strachey hints at Albert's psychosexual inversion (98–9).

governess, Baroness Lehzen, Strachey again seems to offer
within his narrative signal images of his formal method:

> The ascendancy she meant to keep. No doubt it
> was true that technically she took no part in public
> business; but the distinction between what is public
> and what is private is always a subtle one; and in
> the case of the reigning sovereign – as the next few
> years were to show – is often imaginary. (55)

In a sense then, 'the sovereign' here, Victoria, images
Strachey's eponymous Queen Victoria. There are many
instances where Strachey's narration, after zooming in on the
particulars, zooms back out to the more sweeping panoramic
view; this is particularly the case with his thematisation of
Englishness, reprised periodically from near the start through
to the end. In the Chapter on 'Lord Palmerston' the relative
Englishness or foreignness of the Prince Consort is a central
concern (174–6, 182–4). The notion of the Victorian
'gentleman' is a parallel instance here (206). Ending Part VI of
Chapter IV, we read with more monumental intent, sweeping
the age along into the consideration of its eponymous person:

> For Victoria, with all the zeal of a convert, upheld
> now the standard of moral purity with an
> inflexibility surpassing, if that were possible,
> Albert's own. She blushed to think how she had
> once believed […] that one might be too strict and
> particular in such matters, and that one ought to
> be indulgent towards other people's dreadful sins.
> But she was no more Lord M.'s pupil: she was
> Albert's wife. She was more – the embodiment,
> the living apex of a new era in the generations of
> mankind. The last vestige of the eighteenth century

had disappeared; cynicism and subtlety were shrivelled into powder; and duty, industry, morality, and domesticity triumphed over them. Even the very chairs and tables had assumed, with a singular responsiveness, the forms of prim solidity. The Victorian Age was in full swing. (141–2)[13]

In line with what has been suggested about the coalescing of the biographical tale being told and its very framing and formal configurations, it is also the case that there are many instances where Strachey seems to be precociously using literary-critical methods to make historical or biographical judgments. Often enough, he seems to approach the much later-developed technique of eliciting from the forms of statement or their lack, an implied meaning, if not an implied reader (55, 78, 94, 179, 246–7). In tandem with this formalistic note, Strachey also makes dramatic, stage-like, and at times almost choric use of beginnings and endings to his chapters and to the sections within such. This formal selection also tells us more about Strachey's dramatisation of history and biography. Chapter Two, for instance, opens and ends on the note of 'prophecy'. Most of the time, endings and beginnings are used to transition from one demarcated phase of narration to another, thereby indicating a near-modernist sensibility that eludes direct chronological continuity, without being discontinuous – by way of dovetailing, scenic in this sense. Indeed, at times, there is the almost filmic (not to mention musical) intent of a kind of gathering in of previously deployed threads. Among many examples is the actual cadence and close of the work, where Victoria is pictured on her

13. See Strachey for a parallel comment on Victoria embodying the 'Victorian' triumph of the 'middle classes' (28).

deathbed recalling images of her past; in today's context, such a scene would be very aptly portrayed cinematically:

> She herself, as she lay blind and silent, seemed to those who watched her to be divested of all thinking – to have glided already, unawares, into oblivion. Yet, perhaps, in the secret chambers of consciousness, she had her thoughts, too. Perhaps her fading mind called up once more the shadows of the past to float before it, and retraced, for the last time, the vanished visions of that long history – passing back and back, through the cloud of years, to older and ever older memories – to the spring woods at Osborne, so full of primroses for Lord Beaconsfield – to Lord Palmerston's queer clothes and high demeanour, and Albert's face under the green lamp, and Albert's first stag at Balmoral, and Albert in his blue and silver uniform, and the Baron coming in through a doorway, and Lord M. dreaming at Windsor with the rooks cawing in the elm-trees, and the Archbishop of Canterbury on his knees in the dawn, and the old King's turkey-cock ejaculations, and uncle Leopold's soft vice at Claremont, and Lehzen with the globes, and her mother's feathers sweeping down towards her, and great old repeater-watch of her father's in its tortoise-shell case, and a yellow rug, and some friendly flounces of sprigged muslin, and the trees and the grass at Kensington. (309–10).[14]

At this finale two things at the least seem to be happening; the nostalgic gathering in of threads of the dying Victoria

---

14. Another example is on 240.

is at the same time that of Strachey's *Queen Victoria*. More emphatically though, the insinuated idea that at the end of one's life, in oldest age, one's earliest memories people one's mind with more force than otherwise, is a romance-trope, signifying resolution and the coming full circle of the cycle of life. However, it remains precociously filmic. And perhaps Strachey's dramatising methods are more powerfully debunking, more powerfully modernist, in so far as he enacts his critique of the Victorian era, with tenderness, with its own weapons; thus, he is ideologically precocious, again, in so far as he offers us a modernist 'immanent critique', by which limitation (and perspectival delimitation) is embraced as the only the hope for trying to 'transcend' the melee, the 'confusion' of history, and the selves within it, and the selves that partly make it.

Conclusion

If under the modernist dispensation there is no more objective fate that happens to characters, and if, indeed, for the modernist immanent sensibility, fate is character, meaning no more fate in its traditional sense, then perhaps it is a felicitous boon in Strachey's method that he manages to evince both sides of that dichotomy.[15] His peppering of meta-historical comments and images, often invoking concepts like 'omen', 'doom', 'fortune', 'destiny', 'fate' within his narrative is thus a fertile way of saying that he is commander of the drama, commander of prolepsis and analepsis, as well as trying to

15. This rendering of the inversions of the notions of fate and character is derived from Walter Benjamin's own citation of Nietzsche in his 'Fate and Character'. As one example of this collapsing of fate and character into each other, one can think of Ford Madox Ford's modernist classic *The Good Soldier* (1915). Michael Levenson has descried there how character becomes the 'disintegration' of character (102–20).

descry the true meaning of the past as it was lived and felt (9, 22, 35, 109, 213, 219). For just like Strachey writing this history, there is no reason to suppose that historical figures within the tale, and within themselves, did not also turn outwards and think of their dramatic present from the perspective of fate and historical destiny; indeed, this would be more expected of the kind of figures peopling Strachey's tale: all 'eminent', so to speak. Laura Marcus has written with much perspicacity, summarising much of the purport of this paper:

> Strachey, notoriously, drew on published sources alone, which he lists at the end of each life, rewriting written 'lives' and showing how supposedly 'factual' elements can be deployed to quite different ends in different contexts. His emphasis on the role of texts within lives – his biographical subjects are repeatedly depicted in the act of self-portrayal and self- communion through their diaries and letters – reinforces this sense of lives fashioned in and through texts […]. (114)

Textuality and the sense of authority that preceded it thus do a kind of minuet in Strachey's hands; while subordinating the brief of the gods, he still makes use of their jargon.

Works Cited

Benjamin, Walter. 'Fate and Character'. *Reflections: Essays, Aphorisms, Autobiographical Writings*. Trans. Edmund Jephcott. Ed. Peter Demetz. New York: Schocken Books, 2007. 304–11.

Chesterton, G. K. *George Bernard Shaw* [1935]. London: House of Stratus, 2000.

Chesterton, G. K. 'Queen Victoria'. Varied Types [1903]. New York: Books For Library Press Inc., 1968. 225–34.

Chesterton, G. K. *St Francis of Assisi* [1923]. London: House of Stratus, 2001.

Chesterton, G. K. *The Victorian Age in Literature* [1913]. London: House of Stratus, 2001.

Chesterton, G. K. 'William Morris and his School'. *Varied Types* [1903]. New York: Books For Library
Press Inc., 1968. 15–26.

Collini, Stefan. *English Pasts: Essays in History and Culture*. Oxford: Oxford University Press,
1999.

Collini, Stefan. *Public Moralists: Political Thought and Intellectual Life in Britain, 1850–1930*. Oxford: Clarendon University Press, 1993.

Donoghue, Denis. *Walter Pater: Lover of Strange Souls*. New York: Alfred A. Knopf, 1995.

Ford, Ford Madox. 'Creative History and the Historic Sense' [1904]. *Critical Essays*. Eds Max Saunders and Richard Stang. New York: New York University Press, 2004. 4–14.

Ford, Ford Madox. *The Good Soldier* [1915]. Ed. Martin Stannard. New York & London: W. W. Norton & Co., 2012.

Ford, Ford Madox. *Joseph Conrad: A Personal Remembrance* [1925]. New York: The Ecco Press, 1989.

Forster, E. M. *Aspects of the Novel* [1927]. New York: Harcourt, Brace & World, 1954.

Frye, Northrop. *The Secular Scripture: A Study of The Structure of Romance, Charles Eliot Norton Lectures*, 1974–5. Cambridge, Massachusetts and London: Harvard University Press, 1976.

Holroyd, Michael. *Lytton Strachey: The New Biography*. New York & London: W.W. Norton & Co., 1994.

James, Henry. *The Ambassadors* [1903]. Ed. S. P. Rosenbaum. New York & London: W. W. Norton & Co., 1994.

James, Henry. Preface to *The Spoils of Poynton.*
Henry James: The Future of the Novel: Essays on the Art of

Fiction. Ed. Leon Edel. New York: Vintage Books, 1956. 51–3.

Ker, Ian. *G. K. Chesterton: A Biography*. Oxford: Oxford University Press, 2011.

Lee, Hermione. *Body Parts: Essays in Life-Writing*. London: Chatto & Windus, 2005.

Levenson, Michael. *Modernism and the Fate of Individuality: Character and Novelistic Form from Conrad to Woolf*. Cambridge: Cambridge University Press, 2004.

Marcus, Laura. *Auto/biographical discourses: Criticism, Theory, Practice*. Manchester & New York: Manchester University Press, 1994.

McGrath, F. C. *The Sensible Spirit: Walter Pater and the Modernist Paradigm*. Tampa: University of Florida Press, 1986.

Nietzsche, Friedrich. *Twilight of The Idols and The Anti-Christ*. Trans. R. J. Hollingdale. London: Penguin Books, 1990.

Nietzsche, Friedrich. 'On the Uses and Disadvantages of History for Life'. *Untimely Meditations*. Trans. R. J. Hollingdale. Ed. Daniel Breazeale. Cambridge: Cambridge University Press, 2007.

Pater, Walter. *The Renaissance: Studies in Art and Poetry* [1873]. London: Tiger Books, 1998.

Sabbagh, Omar. 'G. K. Chesterton's London: Traversing Therapeutic Space'. *The Chesterton Review* 41.3–4 (December 2015): 507–28.

Saunders, Max. *Self Impression: Life-Writing, Autobiografiction, and the Forms of Modern Literature*. Oxford & New York: Oxford University Press, 2010.

Strachey, Lytton. *Queen Victoria*. London: Chatto & Windus, 1921.

9

Ratiocination in The Old Pretender: Facets of Rationalism in Henry James's *The Golden Bowl*

'And that is what Henry James gives you – an immense body of work all dominated with that vibration – with that balancing of mind between the great outlines and the petty details.'[1]
Ford Madox Ford

Relatively early on in Leon Edel's (abridged) biography of Henry James, it is revealed that at the inception of his writerly career, James's father, Henry Sr. averred that the 'critical faculty' of his son, Henry Jr., was his 'main gift' and the 'dominant feature of his intellectual organization.'[2] Later in said biography, Edel says that for Henry James, critical work was an 'extension' of his other, more predominant, 'creative' work.[3] James is like his character, Adam Verver, thus, who considers his critical, collector's role as equivalent to the original creators or producers of his splendid collection. [4]And finally, regarding the central ground of this paper, Edel writes

1. Ford Madox Ford, *Henry James: A Critical Study* (facsimile, 1913), p. 155. This, even though James was highly dismissive of Ford's book: see Leon Edel, *Henry James: A Life* (Cambridge, Philadelphia, San Francisco, London, Mexico City, Sao Paolo, Singapore, Sydney: Harper Collins, Abridged Edition, 1985), p. 655.

2. Edel, op. cit., p, 163.

3. Ibid., p. 555.

4. Henry James, *The Golden Bowl*, ed. Virginia Llewellyn Smith (Oxford:

of James's *The Golden Bowl* (1904), connecting the biographical life of the author with the plot of his final, finished full-scale novel, that:

> There had always been triangles in James's life. In this ultimate work, they culminated in two joined triangles: father, daughter, and daughter's husband; and husband's mistress, who then marries father and so becomes step-mother of heroine, and mother-in-law of her lover. Everyone begins by having his cake and eating it....[5]

The main tenor of this paper fleshes out, in different ways, the implicit purport, however incidental, of these observations. What all of these observations suggest is that for all his concern with 'felt life,' with experience felt and rendered 'vivid,' with 'impressions,' Henry James was a highly ratiocinative creative artist. Though in his very late memoir (of 1914), *Notes of a Son and Brother*, he recounts his abysmal performance and interest in 'mathematics' as a child and youth, I hope to show in this paper how, as phrased in a slightly later part of that same late-coming memoir, for James, the values of 'life' and of 'knowledge' were or came to be seen by him as coterminous. Indeed, in that same memoir he speaks of coming to the realization of a 'science' of 'impressions.' [6]Phrased there, again – and in other words – he speaks of how, even from that young age, 'impressions of' became for him 'impressions for;' [7]

Oxford University Press, 1999), p. 106. From henceforth, the page references for citations of this text will appear in pursuant parentheses in the main text above.

5. Edel, op. cit., p. 583.

6. Henry James, *Notes of a Son and Brother* and *The Middle Years,* ed. Peter Collister, Charlottesville and London: University of Virginia Press, 2011, ps. 7 & 25.

7. Ibid., p. 24.

just as later, the phenomenon of 'reading into' the experience, however vicarious, of the American Civil War, was re-collected by the very late James as the same as 'reading out' of it.[8]

I will show facets of Jamesian rationalism, first, via the pivotal role of inversions, recursions, binaries, paradoxes and antinomies in the novel which provides the central lens for this take on James's sensibility; second, I will look at some of the imagery and tropes made use of, quite typical of James's rhetoric – specifically, financial, quantitative, arithmetic and/or geometric metaphors, both within and in a manner without the concrete tale, thus linking in a telling way James's predominant mentality as I see it, with the concrete algebra of his production; third, I will suggest how, much like his heroine, Maggie Verver, of whom we are told that while the iconic and pan-symbolic 'bowl' may now be 'broken', 'her reason hadn't' (434) – James evinces a highly redolent unity-of-consciousness in this novel, as elsewhere; but in, I hope to show, many unexpected ways. Like Kant's doctrine of 'apperception,' James's 'I think' accompanies, over-weening-ly, all his 'impressions.' If James was in one manner a founder of (empiricist) Impressionism: he was so in a highly rationalistic manner.

One hallmark of empiricist impressionism, as seen, say, in some of Hume's occasional literary and political essays, is the respect given to the manifold of experience, speaking generally, and the skepticism about abstracting from said manifold in whatever field of life or interest, reducing it to some more fundamental or foundational origin or principle. However, the unifying mentality (the formalist mentality) need not been seen as wholly oppositional to such empiricism; far from it, obviously. Indeed, perhaps the two extremes of

8. Ibid., p. 60-1.

rationalism and empiricism might be seen to be married, determinately yoked, in what Nietzsche, James's close-contemporary, lauded as 'the grand style.'

What Nietzsche called and lauded as 'the grand style,' as parsed at least by Heidegger, involved a 'fundamental condition' – *that of the aesthetic* – where an 'equally original freedom,' reigned, 'with regard to the extreme opposites, chaos and law;' a kind of 'mastery' 'which enables the primal wilderness of chaos and the primordiality of law to advance under the same yoke.' The 'grand ambition here,' according to Heidegger, is '[t]o become master of the chaos one is; to compel one's chaos to become form: logical, simple, unequivocal; to become mathematics, *law*.' This 'grand style,' which I am suggesting is immanent in the late James, involves what Nietzsche sees as a masterful 'calm,' 'by which the antithetical is preserved, i.e., transfigured, in the unity of a yoke that sustains the tension of a bow.' 'The artist – … a designation for the aesthetic state… is love of form for form's sake,' as, '[g]enuine form is the only true content.' For Nietzsche '"[e]stimates of aesthetic value," have as their "ground floor," those feelings that relate to logical, arithmetical, and geometrical lawfulness.' And the 'logical feelings' which Nietzsche invokes are not feelings that are logical, but rather a 'feeling for letting one's mood be determined by order, boundary, the overview.' [9]These (contemporaneous) notions will be shown I hope to be highly pertinent to the sensibility descried here in the late James.

Perhaps, to start briefly with some notes on the (1909) Preface to the novel, it is no accident that James speaks of his work of scenic parsimony as the success of his ability to

9. Martin Heidegger, *Nietzsche: Volume I: The Will to Power as Art & Volume II: The Eternal Recurrence of the Same,* trans. By David Farrell Krell, Harper Collins, 1991, p. 128-29, 136-37 & 119-21.

have 'held' his 'system fast and fondly...the whole thing...'
'... remaining subject to the register, ever so closely kept,
of the consciousness of but two of the characters' (xlii).
Consciousness – *of course* – but more emphatically for my
purposes, a 'system.' And he speaks also of the 'taste of the
poet...so far as the poet in him prevails...' as one whose
truth-bearing priority is 'to hold the silver clue to the whole
labyrinth of his consciousness' (liii). 'System' and 'labyrinth,'
then, as images of, 'clues' to his mentality as bodied-forth.
James also speaks of the 'exquisite *laws*' of '*sovereign* truth –
which decrees that, as art is nothing if not exemplary, care
nothing if not active, finish nothing if not *consistent*...
"connections" are employable for truer purposes than mere
gaping contrition' (lxi, my italics). Indeed, when writing to
Scribner's of this final novel, James says that it was the most
'done,' 'composed', 'complete', 'constructed' work he had ever
done.[10]

Loneliness, we gather from Edel, may well have been the
essential tenor of James's life. [11]But I want, in the main, to
consider that biographical truth through a different, far more
objective, critical modality. More like solitude, than loneliness.
His biographical loneliness, the thoroughgoing Oneness of
his formal conception and method, as well as due thematic
imports, tally with his seminal concentration on psychological
action over material action. And yet, there is more to James
than (empirical) psychology; there is something more
transcendental at play. As Edel notes, nothing really 'happens'
in any conventionally dramatic sense in *The Golden
Bowl.* [12]Much like the relatively-recent Hollywood film,
"Inside Man," James's last completed novel is a tale of one

10. Edel., op. cit., p. 585.
11. Ibid., p. 511.
12. Ibid., p. 434.

operating man, James, who allows all to happen so that nothing, in the end, perhaps, *will have happened*. (A kind of narratological 'I AM that I AM.') In one specific sense, it is a 'vicious circle' (289). And the 'evidence', symbolically speaking, is 'smashed evidence' (436-7). One, final, way of putting it is to say, again, after Edel, that if James was a 'solipsist,' [13] like many of his epigones, such as Conrad and Ford, it *wasn't* necessarily, as is commonly the case, due to a native 'empiricism;' no, I want to suggest that James's aesthetic solipsism was far more transcendental in register than empirical or literal. As Heidegger writes, '[h]ere yawns the abyss of that circularity in which the whole of human Dasein moves. What health is, only the healthy can say….' [14]Which is to say, James names himself in this novel, with every strophe. The tale he's concocted not only emits *from* him but wends back into him as well. He is, as it were, both: judge and judged.

The 'golden bowl,' to put it succinctly at first, is a metaphor for the symbolizing and symbolic mentality arching over the work – which is different to saying it's symbolic of the thematic relationships in the novel. The golden bowl is a metaphor for James's structure of feeling. Charlotte Stant asks if said artefact is '"cut out of" a 'single crystal?"' And the shopkeeper replies that she'll never find '"any joint or piercing"' (85). She continues to ask if it is indeed a 'lost art,' and the shopkeeper confirms it is so. (Indeed, later in this paper James will be seen to be vitally concerned, rhetorically as much as more generically, with *salvaging* operations.) In any case, the interchange continues, '"Does crystal then break – when it *is* crystal?"' To which the charismatic man replies, '"Its beauty is its *being* crystal. But its hardness is certainly its safety. It

13. Ibid., p. 166.
14. Heidegger, op. cit., p. 127.

doesn't break… like vile glass. It splits – if there is a split'"
(87). The idea (already broached) of the complementarity of
thoroughbred unity and the possibility of splitting, will be
significant below, when I begin to discuss James's structuralist
ways, making use of binaries, inversions, paradoxes and
duplicities, whether within or without the art-work.
However, some of the evidence of phrasing within the novel
may emphasize what I'm beginning to suggest.

If indeed, the presiding mentality over the novel is like
the golden bowl, both as supposed and as revealed, then
James's expressions within his tale may well be coded or un-
coded revelations of his aesthetic. So, echoing the shopkeeper's
claim for 'safety' – which, like 'danger', is of course one of
James's central keywords – Charlotte Stant says to the Prince
at one point, "'we're… safe…we're so because they are. And
they're so because they can't be anything else. We hang,
essentially, together'" (251). Towards the end of the novel,
speaking of her own desired end (in both senses) Maggie
wishes for "'a happiness without a hole in it'" (456), which
is a kind of completion of construction. Earlier of course
the Prince had said, speaking of their emergent coterie, that
"'we're of the same connection, of – what is your word? –
the same 'concern'"" (195). These characters are varied and
various effects of James's 'sovereign' imagination – what he
dubs elsewhere, speaking in praise of his own father late in life,
as the latter's 'saving imagination;' [15]they are 'ambassadors,'
perhaps, to 'represent' his own manner, globally-speaking, of
'representation.' A little farther on, thinking of the 'sense of
the past,' the Prince considers that what 'had happened, in
short, was that Charlotte and he had, by the single turn of the
wrist of fate…been placed face to face in a freedom…of *ideal
perfection*, since the magic web was spun, but without their

15. James, *Notes of a Son and Brother,* op. cit., p. 127.

toil, almost without their touch,' (218, my italics). Fate spins by 'the wrist,' much like the pen – even if we know that James was dictating his work by this time. Later Mr. Verver speaks to his daughter, again, of how their coterie moves, 'as a selfish mass' (365-6).

Binaries and dichotomies, essentially ratiocinative features, are redolent throughout the novel. At a generically psychological level, Edel notes how women were considered both worthy of a pedestal and of abject fear, by turns, in James's psyche. [16] In the novel under consideration itself, women are posed as either 'huntress' or 'muse' (36); as 'nymphs and nuns' (139). However, such dichotomies are more widespread than that. Fanny Assingham, we are told, both 'fears' and 'welcomes' 'complications,' (33) much like James himself. In an accurate rendering of, as it were, the paradoxical structure of guilt, Charlotte Stant is split (much like the iconic bowl) between the wish to elide or escape detection, and the wish for a final, thankful, confrontation (182). Just as innocence is guilt, and vice versa (258), so Mrs. Assingham can only show her disinterestedness to the Prince, via an overt engagement with his affairs (247). Maggie says, much later, to the same likable busybody that when the Prince had failed to 'speak' he had in fact done the equivalent of eloquent speech (421). Witness Maggie Verver on two earlier occasions: 'Subsidence of the fearsome, for Maggie's spirit, was always, at first, positive emergence of the sweet…' (312). And Maggie, again, finds the 'quantity of earnest intuition operating… so harmoniously,' as 'the mitigated midnight of these approximations' of hers, which lead her to making out, 'the promise of her dawn' (329). The harmony is a Janus-faced unity.

Such sovereign splitting is redolent, too, in a more mobile

16. Edel, op. cit., p. 16 & 86.

or dynamic way: via the habitual invoking of recursive inversions. Early on, a question is posed: what had happened or gone on between the Prince and Charlotte in the time preceding the opening of the novel. The way it's phrased is telltale: 'nothing except their having to recognize that nothing *could*' (53). Mr. Verver, the oldest character in the relevant coterie is spoken of as 'caught in the act of handling a relic of infancy – sticking on the head of a broken soldier…' (93). And though, 'as much as ever' still his child, 'there were sides on which' Maggie 'had protected' her father 'as if she were more than a daughter' (99; see also, 289).

Indeed, the central, the pivotal affair which spurs the baroque architectonics of the novel is filled with a similar inverting logic. The previous loving-affair between Charlotte and the Prince is the source in the main of all the psychological drama and tension. They, previously, have been doing the 'doing'; however, Charlotte now says that 'it's theirs, every inch of it; it's all a matter of what they've done *to* us…'

> Nothing stranger surely had ever happened to a conscientious, a well-meaning, a perfectly passive pair: no more extraordinary decree had every been launched against such victims than this of forcing them against their will into a relation of mutual close contact that they had done everything to avoid (211).

And then, as a particularly good example of James's dramatizing of psychological paradoxes, psychological inversions, so to speak, the same innocent or wily couple face the following predicament: '[T]hey had to yield to the fear that their showing as afraid to move together would count for them as the greater danger… Their least danger…is in going on with all the things;' the former, as implied, would more overtly or straightforwardly suggest their complicity (383). And at the end of the novel, to reprise an earlier observation, in Maggie's imagination, her father remains, 'always, marvelously, young' (489) – and this: compounding the irony of the paradox of Prince Amerigo's New-World name in tension with his old world lineage; a kind of tango between youth and age, guilt and innocence – a commonplace of course in James's repertoire.

As a final instantiation of this antinomian unity, here are two passages which evince what Daudet first named as the phenomenon of the 'homo duplex,' a term and a technique which later becomes central to the Impressionism of, for one, Ford Madox Ford. Here are two examples of temporal duplicity, or superimposition, or vibration, within, by or through signally unifying minds. Indeed, one might go so far as to say that the analogy of experiences enlisted below is only possible via a characterology that is rigorous and 'consistent' in its unities. Adam Verver, then:

> He had for himself another impulse than to go to bed; picking up a hat in the hall, slipping his arms into a sleeveless cape and lighting still another cigar, he turned out upon the terrace through one of the long drawing-room windows and moved to and fro there for an hour beneath the steep autumn stars. It was where he had walked in the afternoon sun with Fanny Assingham, and the sense of that other hour, the sense of the suggestive woman herself, was before him again as… if it had not yet been… (150).

And then, Mr. Verver's (formal and substantive) counterpart in many senses, the Prince:

> ...he had never so much as during such sojourns the trick of a certain detached, the amusement of a certain inward critical, life; the determined need, while apparently all participant, of returning upon himself, of backing noiselessly in, far in again, and rejoining there, as it were, that part of his mind that was not engaged at the front. (240).

From the internal tropes used in narration, to overall architectonic, James's novel is one grand Identity; one might go so far as to say that nearly all the minutiae are merely micro-logical or microscopic versions (or vehicles) of the import of the whole. James, to my mind thus, evinces a mathematical or abstractive sensibility. He seems, from the pottering of his syntax and prose, to the overall conception and method, to always be whittling a manifold into a more honed, and continuously honing, intention – while still keeping the determinate texture of said manifold.

Briefly now, I discuss some of this reflexive relating of substance and form, inner and outer, via a look at some of James's typical and typifying rhetoric. His continuous concern for 'types,' say, and 'values' – *that abstractive gambit* – is mirrored in some of the financial or broadly-speaking mathematical imagery deployed. James's figurativeness is, to put it tartly, full of figuring and figures.

The least of my concerns has to do with the obvious peppering of formalist tropes within the novel, which of course in a very direct way speak to the intentionality of the author. Whether the terms are 'proportion' (124), 'symmetry of plan' and 'observing the forms' (286), 'precious equilibrium' (310), or an aptitude and preference to 'arrange' (189) – in so far as they are codes for James's mind, they are the least interesting to look at, given his seminal critical contribution, in especial with and for the New York edition. Instead, I want first to discuss some of the figurative import of figuring imagery – financial and, seemingly, strangely quantitative for an author concerned so much and so deeply with the quality of things. As in, again, his *Notes of a Son and Brother,* James's 'interest' is for what 'appreciates,' as much as what he appreciates. Perhaps, speaking of such interest and appreciation, the homonymous paradox of the aesthetic and the financial is encapsulated in his phrases there, discussing such experiential boons as being had and/or rendered 'for human use;' or, in an earlier phrase, for 'a higher interest.' [17] Utility is humanized, thus, while still part of a train of passages in this late memoir, where notions of 'saving' against 'waste,' 'storing up,' 'protecting,' 'hoarding,' 'redeeming,' 'acquiring,' 'profiting,' and having something to 'show for' one's experience, are repetitive, almost obsessive rhetorical gestures in the very late James.

So: Maggie 'appreciates' the non-interference at one point of her princely husband, by thinking how what she now 'owed' him, 'mounted up,' 'like a column of figures' (357). Earlier on, of course, Fanny Assingham had justified her backing of the Prince in his marriage stating her case in a way much like quoting 'from a slate, after adding up the items, the sum of a column of figures' (56). Tropes, to boot, of radical 'calculation,' a kind of mathematical imagery to accompany the cunning (of Reason), are peppered throughout the text (for instance, 9, 18, 20, 92). The Prince takes cognizance of Charlotte's quality, like James's prose; furthermore, in the cited passage below, there is the architectonic symmetry of his figuring with the symmetry of the image at the end going to match Charlotte's eventual husband, Mr. Verver. The Prince's calculation of quality by numbers, put away like objects of

17. James, *Notes of a Son and Brother,* op. cit., p. 171 & p. 84.

art, are a formal parallel to the activity of Charlotte's future husband, Mr. Verver: mathematics within, and without:

> But it was, strangely, as a cluster of possessions of his own that these things, in Charlotte Stant, now affected him; items in a full list, items recognized, each of them, as if, for the long interval, they had been 'stored' – wrapped up, numbered, put away in a cabinet. (35)

Loss and gain, again, a balance-sheet out of the quiddity of persons, nay: women to boot. The free indirect of the Prince, then:

> It further passed across him, as his imagination was, for reasons, during the time, unprecedentedly active, that he had, after all, gained more from women than he had ever lost from them; there appeared so, more and more, on those mystic books that are kept, in connection with such commerce, even by men of the loosest business habits, a balance in his favor that he could pretty well, as a rule, take for granted. (257).

Indeed, the Prince apportions Charlotte early on a 'sort of small social capital' (43), wishing her well, in an implicitly cunning sense, for her to meet some 'capital fellow' (44) – symbolic capital, thus, rendered economic, or, perhaps, to compound the very symbolic register, vice versa; or both, at the same time, a kind of precious (or vicious) equilibrium. Perhaps there's some arcane and beveled sense, 'beyond' the literal or the colloquial in Fanny Assingham speaking of Maggie's having to 'repay' the Prince's sometime 'trust.' 'Trust' is apt for my concerns here, and repayment: both artefacts of, I will now show, a double-barreled 'speculation.' A telling passage, with the Prince and Mrs. Assingham, then:

> ...how strange it was that, with all allowance for their merit, it should befall some people to be so inordinately valued, quoted, as they said in the stock-market, so high, and how still stranger, perhaps, that there should be cases in which, for some reason, one didn't mind the so frequently marked absence in them of the purpose really to represent their price. (196).

Speculation is invoked here. The future value is in a literal, financial sense, beyond the empirical, the future value being within the fiction of what is inveterately as yet the future. However, it is interesting to note that for the 'Idealist,' Hegel, a 'speculative concept' – also 'beyond' or transcending the empirical (much like the uniquely-happy ending of James's end-novel, here, the 'Principino' in-tow) – is beyond the literal by being so thoroughly *through* the literal. But what signifies for me is the idea that these tropes of empirical calculation are transfigured, almost sacramentally, into metaphysical and authorial speculation. The inside is a mirror (in more than one sense) for the outside. What I find so thrilling is that James's speculative mind, method, tale, makes use of, envelops and only *thus*, goes beyond images of self-interest. If renunciation, the possibility of altruism, is perhaps James's most central conceit, it makes use of, operatively, the minutiae of selfishness. Another structuralist facet of the Jamesian imaginary.

And 'imaginary' is significant for what I want to finish with. For the structure of feeling evidenced in this novel as elsewhere, is pre-oedipal, narcissistic, and in the Lacanian sense, a product of a castrated imaginary, rather than a castrated symbolic. My primary point here is that there is an oceanic oneness and stillness (*a lack that is only of the lack of lack*) expressed quite significantly in the osmosis and porousness of all the minutiae in the novel, from imagery to syntax to characterological economy, and so on. James's categorical conception is one 'without a hole in it.' Proto-psychotic, in a way.

Characters in James are always osmotic in their intents. The 'beautiful harmony' (352) continuously evidenced in James makes all his characterological counters part of a seamless identity. When a character, as so often happens, does something 'for' another, we inveterately find, they are, through that action, also doing it, in a substantial sense, for themselves, or indeed for one or more of the others. Which is to say, in this sense, James's characters are not necessarily psychologically realistic, which in one sense of course they are, but algebraic shards making up the sensibility of the artist. For instance, Fanny Assingham, instructing her baffled husband, says, late on, that 'lying for' Maggie Verver is lying 'to her.' This typifies the oceanic effect, happening on nearly every page. Witness how Adam Verver's eyes are described, holding an 'ambiguity,' 'of your scarce knowing if they most carried their possessor's vision out or most opened themselves to your own' (126). Which, by itself, figures the whole purport of this paper: seeing the way James sees his characters seeing: eyes of a certain 'I'.

One way of eliciting my point is to say that the thematic concern with 'charm' is mirrored, by concrete instances of thematic charm, in the implicit magical wish for omnipotence apparent in what might be heuristically construed as James's mathematical mind. Charm is mentioned many times in the novel (for instance, 323, 332-3, 359, 365, 388); and what I want to suggest is that just as empirical 'speculation' speaks signally to a more thoroughbred kind of speculation – physical into metaphysical – so the charms of his little civilized coterie is in a very substantive way the enchanting enchantment of James's (perhaps) infantile imaginary.

> The cage was the deluded condition, and Maggie, as having known delusion – rather! – understood the nature of cages. She walked round Charlotte's – cautiously and in a very wide circle; and when, invariably, they had to communicate she felt herself, comparatively, outside, on the breast of nature, and saw her companion's face as that of a prisoner looking through bars. (466).

This – an apt image of solipsism, a 'prisoner's dilemma' so to speak, so typical of the vicious and hermeneutic circles woven throughout James's oeuvre – also instantiates the kind of eminently *vicarious* experience which goes to make the various sentimental educations in James. Often, doing something, or saying something, to or for one person, is immanently to do or say, or both, to an-other – and, in the end, by implication, *to all*.

One rationalist, to close this paper, namely, Kant, argued that unity and 'consistency,' or cohering integrity, were the index of the normative. But, inevitably (and much like James's insight into the impenetrability of 'death' in his preface to *The Wings of the Dove*) it has been argued by modern Kantians that due to the occlusion of knowledge of the absolute whole, the requirement for moral purpose becomes regulative, rather than categorical. Because, being mortal, we'll never know the *full* moral import of any person's *whole* life – humanity, which is an icon for the realization of philosophy or Reason, becomes something we must continuously strive to keep, rather than reflect as a finished or complete(d) given. Edel ends his iconic biography by speaking of James's 'enduring fame' as product of his ambition to deal 'exclusively with the myth of civilization,' writing of, 'men and women in their struggle to control their emotions and passions within the forms and manners of society.' [18] In (revisionist) Kantian mode, Ermanno Bencivenga writes in his *A Theory of Language and Mind*:

> … one is not "always already" human. Humanity should not be understood as automatically including bodies of a certain shape; "humanity" should not be used in a lazy "referential" way. Humanity is indeed a project: the project of making certain bodies temples of diversity. So, if I favour (and I do) certain bodies, I favour them becoming human (their becoming what they are), their struggling to conquer and maintain humanity, to justify the definition I want to be true of them. I favour the disciplined, painstaking effort of building enough structure so that deviance can happen inside those bodies without taking them apart; ultimately I favour the constitution of a human self – and an arena for transgression that is not purely negative (destructive) of that very self. [19]

18. Edel, op.cit., p. 716-7.

19. Ermanno Bencivenga, *A Theory of Language and Mind* (Berkeley, Los Angeles, London: University of California Press, 1997), p. 54.

10

Heavenly Others: Ford, And The Strange 'Impression' of Transcendence[1]

… And he is indeed, then, homo duplex: a poor fellow whose body is tied in one place but whose mind and personality brood eternally over another distant locality.[2]

[Y]ou remember how Proust, at the end of that great novel, having convinced the reader with the full sophistication of his genius that he is going to produce an apocalypse, brings out with pathetic faith, as a fact of absolute value, that sometimes when you are living in one place you are reminded of living in another place, and this, since you are now apparently living in two places, means that you are outside time, in the only state of beatitude he can imagine. In any one place…life is intolerable; in any two it is an ecstasy.[3]

It is not that body lives in a world of things, and mind in a world of senses; rather, mind and body are two extremes in a continuum of interchange with and manipulation of one and the same reality…[4]

I

Introduction

Ford's prize-winning poem (*POETRY,* 1912), 'On Heaven'

1. The author of this paper would like to thank Dr. Paul Skinner for his input on an earlier version of the same.

2. Ford Madox Ford, *It Was the Nightingale*, New York: The Ecco Press, 1961, p. 217.

is a long poem filled with coherent, cohering paradox.[5] What I hope to show in the pursuant analysis is how, strangely for Ford, and for Ford in this poem especially, Ford's impressionism seems (and seams) to imply and evince forms of 'transcendence'. I say it seems strange, because the doctrine of impressionism is usually associated with British empiricism – with its confutation of 'objectivity', of self, or world. However, as is well-known, in one of his most iconic essays, 'On Impressionism', Ford himself does speak of the duplicity of signal conscious experience; [6]and what I would like to suggest, adapting Ford's biographical intentions perhaps, is that the operative duality in Ford, as read here, is one that makes use of the complements of physics and *meta*-physics – to put it in an emphatic way to start with.

The paradoxes of this poem, this poem described in the dedication to 'V.H.' (Violet Hunt) as a 'working Heaven,' involve mutually in-forming parallel narratives between heaven and earth so to speak; between, as well, as one of the main overt conceits of the poem has it, present and past. From the perspective of redemption, all is overdetermined, because the sum-total of finite happenings are resumed in one justifying infinite moment; from our presents, the world might be viewed to go in any (of a number of) direction(s). This dual perspective on experience, the third person,

3. William Empson, *Seven Types of Ambiguity,* London: Penguin Books, 1995, p. 158.

4. Ermanno Bencivenga, *The Discipline of Subjectivity: An Essay on Montaigne*, Princeton, New Jersey: Princeton University Press, 1990, p. 58.

5. See Ford Madox Ford, 'On Heaven' in Ford Madox Ford, *Selected Poems,* ed. Max Saunders, Manchester: Carcanet, 2003, p. 99-110.

6. See Ford Madox Ford, 'On Impressionism', in *Critical Writings of Ford Madox Ford*, ed. Frank MacShane, Lincoln: University of Nebraska Press, 1964 (p. 41.) See also Ford Madox Ford, *The Good Soldier*, London: Heinemann Educational Books, 1975, p. 97.

'objective,' *God's-eye* view, and the first person one, is illustrated by the contemporary philosopher, Ermanno Bencivenga, as follows:

> A good example of Hegelian narratives: the careful analyses conducted at the end of a game of basketball or soccer, to show how rational and necessary it was for the winner to win. If you were actually watching the game, you often got the feeling that it could have gone either way up until the very end – that it all came down to a few fortuitous episodes. And if it had gone a different way, a different tale of necessity would have been told.[7]

What this amounts to is the idea that from the present, the past may be seen to have been necessary, as that very present wouldn't *be* what it is without it; but in or during the present *of that past*, there is or was no knowing, in any totalized way, what will have or would have happened. If this theory is applied to the long poem in question, it results in the idea that the 'working' Heaven 'works' both as an indication of a planer (or planed) heaven, one that sings through the speaker's at times laconic impressions of romance and loving – the heurism (or 'working'-hypothesis) of a heaven-on-earth; as well as suggesting, in the view of this paper, a heaven that 'works' for, or, thus, *facilitates*, that very secular experience. For the past is only *made past* from an intentional present: looking-on. The (Hegelian notion of the) 'end of history', thus, illuminates Ford's 'Heaven', by showing that it is both a metaphysical 'sense of ending' *and* a logical one. What this

---

7. Ermanno Bencivenga, *A Theory of Language and Mind,* Berkeley, Los Angeles, London: University of California Press, 1997, p. 3.

means is that the 'working Heaven' in question is being written from *and* is being written-up and about. Ford's persona is both inside and outside the frame – if the analysis that follows proves to be in any way a compelling reading of the poem. Fate is fate in this near-epic poem, and at the same time fate is character; [8]the draftsmanship from heaven is of a piece with the draftsmanship of heaven. [9]

The two 'alone' in Heaven in the poem, the two who, *now alone*, thus *enact* that Heaven, can be seen to be part of an emphatically 'metaphysical' poem, thus – in part because, following Donne, no man is an island. In a way (perhaps ultimately trivial) the poem, like all truly great poems, is 'about' it-self; which is to say a poem about 'poesis' or 'configuration' itself – in the sense that it thematizes it-self, in many ways, to be seen. The poem, then, is heavenly by naming itself in the process of naming its contents. Indeed, it is perhaps central to a modernist ethos that any possible transcendence achieved, is achieved as *a processual* by-product of the immanent plane – *not as a given*, anymore at least.

---

8. I am indebted to Walter Benjamin's essay, 'Fate and Character' for this way of expressing the dual perspectives under discussion here. See Walter Benjamin, 'Fate and Character' in *Reflections: Essays, Aphorisms, Autobiographical Writings,* trans. Edmund Jephcott, ed. Peter Demetz, New York: Shocken Books, 2007, p. 304-311.

9. See footnote 16. See in relation to this, Professor Martin Stannard's 'Introduction', in Ford Madox Ford, *The Good Soldier*, ed. Martin Stannard, New York and London: W.W. Norton, 1995, p. xi – Stannard's emphasis: 'Dowell's sign system, the novel of his life, develops its range as it progresses; "knowing" and the capacity for articulation are intimately related. He knows nothing *until* it is written down and composition is not continuous.' See also Ford, *The Good Soldier*, London: Heinemann Educational Books, op. cit., p. 107: 'It was as if his passion for her hadn't existed; as if the very words that he spoke, without knowing that he spoke them, created the passion as they went along. Before he spoke, there was nothing; afterwards, it was the integral fact of his life.' See footnote 22 as well.

One modernist philosopher, conceiving of reflection as narratological or, more emphatically, configurative, puts it like this:

> The specificity of philosophy as a configuration of moments is qualitatively different from a lack of ambiguity in every particular moment, even within the configuration, because the configuration itself is more, and other, than the quintessence of its moments. Constellation is not system. Everything does not become resolved, everything does not come out even; rather, one moment sheds light on the other, and the figures that the individual moments form together are specific signs and a legible script. [10]

> The dialectic's protest against language cannot be voiced directly except in language. Hence the protest is condemned to impotent paradox, and it makes a virtue out of that necessity.[11]

> According to its ideal, philosophical language goes beyond what it says by means of what it says in the development of a train of thought. Philosophical language transcends dialectically in that the contradiction between truth and thought becomes self-conscious and thus governs itself…. [12]

10. Theodor W. Adorno, *Hegel: Three Studies*, trans. Shierry Weber Nicholson, Cambridge, MA and London: MIT Press, 1994, p. 109 and see also, p. 116.

11. Ibid., p. 105.

The 'work' of Ford-The-Father and of Ford-The-Son (forded, fording) will be seen to work in perpetual loop-back with or about each other. [13]There is, I hope to show, transubstantiation between a given, to-be represented world, and the world that is constructed by that very representational activity. It's no accident that among the more pagan images in the poem, the 'little town' near 'Lyons' is famous for its 'silks'; an implicit image, perhaps, of transfiguration. There are many complementary ways in which empirical and transcendental, or physical and meta-physical 'planes' in-form and mingle in this poem. [14]Some of them have to do with differing impressions of place, and some with temporal modalities, in biographical contexts, or, in contexts more strictly reserved for inward-experience and consciousness; and some have to do with the range and/or 'minuet' of different individuals – related or not, speaking or spoken-of. And through all the analysis of these paradoxical and analogizing conceits attention to particularities of phrasing will enhance the arguments of this paper.

12. Theodor W. Adorno, *The Jargon of Authenticity*, trans. Knut Tarrowski and Frederic Will, London and New York: Routledge, 2003, p. 8.

13. To bolster my claim of being *quite serious* with this bold formulation here, with a touch of self-reflexive irony, let me quote Ford – fording between us – himself here: 'For myself I love sweeping dicta; they awaken trains of thought: they suggest; and, the more obviously sweeping they are, the less they need to be taken *au pied de la lettre* and the more they may be refined down until the exact and balanced judgment is arrived at. If you wish to think, you must sketch in a rough design of the region that your thoughts may cover so that you may proceed towards rendering it more exact and more precise.' Ford Madox Ford, 'The Serious Books', in *Critical Essays*, eds. Max Saunders and Richard Stang, New York and London: New York University Press, 2004, p. 193.

14. *Only for the purposes of this paper*, the strictly-speaking different senses of 'transcendent' and 'transcendental' will be conflated. In their respective philosophical context: they *are* different; however, for the more broad-brushstrokes of this paper, they will serve as used.

II

Paradoxes 'About' Heaven

The opening quatrain, close to heroic, typifies in different ways the whole poem. Seasonal rhythms of rise and fall are interlaced with similar rhythms at the individual level. Not only is the cosmos, as it were, resumed by the completion of conceits of 'night' and 'day', but night paradoxically *is*, as it 'turns' out, day. The day 'of the sunlight' is the complement of the union *of lovers* at (amorous) 'night.' And this opening chiasma-tic   structure   may   also   be   seen   to   be: 'charismatic.' [15]The respective totalization of world out there, and world in here, is an image of the union of lovers, of self and other. And subject-object union *just is* a definition of heavenly otherness; and this is because it means the 'Objective Truth' of the world, its total states of affairs, are immanently tallying-with one or some mortal individual subjective perspective. If Christ is both man and God, He is an image of a redemptive totalization of subjectivity and objectivity in this sense.[16]

15. See Ford himself, defining 'impressionism' precisely in terms of (a more quotidian sense of) being 'charismatic': Ford, 'On Impressionism' in *Critical Writings,* op. cit., p. 36; see also Ford's *The March of Literature: From Confucius' Day to our Own*, New York: Dalkey Archive Press, 1998, p. 4-5.

16. See Jurgen Moltmann, *The Crucified God: The Cross of Christ as the Foundation and Criticism of Christian Theology,* trans. SCM press, London: SCM Press, 2001, p. 254-5: 'The concrete "history of God" in the death of Jesus on the cross on Golgotha… contains within itself all the depths and abysses of human history and therefore can be understood as the history of history….' See also Ford Madox Ford, 'The Work of W.H. Hudson' in *Critical Essays,* op. cit., p. 71: 'To be able to perceive a relationship to the Kingdom of Heaven in the tessellated pebbles of a brook; to be able to convey how the rustle of the wind in the dry, false

Both the external seasonal rhythm and the internal individual one, also speak of the relation of past to present. Funnily, and unlike the rest of the poem, at this start, the morrow, on both levels, is bitter; this, in complementary contrast to one of the main themes of the poem in the rest of it, whereby heaven is seen as eminently, and happily, retrospective – the dead as it were, living in the repose of now-made-sense. And that asymmetry between only one of the senses to be elicited from the opening quatrain and the rest of the poem, is also a symmetry; because in a way to be parsed below, there are both themes and forms in this poem which suggest that not all can be resolved; or, better, that all is resolved when one realizes that not all is resolved, or ever will be; rather, it is determined by this poem that over-determination is a flaw. [17]

'…. freedom is… a connective… A variety of

dodder-grass of a down is at one with the thoughts that pass through the mind of a man …. For the poet by rendering the visible as nearly as may be to perfection, sets stirring in the dulled perception of humanity the minute ties that bind us always to the unseen universe.'

17. See Ermanno Bencivenga, *Dancing Souls*, Oxford: Lexington Books, 2003, p. 99-101. These three citations, entered below, are analogously 'modernist' in shape and intention. The basic idea (*greatly simplifying, of course*) behind these reflective articulations is the idea that symmetry and resolution, romance, is *the more itself* when all *is not* resolved, totalized. In other words – and tallying with the shape of the major insight in T.S. Eliot's iconic essay, 'Tradition and the Individual Talent' – the red herring proves the rule. (See T.S. Eliot, 'Tradition and the Individual Talent,' in *20th Century Literary Criticism: A Reader*, ed. David Lodge, London and New York: Longman, 1972, (p. 71-72.)) 'The acting out of articulation is dance. Dance is the pure profile of freedom, for spatiotemporal beings like ourselves…. In dancing we make angles, strange ones, surprising and unfamiliar (to others and to ourselves); we show by doing how far our freedom reaches; sometimes we create new joints altogether…. And all this newly found freedom must be supported by solid muscles….

behavioral structures are appropriated wholesale, and what I am is the particular capacity that belongs to this being... of combining them in certain patterns and not others, of reaching from one to the other along certain specific paths. And my growth, the deepening and expanding of my liberation, consists of appropriating new structures and creating new paths....

'.... to be really playful and creative, one must let automatisms take over, and just intervene at key times to redirect them ever so slightly, to have them cross each other's path.... This of course takes a lot of trust....'

From Part III, then:

> There shall be a little labour and enough of toil
> To bring back the lost flavor of the human coil;
> Not enough to taint it...

The opening heroic quatrain is also the be-all-and-end-all in the Joycean sense, as well as being so in relation to the pursuant poem. The whole of time, cosmos, is covered by night and day. Indeed, straight after the line-break – after, that is, the somewhat comprehensive, near-mythic opening – we enter *in medias res*, with, again, an analogy between the speaker's beloved, 'tall and quaint' and 'a *quattrocento* saint.' The beatified and the mortal; the present and the past – and then following this analogy, or if you like, in-formed by its precedence, the speaker, thus, wishes to 'write about Heaven.' In some ways that 'about' is both: logical and topographical, immanent and transcendent; because one of the main rhythmical principles of this poem is the interlacing of empirical description and more speculative prescription. For example, in the third stanza we move from ten and a half lines of description, starting with 'The Place is small and shaded by great planes', to, 'I'd no wish / To wait for her where it was picturesque, / Or ancient or historic, or to love / Over well any place in the land before she came / And loved it too…' And what I want to suggest is that these two modes, objective and subjective, representationally determined and intentionally free, are one formal way the poem does elicit the work of heaven and the more immanent 'working Heaven.'

Not only does the poem speak of some imagined and configured 'heaven', but the speaker interlaces what we know (from the dedication onwards, or not) as biographical to Ford – such as the amatory complication of his relationship with Violet Hunt – with elements more typically poetic and imagined. Fiction and biography intermingle, poetry and fact;[18]and perhaps, then, it's no accident that the 'nine years' in the England of his former days, is redeemed by the present in heaven – especially as, 'nine years' are a redolent time-frame from the ill-logic of *The Good Soldier.* The reality or unreality of the 'goodly apple' that Dowell ponders on, excruciatingly, is prefigured in this poem – written only a very few years before that more iconic work. [19]

18. Indeed, Violet Hunt's reaction to the poem ostensibly dedicated to her was to call it, among other things, 'A Frivolous Heaven,' 'Love without breadth, or thickness, without dimension…'. *The Flurried Years*, London: Hurst & Blackett, 1926, p. 218-19. Perhaps her report on Ford's poem, as flimsy, might be due to her detecting that it was more about Brigit Patmore than she – Patmore having been present at the personal reading of Ford's working heaven. Professor Max Saunders views the beloved in the poem as more recognizably Patmore than Hunt. I am indebted for this reference, not having (had time to) read the Violet Hunt work cited here, to Dr. Paul Skinner, in an email dated: 25/08/17.

19. See Ford, *The Good Soldier*, London: Heinemann, op cit., p. 18; see also, p. 41.

Indeed, in that last citation, we have an early precursor of Auden's famed 'museum.' Auden's titular conceit, in the wake of twentieth century horrors, is both about value and commemoration, and being 'about' such, is also about the obsoleteness of such. Similarly, the world Ford's persona describes is not a licit world, not as heavenly as all that – *until it is shared* in the midst (the melee, as it were) of passion and earthly love. The world of value is dependent on the world of fact, as much as vice versa, then. The givens of the landscape, the ones we take for granted, *just are not there*, until the impression of love makes them so. God, and the closed book of a representational universe, is made processual, constructed, immanently. Heaven becomes mundane and modernist.

To reprise the note of modernism, the dancer in the dance, [20] here, is highlighted indicatively when the speaker's lover, the lover who is (also) to work-up the incumbent heaven, arrives, only looking at the speaker, 'imperceptibly' and with a 'sideways look.' This ambivalence is a very important feature of the narrative argument of the poem and some of its formal facets. Again, totalization, over-determination, features usually associated with monotheistic heaven, are elided. But there is a rhythmic coherence, as elsewhere, in this very slipshod method. From near the start to the end, lines and phrases, such as, 'the great planes' and many others are rhythmically revisited – both as dovetailing and as a miniature form of Fordian cubism. Which is to say, the periodic resumption of these phrases give further integrity to the poem's argument, as well as suggesting, via repetition, how every progressive or progressing context makes the same objective view, inner or outer, different – a slippery relativism pertinent to Ford's impressionism. The repetitions serve to

20. See citations in footnote 17.

bolster and thicken the representation of heaven, as well as to show its relativity. [21] There is, thus, another way of looking at it, of finding meta-physical content here. For when the repetitions or recitatives are made, they are not done so as exactly on-the-button; no, rather, they are like variations on a theme. This not only highlights the fluid, river-like nature of narrative (see references to the 'Rhone' in the poem,) but also suggests that the work of heaven, as it were, is still to be done; the words after the Word, thus – are both day then night: and night then day.[22]Otherwise-put, heaven is not only the lovers' embrace, not only the poet's incantatory rhythms inspired by that embrace, but the meta-fictional, as it were, content of the form as well. This is to say, like all great poems, subject and object, within the poem's amorous argument, and without, are (analogously) one. Heaven is both in the making, and working in that making.

This coalescing duality is even lived-out in piecemeal phrasing. Often, phrases in the poem, like 'God!' are used both substantively and instrumentally; as idiomatic exclamations and as addressing the Almighty. Indeed, after two or three of these homonymous usages, the liminal conflation is actually named by Ford's use of punctuation. Towards the end of Part II, we read: 'And, thank God, we had nothing any more to think of, / And thank God, we had nothing more to talk of.' The two commas in the first line and the sole single one in the second *might be seen* as a syntactical microcosm and index of both: physical and metaphysical complements. Also, and within the same interpretative rubric, the phrasing

21. See citations in footnote 17.

22. In George Steiner's *Real Presences,* Chicago: University of Chicago Press, 1991, a distinction is made between the ethos of the 'Logos' (pre-modernist) and that of what he calls there the 'Epilogue.' The first intends a world of realism, in which word *follows* already-established reality; the second: is the new sense in which reality is constructed *by* language. See footnote 9.

here might be viewed as *even more* emphatically paradoxical, in that the *quotidian* exclamation speaks of *thought*, and the substantive addressing speaks of word become flesh. (And yet) the antagonistic loop-back 'works.'

To recap, then – there are two parallel 'romances' 'working' in this long poem, that of *eros* and that of, in a manner, *agape*. The notion of wishing for 'remembrance now', which is used in the epigraph to the early Ford-Conrad collaboration, *Romance,* is a constant motif in the rendering of heaven as the (retrospective) day of rest and of quiet after the nine English 'years' of complicated passion. [23]However, to continue the paradox, this dual redemption, remains more potent for being 'thorny.' Not only does one die (or dye) to live in this poem, but the former life, in England, is associated throughout the poem with pejorative imagery, as compared to the (more speculative) life after death ('frost', 'shivers', the 'crawling of the tide'.) The supposedly 'real', truly-mundane life of the stiff upper lip, the 'real' life of repression is deader than the life after life – the strangely super-natural one. In different, analogous senses, both are more real and more unreal than each other. Heaven is a speculative place of repose, but also the place where the detailed passion comes–into–its–own, finds its truer real-ization. In a similar way, God is both spoken-of *and* speaking in this poem. If the speaking persona speaks of himself as hitherto a 'man never fully known, only divined,' as well as more overtly speaking *of* God, 'a kind man',

23. See Joseph Conrad and F.M. Hueffer, *Romance,* London: J.M. Dent & Sons, 1944. The first lines of the dedication here, of the dedication to Ford's and Conrad's contemporary (*romantic*) partners, 'Elsie and Jessie', reads: 'If we could have remembrance now / And see, as in the days to come / We shall…' See also, here, Ford's comment in his essay, 'None Shall Look Back': 'if your approach to horror is not that of the quiet and collected observer and renderer you will fail in attaining to the real height of tragedy.' Ford, in *Critical Essays*, op. cit., p. 320.

an un-blind man, and so on – then, again, the innards of the poem evince a paradoxical coalescing of metaphysics and physics, the 'written' and the writing.

One way of putting this whole discussion into focus, is to compare two more overtly paradoxical formulations. When the speaker speaks of 'Our Lady,' She is spoken of as She who is loved beyond 'all women', but also, beyond 'all love,' even. And when, earlier, the persona speaks of the English past from which he has escaped, dy(e)ing-into France, he speaks of all those 'complications' as an 'impossible heap.' This 'impossibility', the idea that all does not totalize and resolve, is of course central to Ford's lifelong writerly vision, from *The Good Soldier* through *Parade's End.* [24]However, the use of the term 'heap' is suggestive. The paradox of what makes a 'heap' might help to illuminate here. It is a basic pattern of paradox that can be found in many philosophical problems. How long is a piece of string? How many grains go to make a heap, and so on? One example of how this basic complication complicates relates to the debate on personal identity. To put it in a way relevant to Fordian concerns: is the person merely the (working) seat of (Humean) impressions? If he is, well, how does he have any (writerly or not) purchase on any of those impressions? If the self is merely the material reality, be it physical, chemical, biological or psychological, then where does one draw the line at which person becomes non-person? (Am I the same man with no legs and no arms? If so: with only a torso and no chest? And so on. Or, am 'I' only all my conscious states? What of my potential schizophrenic or chronically-drunk ones? How does one, believing solely in

---

24. Indeed, one of the sections of Professor Max Saunders's 'Introduction' to his edition of *Some Do Not…* (Manchester: Carcanet, 2010) addresses this central concern in Ford's literary art.

empirical impressions, differentiate wakefulness from dream? And so on.)

Indeed, the complements of dreamful-ness and waking, (and waking), are also a theme of the poem; for instance, the line towards the end that speaks of how, 'the green world waked, or the black world slept quietly.' Paradox again – the live lush greenness is also busy with a 'wake'; the (pejorative-sounding) 'black world' sleeps and is 'quiet' – that last adjective being, almost, *a (repeated) synonym* for Ford's speaking persona's conception of heaven, and its differing otherness from the impossible, noisome, heap of the past.

'Remembrance now' is in effect the end and quieting of uncertainty; of desire and passion, and of knowledge. The Nietzschean dictum to 'become what you are' might serve as a way of naming the paradoxical weave of subjective and objective stances that have been discussed so far; [25] 'remembrance now,' a strange future anteriority, seems to imply both transcendent and immanent modes – and at the same time. The paradoxical force-field in both these cognate formulations seems to ask the 'impossible' – in that heaven, so to speak, is enticed onto earth…[26]

25. See Friedrich Nietzsche, *Thus Spake Zarathustra,* trans. R.J. Hollingdale, London: Penguin Books, 1969.

26. Prefiguring some of the paradox to come in the pursuing conclusion, and re-collecting some already discussed, here is Chesterton speaking – only *a very few* years before Ford's rendering 'On Heaven' – of the romance, as it were, of not letting all resolve and totalize: 'To accept everything is an exercise, to understand everything is a strain. The poet only desires exaltation and expansion, a world to stretch himself in. The poet only asks to get his head in the heavens. It is the logician who seeks to get the heavens in his head. And it is his head that splits.' G. K. Chesterton, *Orthodoxy,* New York: Dover Books, 2004, p. 10. *Perhaps paradoxically*, see Ford here, speaking, again, of his literary cohort W.H. Hudson: 'I have never had the patience – the contemplative tranquillity – to lie looking up into the heavens.' Ford Madox Ford, 'A Naturalist from La Plata: W.H. Hudson',

III

Conclusion

At the last, Ford's God is more the 'mechanician' than the 'magician' (Part III). He reminds one of one of Ford's contemporaries' creations, 'Father Brown.' [27]Chesterton, the essentialist's, chief irony about his fictional detective is that, as a priest, he uses no magic or invokes no super-natural phenomena to solve the crimes he solves. No, it is the other characters, characters who have not already subscribed to the belief under 'authority' in some supernatural realities, who, when faced by a mystery or what seems like an impossible complication or heap of data, tend to believe *anything, or everything, including magic*. However, because Father Brown knows for himself that there definitely are *some* things which *are* mysterious, and tremendously so, he is able to know equally that and when *they are not*. Hence, he is the most rational or scientific of the characters peopling his tales. Given the above, a parallel and working-duplicity might be

in *The Bodley Head Ford Madox Ford*, Vol. 5, ed. Michael Killigrew, London, Sydney, Toronto: The Bodley Head, 1971, p. 294-5. See, thus, the complement and antagonism of this, and the citation from a different essay in footnote 16. Ford, here, seems to be using the occasion (of writing) of an-other in order to enter heaven.

27. It should be noted that the argument in Hugh Kenner's *Paradox in Chesterton,* London: Sheed & Ward, 1948 (e.g. p. 26 or 30) – perhaps the most insightful, seminal and penetrating of works on Chesterton – is an implicit influence on my treatment of Ford in this paper. I'd also like to note here, for fanciful interest, that though Ford's poem won the *POETRY* prize in 1912, and was published there, that year, it was written in 1911. 1911 is also the publication date of G. K. Chesterton's first volume of 'Father Brown' stories, *The Innocence of Father Brown.*

construed between the Edwardian Chesterton and the modernist Ford.

Both, in this view, analogize, in a highly-operative manner, heaven and earth.[28]God in Ford's long poem is seen, ambivalently, as *either:* a 'lover' or a 'priest', dressed in 'black' as he is. In *The Good Soldier,* Dowell seems to wonder about the inhering parallel between an ascetic-mouthed Ashburnham and his eventually-realized libertinage. [29]The paradox there, as here, is that the ascetic and the libertine are the same person, chiasma-tically arranged; the one takes pleasure in ascetic, religious devotion, the other, makes pleasure his religion. So...

If (in the end: or from it) 'lover' and 'priest' are one – perhaps heaven and earth may (come to) inform each other.

28. Re-calling here the citation in footnote 16 (regarding W.H. Hudson) which shows Ford speaking of the seen / unseen – see Hilaire Belloc, Chesterton's lifelong friend and peer, speaking (posthumously) of Chesterton's analogizing manner, and of hooking the 'unseen' onto the 'seen,' in his *On The Place Of Gilbert Chesterton in English Letters*, London: Sheed and Ward, 1940 (e.g. p. 39).

29. Ford Madox Ford, *The Good Soldier,* ed. Max Saunders, Oxford: Oxford World Classics, 2012, p. 16.

11

Animating Places: Reading Fiona Sampson's *Limestone Country* Beneath a Durrellian Lens

Fiona Sampson's recent *Limestone Country* (Little Toller Books, 2017) proves to be a riveting tour de force. While being, ostensibly, a work that speaks to and of and through the "spirit of place," it manages in a manner to reinvent a genre or genres. Part memoir, part travel-guide, part intimate diary, part dramatic novelistic narrative, part extended meditation, and part exuberant celebration of different "limestone countries" – the writing here eludes categories. It is as various and as variegated as experience itself, without ever losing coherence and the unities that make any work of configuration poignant, redolent and susceptible to being a kind of education for the reader, whether that tutelage is factual, sensual, technical, or philosophical. Sampson herself calls it a kind of "attention" that "is patient and detailed. It's a kind of 'slow knowledge' that is the opposite of generalization" (Sampson 10).

Equally, in the "Introduction" to his (very late) book on Provence, Lawrence Durrell writes, as elsewhere, that "thanks to them," namely, the dramatis personae who happened to precipitate his narrative, then came to inhabit it:

> I can honestly say I have experienced the country

> with my feet as well as my tongue: long walks and
> longer potations have characterized my innocent
> researches, the ideal way to gain access to a
> landscape so full of ambiguities and secrets. (*Caesar's
> Vast Ghost* 6)

Or: if "*Provence is not really a place!*" for Durrell, and if it is
"paradoxical," it is "because of the overlay of different cultures
which are slowly conforming to the genius of the place, but
at different speeds" (32). Similarly, life in Sampson's "limestone
countries" is "messy with overlaps and repetitions" that she
"has simplified" (Sampson 10). Indeed, it was "a shock, and an
epiphany, to realise that they were all made from – and in and
on – limestone. Surely, I thought, this has to be more than
mere coincidence. Limestone," she continues, "has a special
relationship with water, by which it's shaped at every stage of
existence" (8). Hence, we must suppose the supple fluency of
"overlaps" but not repetitions, of dove-tailings and analogies
between her four "limestone countries."

For Durrell, his late work *Caesar's Vast Ghost: Aspects
of Provence* was to be a "compendium of poetic inklings"
comprised of "some history, some myth, some insights and
striking metaphors appropriate to the glorious landscape, the
whole fitted out with the appropriate tourist information"
(3–4). Indeed, describing his earlier travel-book, *Bitter Lemons
of Cyprus*, as an "impressionistic study," Durrell writes how
he had "tried to illustrate" the "Cyprus tragedy" of the early
fifties, "through my characters and evaluate it in terms of
individuals rather than policies" – it not being "a political
book" (*Bitter Lemons* ix). Or, similarly, opening his book on
Rhodes, *Reflections on a Marine Venus*, Durrell outlines and
precipitates his characterological method of illuminating place
like this:

> I have attempted to illumine a single man by a
> single phrase, and to leave him where he sits
> embedded in the slow flux of Grecian days ... a
> good host should ... Gideon with his monocle
> screwed in sitting soberly before a bottle of *mastika*;
> Hoyle winding his enormous watch; Mills talking;
> Sand sucking his pipe; Egon Huber walking the
> deserted beaches hunting for scraps of wood to
> carve, and the dark-eyed E ... putting on a
> flowered frock in the studio mirror with her black
> hair ruffled. I have tried not to disturb them in the
> little eternities of their island life, where somehow
> their spirits mingle and join that of the Marine
> Venus standing in her little stone cell at the
> Museum like a challenge from a life infinitely
> remote.... (*Marine Venus* 2-3)

Durrell's aim is or was (or both, perhaps) to allow the "common reader the feeling of living in a historic present" (*Marine Venus* 4). Indeed, this particular kind of "mythic method," in direct continuum with his novels – where the choice work of the imagination takes the barer (previously-lived, but now quite literally re-collected) reality into the more poignant zone of what Durrell called "reality prime" – is shared in many ways with Sampson's recent Little Toller monograph.

Limestone Country is comprised of a quartet, as it were, of four parts, all representations and reflections of limestone countries: Autumn in "Le Chambon"; then Summer in "Škocjan"; Spring, then, in "Coleshill"; and finally Winter in "Jerusalem." The unruly seasonal chronology is perhaps a wink and a nod to the exigencies of what is eminently *creative* writing, a way to emphasize both: the inherently artistic and selective nature of this kind of life writing, whereby choice configuration, skewing with bold intent the more numb or staple order of things, is highlighted – and a hint at the near-mythic stilling of time, indeed the near-mythic replacement of chronology via a more ecstatic (or paratactic) representation of experience, unified by an inner clock rather than an outer one.[1] This last observation is a small part of the reasons I have chosen to discuss here Sampson's work beneath the lens of one of her modernist forebears, a known influence on her, who excelled and in part himself reinvented writing of and about and through the "spirit of place": Lawrence Durrell. The first paragraph of the first chapter of his Cyprus book, *Bitter Lemons of Cyprus*, reads:

> Journeys, like artists, are born not made…. they flower spontaneously out of the demands of our natures – and the best of them lead us not only outwards in space, but inwards as well. Travel can be one of the most rewarding forms of introspection…[2]

It should be noted from the start that the few travel-books by Durrell mentioned in this paper are in many ways very different, longer on the whole and more copious, than the single Sampson work which is my main purport here. However, for all the differences, I aim to show how both authors animate places in very comparable and quite (literally) brilliant ways. Among other things by the wayside, I aim to discuss and to compare and contrast different aspects of the two sensibilities at work: namely, elements of style and voice that may serve to illuminate each other; aspects of narrative

1. All this said, it should be noted that Sampson's stated reason for the anachronisms is to allow them to be read, if the reader chooses, "separately," rather than as a continuous chronological narrative (Sampson 11).

2. On Durrell's life see, for example, Ian S. MacNiven.

technique and genre; as well as the role of character and dramatis personae as a well-nigh novelistic technique and conduit for illuminating the nature of a place or places. Character after all, is shared by both authors and those they meet, and by the synergy of the two, when welded with expert skill, they quite literally "animate" place; *that*, as much as for both authors, as we will see, place it-self is (already) animate – but waiting for what Sampson would call, musically, the right "attention." Thus, there would seem to be a similar dialectic between place and personhood in both authors' experiences and in the (twinning) work of their recollecting of impressions and the configuring of their representations. In her own Introduction Sampson writes:

> After all, how can we separate what a place is from what it is *for us*? Places are meanings as well as conditions. They act upon us and we act upon them, in the dialectic we call *living*. This is a book about trying on different ways of living – or dying – in limestone country …

2. Synesthesias

The first section (*Santat!*) of Sampson's book opens, much as in Durrell, with a litany or display of dramatis personae being re-collected in their (and Sampson's own) historic present:

> The Savignacs are in the kitchen when we arrive for *un petit apéro*. The stove is lit and, with all five of them already crowded round the table, there's hardly space for us. Heat; noise. Here's Jeannot, the paterfamilias, hitching up his trousers below his belly…. Here's Madame Savignac, monumental and frowning with friendship…. And here is Clarette, with little Josette on her knee. Clarette is

the one who got away, the educated daughter who
works at the *Mairie*.... (15)

So, we enter dramatically *in medias res*. However, the one
glaring feature of the opening section "One Day," where
all these personae figure in ambulant and vibrant ways, is
that the writing is not only filmic, but also that there is the
sense that the writing grows or grew out of the experiences,
much as the limestone detailed in the Introduction waxes and
wanes slowly, with "a particular plasticity" (8). Indeed, the
most striking feature of the writing in and of and through "Le
Chambon" is that it is literally *sensational*. All the senses are
triggered and spurred, with at times synesthetic effect. Here
are some examples of sensual style, where character elicits
place as much as vice versa:

> In fact it's barely dawn. When P opens the
> bedrooms shutters he reveals a velvety blue sky. In
> the west, over the river, it's still night. Only to the
> east, between the Savignacs' barns, can we see a
> smudge of purplish pink. It seems impossible that
> this could become heat and light. The night-freeze
> hangs in the air, missing the yard romantically. A
> white frost stands on every surface, delineating the
> lumpy stones of our garden wall, the corrugated
> lines of the tiled roof. (20)
>
> As we stroll and poke, searching for the dark
> green of this local pottery among the dark-green
> waterweeds, the thawing earthen bank beside us
> gives o a clean clay smell. The paddling dogs kick
> up a faint, greenish aroma from the riverbed. (29)

The provenances of different senses are solicited and
entwined. The writing veers between, welds and synergizes,

what are normally construed as different, or separate, aspects of visceral experience. Smell, touch, sight, taste, hearing, as throughout this opening chapter, *dictate* to the reader a synesthetic world, where the overall effect becomes somehow more than a list of sensations. As in Durrell, to be seen presently, the woken litany is more than its addled parts. Similarly:

> It's quieter on this side of the house, away from the birdcage tangle of our neighbours' trees; in any case the dawn chorus is beginning to dissolve as the morning warms up. Instead we hear the isolated, almost tentative clinks and raps that reveal how the hamlet starts its day. A door opens somewhere. A car drones along the lane from the bridge. A dog bowl is dropped with a bright metallic *twang*! A snatch of children's voices from the schoolteacher's house: abruptly cut o as a window or a door is slammed shut. Someone knocking out the ashes riddled from the overnight stove. Someone, Michel or Marie, coughing down by the river. The distant snarl of a chainsaw at work somewhere in the woods. (26)

This list of sounds (eliciting as it were both sight and insight) reveals how it is "the hamlet" that starts (its day.) Just as Sampson can speak directly of the possibility of "seeing … a taste" (41), so at the chapter's end a noise outside is undecipherable by narrator, partner or pets, as all freeze at the window.

> The noise seems not to come from any one direction but instead to surround the house. Even to call it "noise" seems not quite right: it doesn't have,

> so to speak, discrete edges. It is, rather, *a state of*
> noise; something like air pressure. Still it's getting
> louder and closer. The air vibrates. And now this
> airy teeming begins to make sense, resolving itself
> into a carpet of cries, into the creaking, swiping
> sound of wing beats. It's clearly the sound of birds.
> (56)

Although both writers use verbs, participles in particular, in lmic and painterly ways, perhaps it's no accident that some of Sampson's most poignant passages (and/or as with Durrell: *tableaux vivants*) are to do with sounds, if nearly always parsed by other tactile reservoirs. Sampson has a long history of engagement with the musical, in different modes since the start of her professional life. Durrell by turns, though equally labile across the sensual array and arenas, is more emphatically painterly. To sample here is a dilemma, not because of lack of instances, but because of how proli c Durrell's synesthetic passages are. A few examples here, then; describing the trip by sea to Rhodes:

> The snarling of the great engines wrapped us all
> in a deaf silence – a marvelous brutal music of
> vibrating steel and wood. Behind us we le great
> stains of oily heat upon the waters and a white
> cicatrice which slowly healed again. (*Marine Venus*
> 5)

In that final "healing" image, Durrell, like Sampson, conjoins sight with insight, sensation with its value. In Cyprus, later, while on his way to meet a government o cial, Durrell speaks of the "ugliness of the plain," as "so to speak, at the height of its beauty – a range of tones vibrating with the colours of damson, cigar-leaf, putty and gold-leaf " (*Bitter Lemons* 148).

Even ugly sights are rounded as beautiful – but not beautified. The holism of synesthesia, whether present or merely implicit, is a kind of osmotic gambit, not only for sensual facets to overlap and charge each other almost electrically – but also a space of sensibility, where place and its effects *are effected* in a sweetly over-determining way. Indeed, synesthetic description might be both the sensual equivalent of and an apt modal metaphor for sight (always) becoming insight.

> One day we woke to a sky covered in ugly festoons of black cloud and saw drift upon drift of silver needles like arrows falling upon the ramparts of Kyrenia castle. under clamoured and rolled, and the gape-blue semi-darkness of the sea was bitten out in magnesium ashes as the lighting clawed at us from Turkey like a family of dragons. (*Bitter Lemons* 46)
>
> In the fragile membranes of light which separate like yolks upon the cold meniscus of the sea when the rst rays of the sun come through, the bay looked haunted by the desolate and meaningless centuries which had passed over it since rst the foamborn miracle occurred. With the same obsessive rhythms it beat and beat again on that so eroded point with its charred-looking sand: it had gone on from the beginning, never losing momentum, ever hurrying, reaching out and subsiding with a sigh. (*Bitter Lemons* 178-9)

And perhaps this give-and-take, loss-and-gain, is an apt image for the rhythms in Sampson just as much as in Durrell between immanent visceral impressions and the more transcending reflective bite such impressions trigger in us as realizations – when we pay the right "attention." For, in the passage preceding, Durrell has pivoted between the temporal and the mythically still(ed):

> It was a good idea to surprise the dawn at this forgotten point in history – the hollow curved beach with its great nger of rock raised in patient admonition – and to listen for a while to the oldest sound in European history, the sighing of the waves as they thickened into roundels of foam and hissed upon that carpet of discolored sand. (178)

Typical Durrellian features shared by Sampson in her monograph are adverted to by the animating tropes of persons "surprising the dawn" and the use of soul-fueled words for the sea like "sighing" and "hissing."

Indeed, opening her second chapter in "*Na Zdravje!*" Sampson shows herself an avid avatar and epigone of Durrell, here describing the impression of a cheering drink local to the place – *become, becoming, thus, local to us, too*:

> What we're sampling now … sends a glowing, pleasurable ribbon along the tongue and down the throat. Plum, quince, grape; thyme and apple; hot earth, sunlight and a mountain wind. What would you get if you concentrated and attenuated all these ingredients – distilled them in fact?
>
> If whisky should be cut with water, slivovitz should be cut with air. (Sampson 64)

3. Connoisseur-ships And Conservatives

Another motif redolent in the texture of Sampson and Durrell's prose that speaks both to the tales about and "about" (animating) place, and to the authorial intentions and methods of each, is the gesture of connoisseurship. Durrell calls himself a "conservative," but the political tales he tells in his ction or in his (creative) non-fiction are never trenchantly political. His mythic and mythopoetic sensibility would deem a direct temporal take on politics, one not steeped in the more lasting and self-forged verities of character and place, as in bad and truncated taste.

It seems clear that one of the most overt ways in which Durrell is a conservative, both formally (narrative framing) and in content is that he is always like an avid collector – in fact, a recollector – of curios, whether it is aspects of characteristic presences, personae, of national ethos or identity, of food and wine, of types and timbres of crucial experience, like love or death, and so on. In short, Durrell's is not only a "style" impregnating his prose, but also this style is the stigma or symptom of a more global search for and conservation of "style" in sucking the marrow out of a life. When Durrell writes of his friend Austen Harrison that he "represented that forgotten world where style was not only a literary imperative but an inherent method of approaching the world of books, roses, statues and landscapes" (*Bitter Lemons* 89), he is, like a true impressionist, speaking of himself as well. Durrell abounds in types and typologies; he makes as T.S. Eliot would say, nice distinctions. So, here, speaking of the British failures in that troublesome time for Cyprus, he speaks of the failure in the British "angle of vision" (painterly even here!):

> Colonial officials, trained to direct rule, will always nd this di culty in dealing with problems outside the rule of order…. those who work in sovereign territory have to cultivate a suppleness and dissimulation, a tactical mind and a reserve because no issues can be forced: they must be engineered. The difference is between the craft of a fly-

fisherman and someone who dynamites from a
rowing boat. (151)

This is a reflection on politics. But it is also a way, intimate to
an aestheticist sensibility, of classifying types: and even if it has
political provenance, it is a very apt illustration of how Durrell
goes about feeding from his experience and impressions.
Similarly, discriminating between the Cypriots and the Greeks
of the mainland, Durrell adjures:

> A *feeling* of foreignness, of alienation from
> themselves, persisted: somewhere, dimly, they felt
> that this weird, padded, essentially suburban life
> was not theirs. Somewhere the values they sought
> would be found to depend on the spare, frugal
> Mediterranean pattern of things – the light-
> intoxicated anarchy of Greece always leaped at
> them like a panther. (139)

A situation is animated by distinctions of national ethos.
Persons are (soon to be) determined by the skyscape and sea
of the Mediterranean. It is a "feeling" that is being gauged.
And in that dim and repeated "somewhere" the hallmark of
a rabid impressionist makes itself felt. The "panther" is not
only a brilliant touch, but is, again, an overt stigma of how
different areas of animation may (come to) "light" up each
other. Indeed, if Durrell's style is bold, muscular while
remaining highly sensitive, his voice always incurs a sad touch
of irony, a light(er) touch. ere is always the sense that for all
the strumming of the deep-bellied cello-like notes, laughter is
not far away.

In parts of *Limestone Country*, the same could be said of
Sampson. However, in the opening of the second Chapter:
"Elegies and Ballads," romance and loss are evinced in a section

very different in narrative technique to the first. If in the first there is a sense (actually less like Durrell's commanding recollecting mode) of the writing being wholly immanent to itself, reflecting and reflected moment to moment as it were, here in line with the romance notions of the title, there is closure from the beginning. In other words, there is an overtly-worded story-arc of a beginning, middle, and end. I will cite here the opening and closing of the chapter:

> This is the story about the former Yugoslavia, and about how sometimes it becomes necessary to visit a place only a er you've fallen in love with it. Or maybe it's about how narrow the gap is between the people we love and the places where we love them. Or else this story is about how ideas and dreams, stories and proverbs, create the places that mean something to us. It's certainly the story of how a particular place is highlighted and shadowed by death... the high, half-forgotten limestone country that the tragic Slovenian poet Srečko Kosovel made his own a hundred years ago.

We have jumped back in time with this chapter. But we are overtly told so: the writing is valedictory not only in content but in temporal mood. She starts the next paragraph: "To begin with though, it was just a dream of the good life. My lover S was Macedonian but I worked in London, and we used to fantasize about ways to stay together" (65). And the last passage of the chapter runs: "As we lie in the late sunlight that warms the pebbles of the riverbank, what we feel is a kind of fullness; as if the things we need in life might all, for once, have come together here." (113).

At a purely formal level, the reader will observe how the beginning opens on a tragic note, the ending on one close to that of plenitude. Both modes and both modes conjoined at either end of a more controlled or controlling narrative (than the first chapter) are romantic. And in this chapter, with the very executive conceit of telling a nished or already-made story, Sampson shares with the Durrell of the travel-books made-use of here a kind of metafictional conceit, where the author is both inside and outside the frame of then, as now. Indeed, in *Caesar's Vast Ghost, Reflections on a Marine Venus*, and *Bitter Lemons*, Durrell's narrative persona (unlike in his novels, to a certain extent at least) is very much himself, and he often prefaces those narratives with meta ctional talk, *metafictional planning*, about and "about" the very work underway beneath the wave-strokes of his pen. In this sense, *both* Durrell and the Sampson of the Summer in "Škocjan" are conserv-atives.

Like Durrell, Sampson makes use here as elsewhere of historical contexts like wars and the experience of wars, within a more global piece of (personal) memoir. Larger contexts are compounded of course with even larger near-mythical contexts; the blurring of boundaries (already detailed in part) of persons and place, persons and their intra-personal spaces over time, persons and others, and these with or against historical and political contexts, are all uni ed and resumed in the authorial take of things by the repeatedly-mentioned "bowl-shaped" topographies endemic, we gather across the work, to "limestone countries." Indeed, all the above dramatic and dramatized tensions typify the lessons one might give about how to write creatively. One might almost say that there is thus a more than trivial sense in which creative writing and nonfictional writing bend and swerve into each other in Sampson, as in Durrell.

That said, Sampson is also interested in facts; indeed, one instance made use of as a unifying literary device, one of a won or newly-won connoisseurship, is the way in which Sampson peppers her mix of memoir, diary, meditation, storytelling, and her eliciting throughout the genii of places with Latinate names for all the ora and fauna she comes across. ese discoveries are, as it were, *in Latin*: a romance, then, of nding romance there, waiting, for or with the right "attention."

> I like the way the Coleshill snowdrops don't know whether they're wild or cultivated. *Galanthus nivalis* is regarded as naturalized in Britain now; but it's not native here as it is on the European mainland. e dri s of bulbs we're here to see, spreading for yards between the trees of this elongated little copse, were originally planted by gardeners for the Coleshill Estate – how many centuries ago? One? Two? Even three? I touch down on the driest slope I can find to try and catch their perfume. e dogs wonder what's going on. They push their muzzles in my face, giving me quick interrogatory licks. But what interests them more are the innumerable, much stronger odours that the February damp has loosened. Rabbit, fox, rat? We guess – and they know. (135)

It's not the interested, interrogating dogs that tell here, so much as the snowdrops that beg to know if what they are themselves are wild or cultivated. Indeed, we might infer from this and all noted so far, that just as both authors use dramatis personae as conduits to illuminate place, the very continual gesture of ventriloquism, vicarious staging, is as it were a writer's way of eliciting for him and/or herself insights and expressions of insights that take wing and are somehow more to the person than the erstwhile person. It is magical, alchemical, or, as Durrell would say: "heraldic."

Indeed, echoing (layering, "overlaps" again) with apt

tension the already-cited opening of the second Summer section – opening the third, in "Spring" again, at "Coleshill," we nd the following passage; it echoes as I say, but in a different way, the mutual play of two kinds of romance – between the gasp of shock and the gasp of relief. "Parish Map" opens:

> Being a tourist is easy enough. But how do we map the localities we know really well, the ones we don't choose to explore but where we nd ourselves – often with a slight sense of surprise, as if waking up from some long sleep – spending our actual lives? (119)

Sampson is overtly a connoisseur of the place here. And yet: Spring here follows Summer; *and yet*, the opening passage is phrased as *a question* – perhaps for a reason? *And yet*, that is, there is more to be said …

4. Conclusions: from "Parish Map" to "Jerusalem" or, closure and exile

> I force myself to concentrate. You're saying how much you'd love to go to Jerusalem. e place itself, you're saying: all those layers of settlement like sedimentary rock formation. You think it's the sort of city photos tell us almost nothing about. It's not the facades that matter, you insist, it's what's underfoot. (117)

This passage, starting the third, "Coleshill," section is exemplary of Sampson's technique for many reasons. e reader sees the note of the culture and of cultivation meeting, place and personhood, again; the return, checkered, to the temporal mood of the first chapter, skipping over the head of the second, which was more emphatically a story related from a distance; and, perhaps most importantly, if we're scenting out a modernist animus against chronology in favor of a historic consciousness that involves parataxis and dovetailing, analogies and juxtapositions – this nod to Jerusalem comes a section before the section so-named, as though all the four "limestone countries," being of the same rock, interpenetrated each other in the personal experience as much as in any global sedimentary community. Also, by thematically jumping between this third chapter, a "Parish Map," and the fourth to-come, at "Jerusalem," we would seem to have a comprehensive gesture; just as much as the first section, "One Day," is by titular trope here and execution, proto-Joycean, so the titular move from a "Parish" to a world-pivotal place like "Jerusalem" would seem to be a gesture of totalization and resumption – if with a light touch …

In "Parish Map," then, first, Sampson again reflects between the gasp of shock and the gasp of relief; exes between the romance of what we, questing, may nd, and the more conservative romance of knowing where we stand, mapped as we are, by and with quiddity.

> We can locate ourselves: on the weather map, in the train timetable, by the echo chamber of local accents and familiar voices. Some of this is yawningly familiar; some of it we don't even recognize we know. (117)

And again we see the breeding liminal ground where person and place in-form each other. Then, here are two passages in the tradition of the Durrell elicited so far. First, and like Durrell, Sampson names the complementary sedimentation, complementary to that of juxtaposed limestone countries, of culture in a place, its burdens of animus or anima; second, the motif of "map" and "mapping" becomes, as in Durrell, a metaphor for self-discovery, a trajectory of self-realization(s):

> …What I really think is that this village I know so well is less a vital, living ecosystem than a map of its own history and geography – of how it was made. (120)

> Ownership imposes limits, something English hedges ('vegetable walls', as a Romanian friend calls them) have long marked out on the landscape. In a way maps limit us too. To be 'o the map' is not to count: to be mysterious, unknown, forgotten. e edge of the map is the limit of the known. And yet. To map is to unify, to draw together the disparate pieces of knowledge that make up a place. at delightful arcana of Ordnance Survey symbols – windmills, cuttings, and contour lines – says, in part, there are all these things making up a landscape. And browsing a map is one of the most pleasurable forms of reading; a way to take an imaginary journey through a place you don't yet know. (121)

To recap, the discernment and the pleasure here are ones of (incumbent) connoisseurship. As with Durrell, there is the sense of discovering, realizing new senses; but senses that, for all their brilliance and quested-signi cance, were perhaps always there – waiting for the right "attention.":

> The fossils I have always picked up and discarded when we walk our local elds in spring are like

nothing so much as rumours, hints of a radical past
in which countries rose from the water and fell back
into it. (164).

As with Durrell, the wax and wane, the wavy transpiration of
geography and topography, are metaphors, dialectical images,
almost, for the self: engaged with and about and through
them. It is a kind of mythic or at least mythopoetic method.
The Coleshill section closes with the observation, "the only
barn owl from Middle Leaze… maps her hunting ground
methodically, up and down over the dark acres …. It's not
so bad, after all, to know that she'll still be here when we are
gone." (169)

    And it goes without saying that Durrell's list, cited earlier,
his almost shopping-list of what was to be included in his
Provence book, myth, history, metaphor, insight, travel-
guide, and so on – is both named and spent through Sampson's
own descrying of the genii of place. Indeed, this mapping
chapter is the most overtly as it were factually informative
– as though to o er a long and enduring geography (and
history) lesson were a way, like Durrell's own travel, of and
for "introspection." Even the sensations of the weather are
maps of personal experience and personal realization: "In the
brisk early-spring air, everything ought to feel as though it's
starting. But today even the dampish, earthen twang to the
wind no longer smells of possibility, but loss" (Sampson 121).

    And speaking of possibility, of loss: now, at the close
of the nal chapter, "Winter" in "Jerusalem" – winter before
spring, as it were – we read of hope and of its dire slippage:

    The light makes everything dreamlike. There's
    haze: a dustiness settling at the bottom of the sky.
    In this version of limestone country, it's impossible
    to see anything clearly. Still, the light says: hope.

> What can we do but hope? From far away, it is
> what Jerusalem represents. For those who live at
> close quarters, that hope is mixed… (228)

The liminal mix, the back-and-forth, the give-and-take, the dialectic of how things – this thing (called) "living" – transpire, is lived out by sights and by their entailed, incumbent insights. As with Durrell, both in general, but also peppering his books of place – Sampson, a prolific and distinguished poet in her own right, ends with the quotation of a poem by Mahmoud Darwish, translated by Fady Joudah. The last line reads: "I said: You killed me… and I forgot, like you, to die" (229). To paraphrase part of the opening cadence of Durrell's major fiction, the *Alexandria Quartet*: in the midst of winter we can feel the inventions of spring… At the conclusion, then: an image of closure; and yet, an image of prolific exile, as well.

References

Durrell, Lawrence. *Bitter Lemons of Cyprus*. London: Faber & Faber, 1957, rpt. 2000.

Durrell, Lawrence. *Prospero's Cell, and Reflections on a Marine Venus*. New York: Dutton, 1960.

Durrell, Lawrence. *Caesar's Vast Ghost: Aspects of Provence*. London: Faber & Faber, 1990.

MacNiven, Ian S. *Lawrence Durrell: A Biography*. London: Faber and Faber, 1998.

Sampson, Fiona. *Limestone Country*. Dorset: Little Toller Books, 2017.

12

Facets of Exhaustion: The Mystic Antagonism of T.S. Eliot's 'Music'

'To accept everything is an exercise, to understand everything is a strain. The poet only desires exaltation and expansion, a world to stretch himself in. The poet only asks to get his head in the heavens. It is the logician who seeks to get the heavens in his head. And it is his head that splits.'
G. K. Chesterton, *Orthodoxy*[1]

'My smile falls heavily among the bric-à-brac.'
'Portrait of a Lady,' III, 9

'These fragments I have shored against my ruins.'
The Waste Land, V, 430

In a recent review-essay triggered by the occasion of the recent publication of volumes of T.S. Eliot's *Letters*, Stefan Collini speaks of early periods in Eliot's life when he was faced by many kinds of impending ruin – social, economic, spiritual and sexual; against such threats, Collini speaks of the 'pit-props' Eliot came to use by the late 1920s to shore himself against such ruin. [2] 'Disguise, camouflage, adaptation: Eliot was rich in the strategies of self-protection.' [3] It is well-known of course that in the years 1921 and 1922, when Eliot

1. G. K. Chesterton, *Orthodoxy*, London: Dover Publications, 2004, p. 10.
2. Stefan Collini, *Common Writing: Essays on Literary Culture and Public Debate*, Oxford: Oxford University Press, 2016, p. 37-63 (p. 63).
3. Ibid., p. 52.

was composing his first major work, *The Waste Land,* that he (along with his then-wife, Vivien) suffered from exasperated neurasthenia.[4] And this commonplace in Eliot lore finds itself posthumously reflected-on by Eliot himself:

> It is a commonplace that some forms of illness are extremely favourable, not only to religious illumination, but to artistic and literary composition. A piece of writing meditated, apparently without progress, for months and years, may suddenly take shape and word; and in this state long passages may be produced which require little or no retouch. I have no good word to say for the cultivation of automatic writing as the model for literary composition; I doubt whether these moments *can* be cultivated by the writer; but he to whom this happens, assuredly has the sense of being a vehicle rather than a maker... You may call it communication with the Divine, or you may call it a temporary crystallization of the mind...[5]

This was written in 1931. In 1933, he wrote in a similar vein:

> That there is an analogy between mystical experience and some of the ways in which poetry

4. That said, Collini records in his essay how Eliot in 1925 found himself 'at the blackest moment of my life.' Ibid., p. 46. See *The Poems of T.S. Eliot, Volume 1: Collected and Uncollected Poems,* ed. Christopher Ricks & Jim McCue, London: Faber & Faber, 2015, p. 548, where his wife Vivien is recorded as saying in a letter to Bertrand Russell on November 1, 1921: 'Tom is having a bad nervous – or so called – breakdown.' Or, Ibid., p. 557, Ezra Pound to Harriet Monroe in March 1922: 'Eliot is going to pieces physically. He had a breakdown a few months ago, went to Switzerland, recovered, sufficiently to do probably the most important modern poem of its length (19 pages) that there is ....'

5. Ibid, p. 686-7.

is written I do not deny… I know, for instance, that some forms of ill-health… may… produce an efflux of poetry in a way approaching the condition of automatic writing… it gives me the impression of having undergone a long incubation, though we do not know until the shell breaks, what kind of egg we have been sitting on.[6]

Indeed, this sudden 'efflux' had occurred quite a few times in Eliot's poetic career to date, namely, the fifth section of *The Waste Land,* and the far shorter and less copious 'Journey of the Magi,' written in three quarters of an hour one afternoon.[7] However, though it is a commonplace – another one – that *The Waste Land* reflects some vision of Eliot's of civilizational barrenness and collapse, on a number of occasions Eliot wrote that the work was not composed as social criticism, and did not attempt to reflect a social crisis; rather, it was a spiritual malaise which stimulated this now iconic work. When E.M. Forster, for instance, invoked the impact of the recent First World War, Eliot replied, 'The War crippled me as it did everyone else; but for me chiefly because it was something I was neither honestly in nor honestly out of; but the *Waste Land* might have been just the same without the War.'[8] Close to this time, Eliot wrote: 'To me it was only the relief of a personal and wholly insignificant grouse against life; it is just a piece of rhythmical grumbling.'[9] Indeed, later, regarding 'The Hollow Men,' Eliot responded on January 29th 1936 to one

6. Ibid., p. 687.

7. See Ibid., p. 686 & p. 760.

8. Ibid., p. 592.

9. Quoted in Robert Crawford, *Young Eliot: From St Louis to The Waste Land,* London: Jonathan Cape, p. 423.

Mrs. Yeo, that the poem was not to do with 'Social Disease', rather, 'Spiritual Disease'.[10]

I want to argue in this essay, that whether to do with personal crisis, or with civilization generally, Eliot's work expressed, by the wonderwork of all its facets, and in different ways across the decades of his oeuvre – the boons and the banes of an aesthetics of exhaustion, and a music of mystic antagonism. The mystic inkling (more redolent perhaps in mid-late Eliot, i.e. from 'Ash-Wednesday' through *Four Quartets*), whether we call it such or not, occurs as and when a mind, particularly keen in the analytic sense – and Eliot was of course close to becoming an academic philosopher – stretches itself to exhaustion-point; the result is the efflux of reactive material which has none of the continuity or close, de-limiting boundaries of ego-organizational control; as though to weave what is or was disparate were a way of relaxing the previous exasperation of the too-honing-mentality. For my purposes here, I make no distinction between, or rather choose to combine and conflate, an un-controlled relaxing of the mind and a very controlled artistic purpose attempting to effect the reflection or representation of that very deflationary movement, and/or its process. The notion above (to be revisited) of being more a 'vehicle' than a 'maker' is apt here; indeed, for Eliot, 'humility' and 'freedom' – the freedom of acceptance – amounted to the same thing.[11]

10. *Poems of T.S. Eliot,* op. cit., p. 714. Ibid.: Eliot to Henry Eliot on 1 January 1936 called the poem 'blasphemous' because 'it stands for the lowest point I ever reached in my domestic affairs.'

11. Discussing 'Ash-Wednesday' in a letter to Stephen Spender on 9th May, 1935, Eliot wrote that the poem 'is an exposition of my view of the relation of *eros* and *agape* based on my own experience... One has got at the same time to unite oneself with humanity, and to isolate oneself completely; and to be equally indifferent to the "audience" and to oneself as one's own audience. So that humility and freedom are the same thing.' Ibid., p. 732.

Whether it's the very process of composition, choppy to say the least, of either *The Waste Land,* or, say, *Four Quartets,* or the exasperated mind of the bard under discussion;[12] or indeed, whether it's the aesthetic structure of feeling evinced within and by the poetry; or the philosophic thought expressed therein; or finally, whether it is the poetry's reflection of the human condition – which we will see to be that of a 'whole' that is radically un-resolved, an un-whole whole, essentially antagonistic – I find that the trope of exhaustion and its correlates provide a good reading direction through and across the poetic oeuvre. The musical patterning, equally, is there to stretch sensibility and comprehension towards the cusp of the real, on the other side or underside, that is, of indicative words. The beauty in Eliot's verse is the resolute beauty of a knowing-failure: his 'bang' to *our* 'whimper':

> Trying to learn to use words, and every attempt
> Is a wholly new start, and a different kind of failure
> Because one has only learnt to get the better of words
> For the thing one no longer has to say, or the way in which
> One is no longer disposed to say it.
>   'East Coker,' V, 3-7

The 'thousand sordid images' of which he 'was constituted;' the Eliot who 'moved' like an 'infinitely gentle / Infinitely suffering thing' is also the Eliot (still in part III of his 'Preludes') who 'had such a vision of the street / As the street hardly understands.' Ending 'Portrait of a Lady,' the poetic voice

---

12. See *The Annotated Waste Land with Eliot's Contemporary Prose,* ed. Lawrence Rainey, New Haven & London: Yale University Press, 2005, p. 17-24 (p. 22-23); or *Poems of T.S. Eliot,* op. cit., p. 557-560 & p 883.

liberates itself by questioning itself, 'And should I have the right to smile?' Or, at line 33 of 'Gerontion,' we read an even more blatant signal: 'After such knowledge, what forgiveness?' And then, many years later, in *Burnt Norton*: 'But to what purpose / Disturbing the dust on a bowl of rose-leaves / I do not know.' As 'Only through time time is conquered' (*Burnt Norton*, II, 43), Eliot's wisdom entailed the acknowledgment that to reflect 'impersonality' – his neo-classicism – meant the most arching, taut and purposive use of his poetic skill and control. In true Hegelian manner (Hegel being the master of Bradley), to willfully show the inhering limitations of the self was for him the only way to immanently transcend that very self. Just as line-endings and line-breaks – those sculpting de-limitations on the page – when cannily deployed, chisel verse-intents in a way that makes their senses greatly amplify, so Eliot seemed to believe that to re-cognize the limits of the human understanding was, immanently, to go beyond it.

For Hegel, the Idealist, to understand some-*thing*, a tree, say, was one thing; but Reason was a higher power than mere 'understanding.' Reason was more than the consciousness of some-*thing*, 'out there'; it was the consciousness *of that* consciousness, and mystical thus – in the following sense. Mysticism can be defined as the experience of the infinite, the transcendent, within the medium of the finite, the immanent; the experience of a mortal – *of the immortal*: the 'timeless' in the 'times', a veritable 'still point,' indeed. And for the mystic Hegel, thus, like Eliot, at times, the consciousness *of* consciousness, the thought, not only of *some-thing*, objectively 'out there' – but beyond that: the thought *of that very thought*, was a way of being at-one with Being, God (or, if you prefer, the 'Absolute'). Experiencing the Absolute, and/or reflecting that experience in verse, meant, thus, experiencing or reflecting the Objective Truth within one's own (de)limited subjective prison; experiencing or reflecting God meant that (the poet's) consciousness not only faced an object world; but that that consciousness *became* the object-world – which is a very redolent motif for a 'modernist' sensibility. The point to be elicited here is that this de-limiting of the self or subject was seen by Eliot – again, in both argument and, much of the time, in verse-con-figuration – as the sine qua non of access, however fleeting, to that, or the, ultimate '*omphalos*' of Truth; be that Truth poetic or otherwise.

Matching the pattern, or (mystic) music, of these ruminations (about a snake eating its own tail), Kenner is in one sense right to aver that: 'Eliot's poems differ from reader to reader to an unusual degree, posed between meaning nothing and meaning everything.'[13] In 'The Love Song of J. Alfred Prufrock,' after the poetic voice's self-disparaging disavowal, we read the almost-random line:

Shall I part my hair behind? Do I eat a peach?

Or, earlier, similar disjunctions served on both sides by line-breaks:

In the room women come and go
Talking of Michelangelo…
      I should have been a pair of ragged claws
Scattering across the floors of silent seas…

The knowing superimposition-effect of the first is a savvy scattering of univocal continuity, and though there's an end-rhyme the couplet remains a telltale shard, if picked up contrapuntally; the internal rhyme, in the second couplet, of 'claws' and 'floors', rather than a resolute end-rhyme is

13. Hugh Kenner, 'Bradley' in *T.S. Eliot: A Collection,* op. cit., 48.

expressive of both: the lack of self-knowledge, the lack of real depth of the voice's identity, and of the self behind the persona, arranging his words for this very effect. And the two instances combined in the same poem, among others, only exhaust the effects.

Another way to invoke this idea, that the I is the 'I am here / or there, or elsewhere', ('East Coker,' I, 49-50), is to advert to the opening stanza of 'East Coker,' whose major conceit to my mind is the liberating notion of the interpenetration of all things: pastoral, urban, human, animal, or plant. That all is itself and other at the same time; just as much as later in the same section, there is 'coiunction' and 'concorde,' at a formal or structural level, with the glaringly-referenced Sir Thomas Elyot of *The Governour.*[14]

And once we appreciate the knowing mixture of the random, the contingent, with the more continuous and seemingly-necessary – a lesson Eliot admitted he'd learnt in part from Baudelaire – it's little wonder to learn that the 'Notes' published in the book version of *The Waste Land* were often, as by Arnold Bennett, taken at the time to be a lark, a skit, a hoax.[15] It was as if the magic and the realism of the verse were joined by the very fluid awkwardness of their conjunction. Kenner writes how 'Prufrock' is just a name and a voice, without depth of individual or individuated 'character.' Prufrock is a mere vehicle – what Lacan would call an 'empty signifier,' – merely 'the name of a possible zone of consciousness where the materials can maintain a vague contiguity.'[16] Or:

...music heard so deeply

14. See *Poems of T.S. Eliot,* op. cit., p. 933.

15. See Ibid., p. 415 & p. 569.

16. Kenner, op. cit., p. 36.

That it is not heard at all, but you are the music
While the music lasts…
    'The Dry Salvages,' V, 27-29.

Or take perhaps one of the most quoted, known, and famed of Eliot's similes, from the opening of the same 'Prufrock:'

When the evening is spread against the sky
Like a patient etherized on a table…

This early, iconic image encapsulates the antagonistic ethos of Eliot's modernism. The evening 'spread,' *by being 'spread*,' actually jars against the sky – where normally, or literally, such a spread would be automatically matt. Then the startling, the shocking simile only exacerbates or exhausts this effect. What is happening is that the literal words, the letter, and the symbolic will behind them, clash, alienating the reader into new sensations. There is patently, here, both antagonism and poetic fluency, and the two, together resolve to be unresolved. Eliot's sensibility, communicates a kind of solipsism. He addresses an audience sundered from him, as much as he is (pace Kenner) from himself. Opening part II of 'The Hollow Men':

Eyes I dare not meet in dreams
In death's dream kingdom
These do not appear:
There, the eyes are
Sunlight on a broken column…

Eliot wasn't unaware of the pun of 'eye' and the principle identity, 'I'; in the Platonic tradition the 'eye', manumitted by light, is considered the most spiritual of the senses, the closest to mental capacity. Perhaps it's no accident that the light, for the eye, falls on a 'broken' 'I'.

Indeed, Paterian impressionism was recognized by Eliot later in life as a major influence. Pater had written in his renowned *History of the Renaissance* book, that 'Experience… is ringed round for each of us by that thick wall of personality through which no real voice has ever pierced… each mind keeping as a solitary in its own dream of a world.'[17] Though Eliot disclaimed speaking of himself as a mystic or contemplative [18], there is in his understanding of mystic attitudes a cognate coincidence of oneness and radical otherness. He writes in 1949 of how 'to many people, every writer on mystical subjects appears not only to be saying the same things as other writers, but himself to be saying the same things again and again;' and in 1940, he'd written: 'I may often repeat what I have said before, and I may often contradict myself.' [19] These latter citations, combined here, are surely redolent for some of the patterns, recursions, disjunctions in *Four Quartets*, as elsewhere. Eliot's selves self-question themselves, but with real will and purpose: 'And should I then presume? / And how should I begin?' ('The Love Song of J. Alfred Prufrock,' 68-9.)

Tying-in with all this, Allen Tate once wrote of the opening of 'Ash-Wednesday' that the self-questioning banality of liturgical reference in the first stanza was an irony that betokened deep humility. Tate sees the self-ironisation

17. This quote is a reference in the editorial commentary of *Poems of T.S. Eliot,* op cit., p. 703, to *The Waste Land,* V, 413. Indeed, on p. 386 (again, part of the editorial commentary in this volume, but this time regarding 'Prufrock') we have an excerpt of a letter from 12 August, 1953 to William Blisset, where Eliot writes: 'Pater had a much greater influence upon me at one period of my life than any reader would gather… At the age of sixteen or seventeen, I was fascinated… and I think I read all his work – some of his books several times especially *Studies in the Renaissance, Marius the Epicurean,* and *Imaginary Portraits.*'

18. *Poems of T.S. Eliot,* op. cit., p. 985.

19. Ibid., p. 944.

of that opening stanza as leading to the implication of a de-personalized humility – derived as a form of 'self-respect proceeding from a sense of the folly of men in their desire to dominate a natural force or situation.'[20] The process is eminently Socratic, and reminiscent of the central figure of 'Tiresias' in 'The Fire Sermon' from a decade earlier:

> I Tiresias, though blind, throbbing between two
> lives,
> Old man with wrinkled female breasts, can see…

The gift of seeing sight, like the gift of poetry, is a sigil conferred on a ruined self. Or in Part V, 'What the Thunder Said:'

> Who is the third who walks always beside you?
> When I count, there are only you and I together
> But when I look ahead up the white road
> There is always another one walking beside you
> Gilding wrapt in a brown mantle. Hooded
> I do not know whether a man or a woman –
> But who is that on the other side of you?

This unanswered and unanswerable self-questioning is a microcosm of what I have suggested is the beauty in the failure of Eliot's (successful) poetic vision. The androgynous seer is 'hooded;' we see that he sees, but not what he sees.

> For hope would be hope for the wrong thing; wait
> without love
> For love would be love of the wrong thing; there is
> yet faith

20. Allen Tate, 'On *Ash-Wednesday*' in *T.S. Eliot: A Collection,* op. cit., p. 132-3.

> But the faith and the love and the hope are all in the
> waiting.
>> 'East Coker,' III, 24-26.

Eliot, following F.H. Bradley (on whom he'd done doctoral research before arriving in England), offers no finished or resolved answers[21]; the questing, searching process, as much as the form and patterning (discussed further below) just is the thing, the content. On 9th August 1930, Eliot wrote to the poet William Force Stead:

> Between the usual subjects of poetry and "devotional" verse there is a very important field still unexplored by modern poets – the experience of man in search of God, and trying to explain to himself his intenser human feelings in terms of the divine goal. I have tried to do something of this in *Ash-Wednesday*.[22]

Indeed, this notion is overtly articulated in a well-known part of *Burnt Norton*:

> Words, after speech, reach
> Into the silence. Only by the form, the pattern,
> Can words or music reach
> The stillness…

To Cleanth Brooks, on 15th March, 1937, Eliot wrote:

> The conscious problems with which one is concerned in the actual writing are more those of

21. See Kenner, op cit., p. 36-57, for many reflections on this notion inherited by Eliot from Bradley.

22. *Poems of T.S. Eliot,* op. cit., p. 731.

a quasi musical nature, in the arrangement of metre
and pattern, than those of conscious exposition of
ideas.[23]

In his 1924 'Brief Introduction to the Method Of Paul Valéry'
he wrote of: 'a recognition of the truth that not our feelings,
but the pattern we make of our feelings, is the centre of
value.'[24] Or later, in 1941, Eliot expressed his view that
'Imagination' was a 'capacity for experience… in which
"experience" is spiritual experience,' and as a capacity for
experiencing not merely the immediate but the immediate
with its relations – so that the highest imagination will
combine the maximum of immediacy with the maximum
implication of pattern.[25]

I knew that a poem, or a passage of a poem, may tend
to realize itself first as a particular rhythm before it reaches
expression in words, and that this rhythm may bring to birth
the idea and the image. [26]

Pater was famed for saying that all arts aspire to the
condition of music. Eliot agreed, but averred that the analogy
of poetry with music was dangerous if pressed too far.[27] While
Eliot was quasi-aestheticist in thinking that the poem is the
poem for its own sake, like a dancer in the dance, and not
made for some consequential or didactic end;[28] and while he
could never conceive of good or worthy poetry not having
a presiding sense for the ear; [29] while he was even reported
as having never been able to write a poem 'unless he tricked

23. Ibid., p. 575.
24. Ibid., p. 955.
25. Ibid., p. 956.
26. Ibid., p. 978.
27. See Ibid., p. 893.
28. See Ibid., p 917.
29. See, for instance, Ibid., p. 388.

himself into the belief that it was only a technical problem to be solved;[30] yet he always claimed that his art was at the service of his morality. 'My own "art" (such as it is) has always been at the disposal of my moral values.'[31] That said, following the likes of Arthur Symons from the decadent 'nineties, Eliot made use of musical tropes overtly and eponymously across his oeuvre (as in 'The Love Song of J. Alfred Prufrock,' 'Preludes,' 'Rhapsody on a Windy Night,' '*Four Quartets*'.)

And Eliot was at-one with Virginia Woolf in this. Writing of *Burnt Norton* and the *Quartets* on 3rd September 1942, Eliot spoke of 'the set form which I have elaborated.' He spoke of his titular choice of 'quartet' as suggesting to him, 'the notion of making a poem by weaving together three or four superficially unrelated themes: the "poem" being the degree of success in making a new whole out of them.'[32] In *Craftsmanship,* a few years earlier, Woolf had written:

> You cannot use a brand new word in an old language because of the very obvious yet always mysterious fact that a word is not a single and separate entity, but... part of a sentence... How can we combine old words in new orders... That is the question...[33]

Tallying with all this 'agenbite of inwit,' Eliot had a musical notion of what, since *The Waste Land,* he'd become famous for: namely, peppered references and shards of quotations woven into complex and composite verse. Part of the reason he added the 'Notes' to his 1922 mini-epic was to pre-empt critics who'd previously suggested plagiarism. In 1932 he wrote:

30. Ibid., p. 964.
31. Ibid., p. 732.
32. Ibid., p. 893.
33. Ibid., p. 1040.

You cannot effectively 'borrow' an image, unless you borrow also, or have spontaneously, something like the feeling which prompted the original image. An 'image', in itself is like dream symbolism, is only vigorous in relation to the feelings out of which it issues, in the relation of word to flesh. You are entitled to take it for your own purposes in so far as your fundamental purposes are akin to those of the one who is, for you, the author of the phrase, the inventor of the image; or if you take it for other purposes then your purposes must be consciously and pointedly diverse from those of the author, and the contrast is very much to the point; you may not take it merely because it is a good phrase or a lovely image…[34]

The opposition phrased in this rumination captures perfectly the simultaneous oneness and many-ness that has been the main purport of my reflections here. Whether we read Eliot's now-notorious mosaics as timely, coming at a time when modernity was at the start, or end of a certain exhaustion, aesthetic as otherwise; or whether we see him as truly possessing a 'historic sense,' in which he was continuing the past by new, discrete means – his facets are facets of exhaustion. And yet, either way, his music of mystic antagonism was and remains 'a still point in our turning world' where 'right action is freedom / From past and future also' ('The Dry Salvages,' V, 41-2) and where '…History may be servitude / History may be freedom…' ('Little Gidding,' III, 13-14).

34. Ibid., p. 401.

13

Good Neighbours: Reading Love and Loss in Basil Bunting

> 'It was not so,
> scratched on black by God knows who,
> by God, by God knows who.'
> 'Villon,' I, 12-14

> 'He has untied the tape
> of her striped flannel drawers
> before the range. Naked
> on the pricked mat
> his fingers comb
> thatch of his manhood's home.'
> 'Briggflatts', I, 99-104

> 'Days jerk, dawdle, fidget
> towards the cesspit.
> Love is a vapour, we're soon through it.'
> 'Briggflatts,' II, 66-68

At the close of one of his poems, 'The Good Neighbour,' John Burnside writes, in *propria persona* – or not – of how:

> my one good neighbor sets himself aside,
> and alters into someone I have known:
> a passing stranger on the road to grief,
> husband and father; rich man; poor man; thief.

From the biblical reference in the title, through to this closing,

Burnside's poem is a metaphor for how self and other in the good world are imminently and immanently neighbours. Just as love and loss are indicated by these lines, so the metonymic use of 'rich man; poor man' to stand-in for 'Everyman', is for my purposes here an interesting way, I hope, into a consideration of this new volume: *The Poems of Basil Bunting*, edited, introduced and annotated by Don Share. What I intend to show here are the different ways in which Bunting's work, and Bunting's work as arranged here, copiously supplied with scholarship, evinces formal as well as discursive senses of (what are in the end, good) neighbouring. Though love—and in many ways its mirror and complement, loss—proves to be one of the main presiding tenors of Bunting's work, let me begin by listing some of the other ways in which Bunting's poetry, as presented in this volume, offers the reader ways of being his 'semblables.'

From the start of his career, in 'Villon' (published in *Poetry* in 1925,) Bunting often uses archetypal, complementary binaries in the very verbal texture of his verse. However, after a canny reading of this annotated volume, we can discern other binaries. Like Eliot and Joyce, among others, Bunting makes use of a 'mythic method', anchoring contemporary contingent experience with incisively-portrayed mythic parallels, making use of mosaics of quotation, translation and reference. Part of the biographical context we learn of in Share's edition informs us about how Bunting often offered parallels between east and west, orient and occident (the most pressing example being 'The Spoils' (1951)). We can also see ways in which Bunting is ekphrastic, mixing media, especially poetry with music.[1] As mentioned, throughout his oeuvre,

---

1. See for instance, *The Poems of Basil Bunting,* ed. Don Share, London: Faber & Faber, 2016, p. 326. Speaking of the composition of 'Briggflatts,' Bunting relegates content or argument in his working-method to his inklings of 'rhythm'

past and present seem to marry in concord and discord via his juxtaposition-ing of autobiographical experiences and mythological parallels, both pagan and Biblical. However, as lit-up so copiously by Share, in Bunting's work past and present also mix, via the evident poetic schooling from the possession of an absurdly polyglot poetic past (from Horace, Catullus and Longus, to Chaucer, Dante, Malherbe, Villon, to Gibbon and Byron, Swinburne and Tennyson; and so on…). And finally of course, above all of these neighbourings, indeed, facilitating their very construal, we have the basic architecture of the volume, between the work of the poet and that of his newest, latest editor.[2]

In his helpful but spare Introduction, Share offers his rationale for the production of this edition—in particular, to ratify it after the not-too-distant Bloodaxe edition, published at the turn of the century. First, this edition 'presents and corrects poems Bunting published or intended to publish during his lifetime,' as well as poems published posthumously by previous editors, such as Richard Caddel. It also offers a selection 'of fragments, drafts or variant versions of poems published in works (including facsimile) by others, or hitherto unpublished.' Second, it supplies a publication history of all Bunting's work, often fascinating insights into Bunting's composition processes across his career, as well as a comprehensive amount of annotation to the poetic work, ranging from poetic wholes to specific lines or groups of such (in a manner to quite match the recent Faber volumes of T.S.

and 'mood.' There is also, as mentioned later in the main text, the fact that, along with 'Sonatas,' much of his works are 'Odes' and 'Limericks.'

2. As well as the densely annotated commentary to all the published, unpublished, uncollected and drafted versions of the oeuvre, the volume also contains at the end significant sections of 'textual variants' to all the poetry collected, as well as a clutch of 'Appendices,' such as a supplementary essay on 'Bunting's Interest in Persian Poetry,' or, a selection of 'Bunting's Prefaces.'

Eliot's work, edited by Christopher Ricks and Jim McCue). As with these latter, recent, Eliot Faber editions, the annotations and the textual variants are indicated page by page beneath the central work presented, offering immediate access to the reader of insight of a biographical, contextual nature, as well as, if far less copiously, of a more objective, critical nature. Finally, the edition offers textual variants from printed sources, seen to be especially necessary given what we learn about how little control or input Bunting had over his published work throughout his life.[3]

Having introduced the main purposes of this new scholarly edition, I will now turn to two basic case studies, pitting Bunting's earliest published poem, 'Villon', 1925 (in *Poetry*), with 'Briggflatts,' his major work from far later in his career, in 1965. I aim to discuss the poetry in detail, making telltale use however of the scholarly accompaniments. Through an examination of these two poems, in the main, I hope to open a brief window for readers, new and old, to Bunting's work, by offering an interpretative consideration that at the same time highlights the illuminating purport of this scholarly edition. As I've already made mention of his major contemporary on the British scene, T.S. Eliot, that's where I'll start.

On the first page of Share's substantial commentary, introducing the first chapter as it were of collected work, the 'Sonatas' (as against, say, later sections of 'Odes' and 'Limericks') we read a quote from Bunting late in his life, where he reflects on how central (much as with Eliot) musical forms were to his poetic career and, more emphatically, method.[4] However, towards the end of this citation he's

---

3. *Poems of Bunting, op. cit.*, p. xx.

4. See reference in footnote 1. See also reference in footnote 5. For one example of Eliot's invoking of musical form(s), see *The Poems of T.S. Eliot, Volume 1:*

shown to have ruminated, contrasting his manner with Eliot's, in a way I hope to ratify with concrete analysis, below.

Eliot… show[s] prodigious skill in fitting words to a prearranged pattern, very admirable: yet [he doesn't] do it without losing some suppleness […] Critical notions are in control from the outside so that the poem is constrained to meet them, as though it had never been conceived in the form it wears… My matter is born of the form – or the form of the matter, if you care to think that I just conceive of things musically. There's no fitting, at least consciously. Whatever you think I am saying is something I could not have said in any other way.[5]

Apart from the odd parody of the (after all) chronologically-preceding Eliot (noted, for one instance, in the commentary to 'Attis: Or, Something Missing' (1931))[6], we can directly compare snapshots of verse with cognate arguments which show Bunting's reflection to be quite close to the mark.

From 'Burnt Norton,' Eliot, then:

'Time present and time past
Are both perhaps present in time future,
And time future contained in time past.
If all time is eternally present
All time is unredeemable.

Collected and Uncollected Poems, ed. Christopher Ricks & Jim McCue, London: Faber & Faber, 2015, p. 575. In a letter to Cleanth Brooks, cited there, from 15th March, 1937, Eliot writes: '[T]he conscious problems with which one is concerned in the actual writing are more those of a quasi -musical nature, in the arrangement of metre and pattern, than those of conscious exposition of ideas.'

5. *Poems of Bunting, op. cit.,* p. 275. This citation in the annotated commentary is taken from a letter to Bunting scholar Victoria Forde on 23rd May, 1972.

6. See for instance, *Ibid.,* p. 286.

What might have been is an abstraction
Remaining a perpetual possibility
Only in a world of speculation.
What might have been and what has been
Point to one end, which is always present.
Footfalls echo in the memory
Down the passage we did not take
Towards the door we never opened
Into the rose-garden. My words echo
Thus, in your mind…
(I, 1-14)

And then, later, a just as-well-known snippet:

… Words, after speech, reach
Into the silence. Only by the form, the pattern,
Can words or music reach
The stillness…
(V, 3-6)

Roughly twenties years later, Bunting writes in his (archetypal, I'd say) 'Autobiography', 'Briggflatts:'

Fierce blood throbs on his tongue,
lean words.
…
In such soft air
they trudge and sing,
laying the tune frankly on the air.
All sounds fall still,
fellside bleat,

hide-and-seek peewit.
(I, 66-67 & 73-78)

'Snow lies bright on Hedgehope
and tacky mud about Till
where the fells have stepped aside
and the river praises itself,
silence by silence sits
and Then is diffused in Now.
(V, 55-60)

I'd say that the small typographical difference, of lines
opening in uniform Upper Case, and those not, is a symptom
of two different sensibilities. The one: more overtly oracular,
the other – though doing similar juxtaposition-ing and super-
imposing work – far more concrete and intimate. Both poets
were radically against the confessional mode,[7] but one finds
a certain truth in Bunting's comment cited above. Put in
another way, where often, Bunting portrays personal loss,
as we are to see, he does so without loss of spontaneity. In
this sense, Eliot inherits from Arnold his reflective mode; his
representation of experience, and indeed loss, reflexive in a
way which seems to render his verse, like Arnold's, detached
and (literally) re-flective; overtly intellectual.[8] While quite a
lot of the time equally reflecting loss, Bunting on the other

7. See *Ibid.*, p. 277, where Bunting writes of his lack of use of both, 'personae,'
as in Browning or Pound, and direct confessional reference. The excerpt alluded
to here is from an interview with Dale Reagan, published in *Montemora 3*, Spring
1977.

    8. I should say that I was spurred to this critical analogy by Stefan Collini's
Arnold, Oxford & New York: Oxford University Press, 1988, p. 25-45. Though

hand, never loses the texture of the actual experience – however much it is indeed being looked-upon. In a sense, Bunting makes more use of what Wallace Stevens called 'the irrational element' in poetry.[9]

For all his educative range and sophistication, from the start Bunting was a Northumbrian poet. Not only does he make use of mythoi from that past (like 'Bloodaxe' in 'Briggflatts'); and not only, as we learn from Share's commentary was he often dismissive of 'Southron' readings of his verse, which he, by contrast, often sang in dialect and in dialect's music;[10] but he peppers his verse with words less stately, such as, opening 'Villon' in a mildly heroic manner, when he speaks of: 'He whom we anatomized…/ speaks / to us, hatching marrow…' This is a nice and poignantly paradoxical image, living-out much of the purport of the poem, between life and death. But we also learn from the commentary of how the word, '*marra*' in dialect meant 'peer' or 'friend' – making the play of neighboring not just between reader and writer, then and now, but also signaling the mythic method, between Villon and Bunting, via very concrete signals. Even if the walls of the prison where Bunting, we learn, was reading Villon – himself once in the same kind of

---

Collini makes no mention of Eliot here, the analogy none the less suggested itself to me.

9. See for instance, Joan Richardson, *Wallace Stevens: The Early Years, 1879–1923*, New York: Beech Tree Books & William Morrow, 1986, p. 66 and p. 70. This latter coinage allowed Stevens to distinguish between the literal words bodied-forth, the 'poetry of the subject' and the symbolic will beneath, the 'true subject.' This distinction allowed Stevens to articulate how he was able to smuggle-in the messiness of his true or real self into a poetry that was nonetheless eminently ordered and fluent. Indeed, to continue the heuristic parallel, Harriet Monroe, editor of *Poetry*, first published Stevens in 1915, a neat decade only before Bunting.

10. See *Poems of Bunting, op. cit.*, p. 327.

prison – are 'unresonant' to the poet's or his (neighboring) persona's 'hulloing'; and even if, still in prison, 'eyes lie and this swine's fare bread and water / makes my head wuzz…'; the 'wuzz', and words like it (parsed in Share's commentary) from across his oeuvre, is quite alive. Alive while, *again*, like Villon, and like 'Villon' he remains: 'in the dark place, in the grave / fettered to a post in the damp cellarage' (II, 5-6).

In that first poem, as later, Bunting is critical of hard science, of its claims to comprehend reality by measurement.

> My tongue is a curve in the ear. Vision is lies.
> We saw it so and it was not so…
> (I, 7-8)

Or, below:

> To the right was darkness and to the left was
> hardness
> below hardness darkness above
> at the feet darkness at the head partial hardness
> with equal intervals without
> to the left moaning and beyond a scurry.
> (I, 29-33)

The recursions re-call Eliot, but where Eliot is unlike Bergson,[11] in a way spatializing his experience across the page, Bunting seems to be critical here, in argument and in configuration, of the visualized or spatial – as against the immanent or seamless being of music. Indeed, towards the end of part II, he criticizes police methods, police methodology, almost, whether now or then:

---

11. See Henri Bergson, *Time and Free Will,* trans. F.L. Pogson, London: George Allen, 1913.

What is your name? Your maiden name?
Go in there to be searched. I suspect it's not
your true name.
Distinguishing marks if any? (O anthropometrics!)
Now the thumbprints for filing.
Colour of hair? of eyes? of hands?…
(II, 33-37).

And thankfully, Share's commentary allows us insight into this poetic or concrete criticism. In 1927 (two years after the publication of 'Villon'), Bunting writes of his scorn for the modern pretensions of modern science. It pretends to exhaust with:

its universe of exact measurement and strict logic,
all the subjects of thought and knowledge…. There
remain two realms at least that cannot be explored
by scientific methods, that of Religion n the one
hand, and that of Art on the other; both wide
regions in which the mid must wander without a
chart, in which the dominant mode of thought is
not logical but intuitive…[12]

This tallies with what I've intimated above; what you cannot (spatially) 'chart,' is precisely the matrix of real feeling and true spontaneous experience.

If love and loss now become the dominant theme of the last third of this review-article, it is not only because it happens to be a dominant thematic coupling in Bunting's imaginary; but also because, in a sense, love just is death, for a poet, thinking poetically. Love, in its truest sense, is vulnerability, susceptibility, susceptibility to experience; at the

12. *Poems of Bunting, op. cit.,* p. 283. This comment was part of an article,
'Philosophic Criticism,' published in *The Outlook* 60, on 6th August, 1927.

farthest extreme of this experiential de-limitation, is death. 'Hatching marrow,' indeed.

In 'Villon', like 'Villon,' then: '….these things are not obliterate. / What gobs spitten for mockery; / and I too shall have CY GIST written over me' (I, 39-41). Being written over, here, is being written over.

Or, in the second, more periodic half of this same opening part, from a series of neat iambic octosyllabic verses:

> Worn hides that scarcely clothe the soul
> they are so rotten, old and thin,
> or firm and soft and warm and full –
> fellmonger Death gets every skin.
>
> All that is piteous, all that's fair,
> all that is fat and scant of breath,
> Elisha's baldness, Helen's hair,
> is Death's collateral:
>
> Three score and ten years after sight
> of this pay me your pulse and breath
> value received. And who dare cite,
> as we forgive our debtors, Death?
> (I, 46-57)

The neighboring of mythoi, past and present, pagan and Biblical, mirrors the play-like quid pro quo between death and life. Even if the value is 'received' only 'after sight,' suggesting in the verse posthumous re-flection – none the less, the use of fluid enjambments suggests a truer because messier recognition. And then, closing this opening section at the inception of Bunting's poetic oeuvre, 'a word, a tint, a tone, / insubstantial-glorious / when we are dead and gone / and the green grass growing over us.' Death: for green; and glory for the insubstantial; binaries, neighbors, again. Indeed, because of 'the beauty of Helen,' Bunting's 'precision' clarifies 'vagueness; / boundary to a wilderness / of detail; chisel voice / smoothing the flanks of noise' (III, 27-29). And if Bunting's persona's penultimate line questions: 'How can I sing with my love in my bosom?' the question is incumbent, both literally and figuratively, on the preceding three-line stanza, running:

> The sea has no renewal, no forgetting,
> no variety of death,
> is silent with the silence of a single note.

However, the poem dies, quite variously (and in ways comparable to parts of Eliot's 'Prufrock'), with the persona dubbing himself: 'Unclean, immature and unseasonable as salmon.'

In true modernist fashion, seasonal rhythms are central to much of Bunting's imaginary and much of his imaginary output. In his major work from 1965, 'Briggflatts', which opens heroically, much like 'Villon', with 'Brag, sweet tenor bull,' the 'bull' as much as the overt references to spring and May below,[13] is referenced multifariously in Share's commentary as a (personal) symbol of Spring. Punctuating the opening section, across different staggered stanzas, we read music like:

> 'May on the bull's hide
> and through the dale
> furrows fill with may,
> paving the slowworm's way.
> (I, 10-13)

13. Indeed, Bunting's 'May' comes chronologically after Eliot's cruelest 'April.' But one might say: *only according to the calendar*. Bunting's verse, as read here, differs greatly in many ways from Eliot's, despite many parallels.

The solemn mallet says:
In the grave's slot
he lies. We rot.
(I, 24-26)

Wetter, warmed, they watch
the mason meditate
on name and date.
(I, 89-91)

For when 'Love murdered neither bleeds nor stifles / but jogs the draftsman's elbow' (I, 125-126), it's no wonder that: 'Dung will not soil the slowworm's / mosaic' (I, 144-145). Indeed, to complement this notion, the end of the earlier 'The Well of Lycopolis' (1935), runs: 'The surface sparkles and dances with their sighs / as though Styx were silvered by a wind from Heaven.' And in Share's annotated commentary we find Bunting discussing how this ending plays on, and hopes to redeem, Dante's hopeless damning of those 'helpless victims of accidie.' And this because, it was 'a sin,' Bunting records, 'I feel myself much inclined to, to be cured or nullified by the epicurean slowworm.'[14] The poetic music aims for what Heaney called 'redress;' and Bunting's neighboring persona reflects himself, Dante, those condemned by Dante, and the various processual and dynamic neighborings between them.

Making use of the mythoi of Alexander and Bloodaxe, among others, Bunting's 'Autobiography', 'Briggflatts' recalls among other things the experience of first love. The 'mason' in this poetic mosaic seems to represent the poetic or musical artist. 'The mason stirs: / Words! / Pens are too light. / Take

14. *Poems of Bunting, op. cit.,* p. 306. This comment comes from a letter to Bunting scholar Peter Makin on 3rd December, 1985.

a chisel to write' (I, 115-118). The chisel, one feels, is not only subject to and of 'dialect,' but seems to represent the poet's more globally ruddy intents. The mason 'says: Rocks / happen by chance. / No one here bolts the door, / love is so sore' (I, 36-39). And the mason laments: 'What can he, changed, tell / her, changed, perhaps dead? / Delight dwindles. Blame / stays the same' (I, 127-130). And the mason reflects how, though it 'looks well on the page,' it is: 'never / well enough. Something is lost / when wind, sun, sea upbraid / justly an unconvinced deserter' (II, 93-96). *None the less*, we end this second part of this tale of loss-in-love and woe, of less, with the 'glory' 'in unlike creation.' Quiddity: in a word. And then, musically-redolent, contrapuntal, at the ending of part IV, we read an island of three short lines, 'Stars disperse. We too, / further from neighbours / now the year ages.' Finally, wending towards the end of the fifth and final section (before the curt coda):

> …The star you steer by is gone,
> its tremulous thread spun in the hurricane
> spider floss on my cheek; light from the zenith
> spun when the slowworm lay in her lap
> fifty years ago….
> (V, 92-96)

> Fifty years a letter unanswered;
> a visit postponed for fifty years.
> She has been with me for fifty years.
> Starlight quivers. I had day enough.
> For love uninterrupted night.
> (V, 107-111)

Love and death, love and loss, neighbor each other, here, as elsewhere: by God, by God knows who.

14

Fathering Sons[1], Or, Re-Hearsing His Race: On Don Paterson

His face is tilted upwards, heavenwards,
While the skull, in turn, beholds his upturned face.
'Phantom, II'

The dream is taxed.
'The Circle'

He proves by algebra that Hamlet's grandson is Shakespeare's grandfather
and that he himself is the ghost of his own father.
James Joyce, *Ulysses*

... we shall never see his like again...
William Shakespeare, *Hamlet*, I, ii

Permit me this fiction. Imagine that Jorge Luis Borges was to have a lovechild, out of (novelistic) wedlock, necessarily, with Kazuo Ishiguro. That is fiction. N o w to poetry: their child might be the eminent/eminently gifted poet under discussion here.

First things first (so t o s peak) ... B y w ay o f introducing the major tenor of this article, let me adumbrate (or

---

1. Apart from the obvious and parsimonious puns of/in these titles, the meat of my thesis in this article is: not only that Paterson is a universally-redolent poet, but also that in the uni-verse of his whole oeuvre, there is a uni-vocal be(e)line, "to be" elicited ... (a boldness, and a subtlety ...).

enumerate) some of Paterson's titles: *Nil, Nil* (1993), *God's Gift to Women* (1997), *The Eyes* (1999), *Landing Light* (2003), *Orpheus* (2006), *Rain* (2010), and now *40 Sonnets* (2015).

Note the bold gambits implicit in these titles. Archetypal elements, archetypal organs, the invoking of the Everything and the Nothing – light and dark, the feminine, the masculine: landlubb-ing and the oneiric. (Forty, of course, is a Biblically-metonymic number.) Borges has a famous two-page skit titled "Everything and Nothing". The short tale is a metaphor for how, without de-limitation, the human animal, like Paterson's "Tony Blair" in 'The Big Listener' (in his latest work, *40 Sonnets*), is soulless. The thespian narrating the tale has acted all the major leading roles – except himself. There is something of this, but in a highly acutely-knowing manner, in Paterson's latest book – as elsewhere, earlier. In a way, Paterson is a ventriloquist of himself; thus, a ventriloquist who is not one.[2]

Like Borges, Paterson is deeply metaphysical, incisive, in-sight-ful. Not only does he make use of metaphysical conceits, and with a light touch, thankfully – making him exemplary as a lyric poet representing human(e)[3] conditions – but there is also something re-cursive and re-hearsing in this latest collection; something, dare I say it, highly reflexive, like Borges. In a way, in this more simply or minimalistically-titled book of sonnets, Paterson is doing a rendition of Paterson: doing renditions. Many of his most powerful and memorable pieces of work are lit up, if not intentionally adverted to in this, by turns, whimsically funny and dreadfully serious book. What I want to suggest throughout is that Paterson seems

2. See the prose piece in *40 Sonnets* titled 'Version', after Nicanor Parra (a reference about which I am ignorant, I'm afraid); and yet it is also a "version" after himself, to boot, given his stellar career before this collection. Both: father and son, then.

3. More on this, the most-used letter in the alphabet, below.

to rehearse (his own) essential situations, whether demotic or hieratic, of everyday living – except tuned (turned) by the vehicle of a highly intelligent poetic mind.

Take the central idea in his 'Letter to the Twins' (from *Landing Light*), the idea that ontogeny needs must fall from the womb and rehearse ever and again phylogeny; this serious-minded idea, yes: but with the opening and closing ironies about the identity of the twins' mother, or speaking father. That is where my heurism, my fictional Ishiguro, comes in. Not only is Paterson a wonderfully laconic story-teller, with all dues paid to form, as a matter of course, but like the fictions of Ishiguro, his effects, however powerful in effect, are achieved in an extremely subtle way. When we read Ishiguro, it is sometimes a single off-word, or a single off-passage, that, seen in reader-ly retrospect, holds the hidden source of his tales' acute dramas. The ironies and the tragedies of his stories lie somewhere in the interstices of the lines. This is something Paterson does too; his lines speak between themselves, as well as more obviously or overtly in and on themselves. And so that is where we shall start …

To open my opening, dominant theme: take the opening and the closing of Paterson's previous collection, *Rain*. In a way, what I am about to show, qua structure of feeling, of both poet and poems, is Paterson's signature. I presume the "Miguel" of 'Two Trees' is the Michael Donaghy of *Rain's* longest piece, the late-coming elegy 'Phantom.'[4]

This poem (like my current explanation) evinces what I believe is called a *piano nobile*. Two stanzas of 12 lines each (making 24, all things) which taper outwards then inwards

---

4. Among other things, Paterson is the (posthumous) editor of Donaghy's work; he also recently published a work of commentary on Donaghy's poetry, Smith: A Reader's Guide to the Poetry of Michael Donaghy (2014); neither of which I have read, as yet.

like that very notion of a rounding musical staircase. The first stanza involves our"Don Miguel" getting "out of bed". The second stanza, by turns, speaks of a second person (the survivor) who bought our eponymous-posthumous hero's house having "no dream". The first stanza is a quotidian tale; the second, where the magic dies, is told in a more magical and richer register. The story told, about Donaghy or beyond him, is to do in the main with poetic inspiration, spirited or spiritless. The poem ends laconically about the soullessness of simple trees, "trees" being the sole things the poem is"about" (meant topographically as well as logically).[5]

Moving on, the end poem of the collection, 'Rain', ends with the Auden-esque (second [penultimate] part of an elegy for Yeats, like Paterson's penultimate Donaghy elegy) idea that all this poetry, gone before and to come, does not "matter". But of course it does. But off course, it does. Indeed, the epigraph to *Rain*, from Antonio Porchia, about man being "air" and having to "fall" to no longer be "air", mirrors the epigraph of *40 Sonnets*, from the same source. What might this mean? That *Rain* and *40 Sonnets* have the same source: that Paterson and Donaghy do (indeed, note that the Donaghy elegy has seven parts; seven being half of the sonnet's 14); [6] that Paterson and Rilke do? (The letter "e" [missing from 'Rain'] is another "everything" – the most used letter in the alphabet.) And so on. (That was me doing a Helen Vendler on Paterson – Paterson's edition of Shakespeare's Sonnets having been, I was told by a knowledgeable acquaintance, a riposte

---

5. There is also of course the more overt sense of the two trees being "Don" and "Michael".

6. Another possible reading is the arithmetic as it were of the first poem, where the "M" and "D" of Michael "Don"aghy are inverted – signalling perhaps a subtle intention to "invert" the "nothing-matters" of this first poem's "end" counterpart, complement, 'Rain'.

to the well-nigh cabalistic baroque of Vendler's work on those same sonnets. [7]

Now back to demotic, Paterson as Ishiguro.

Staying with the Donaghy elegy from Paterson's penultimate collection, the persona addresses his addressee with lines (in admiration) invoking him to "strike one match, and then another – /

> not to light these rooms, or to augment
> what little light they shed upon themselves
> but to see the kind of dark I laid between them.

Interstices, again; layers of dark between the positives of the world of light (landless-ness, rather than *Landing Light?*) The final poem, 'Rain' again, is also redolent with the matter and its ante.

We are told in a down-to-earth tone, opening the poem, "I love all films that start with rain", and later how "such a film can do no wrong". And yet, the poem also, and at many levels, is a tale of woe, and more emphatically: privation. Like the opening and closing of *40 Sonnets*, 'Here', and then, by the time we get to it,'The Roundabout'; like the already mentioned 'Letter to the Twins' – one of the most moving poems in that penultimate collection is titled 'The Circle', and is, again, fathering sons. His son's draftsmanship fails (to close

---

7. I was informed of this by W. N. Herbert, close to the time Paterson's edition of Shakespeare's Sonnets was released. I should say that in my view (and I am certainly no Shakespeare scholar) Vendler's book on Shakespeare is superlative, and deeply enjoyable for a thinking mind. Paterson's Shakespeare book is very down to earth by comparison, rigorously playing down the fetish or hypostatization of the iconic bard. There are senses, then, in which both Paterson and Vendler are radical or complex: Paterson for taking a contemporary, quotidian approach; Vendler for doing a Renaissance Shakespeare. Two kinds of (complementary) immanent critique, then.

the circle); yet closing the poem we sing with the mention of implicit"rain" "singing under everything". Like Raine, again, Paterson is not only writing for, to, and about a son; the son is the father; and *vice versa*. Even if the "dream is taxed" ('Phantom'); and even if this fee goes against"one great heavenly design" ('The Circle'), speaking to the craft of a son again in the same "penultimate"collection:

> the whole man must be his own brother for no man
> is himself alone;
> though some of us have never known the one
> hand's kindness to the other.

Much like his versions of Machado, here ('Correctives') Paterson is aphoristically taut; rhyming a controlled reflection; [8] in some ways similar in this short piece to some of Michael Longley's short pieces, as in, recently, The Stairwell.[9]

From aphoristic rigour, now, to a more Hardyesque tale-telling, witness: 'The Story of The Blue Flower'. This tale of fantasy, nightmare, dream, and its wakening is roughly halfway between the tales of 'Don Miguel' and 'Phantom'; it is constructed like a pulley between centrifugal and centripetal energies, in the tale told and in the way the tale is told. In fact, and now before I come to a more detailed look at his latest,

8. In an earlier version of this essay, this last-mentioned poem ('Correctives') was "incorrectly" attributed to Paterson's latest collection, rather than, as now corrected, his "penultimate" one. Without this footnote and the corrective work it adverts to, the former erratum may well have still been legitimate, given the overall gambit of this essay – a little red herring, or exception, to prove the rule. At the last, it is up to the reader to decide whether this footnote exists or not. (And so on[e] ...)

9. Allying this comment with other comments here, to do with Paterson's "lyrical" mathematicity, it should be noted that Paterson has also published volumes of, precisely, aphorisms.

40 Sonnets, that last piece ('The Story of The Blue Flower') holds an argument in line with the paradoxes of mattering and its mattering or ante. In a way, the conceit is, again, of everything and nothing – much like the recent Hollywood film *Inside Man*.[10]

It is a tale filled with matter (two pages and four longish stanzas);[11] a tale too, we realize at the tail, that just never happened. Perhaps the answer, against bitty particles, is "waves" – epigones of womb-ocean, and yet connected to land. And this last serves as a bridge to a theme rhythmically-redolent in Paterson's latest book, *40 Sonnets*, now to be addressed.

As already adverted to, Paterson is a past-master, as poet and as editor, of the sonnet form.[12]

So we might say that (as in my opening) Paterson here is a "self-illuminate", like the title of a poem dedicated to the memory of Peter Porter, which ends with "a portable altar ". (In his notes to his Rilke versions, Paterson speaks of

10. Pun not intended, at first at least; now however, I shall claim it.

11. Significantly or not, a witting or unwitting prolepsis, the total line count of this poem is "40".

12. As well as his Reading Shakespeare's Sonnets (2010), Paterson edited another Faber volume, an anthology titled 101 Sonnets (1999); indeed, his powerful introduction to the sonnets and the sonnet form in this edition ratifies some of my formalistic ways of reading Paterson, including rum numerology. And this is because, among other things, Paterson invokes mathematical speculation about the origin of the topography of the sonnet form. Furthermore, I recognize a fellow-ratiocinative spirit in Paterson; for example, his two-part essay, on the sound of sense and the sense of sound, 'The Lyric Principal', published in Poetry Review (2007), as well as his fantastic, taut 'Fourteen Notes on the Poetic Version' which close his Rilke versions. In these latter texts – as well as, as another instance, the critical paraphernalia that accompanies his afore-mentioned Shakespeare book – Paterson reveals a highly-gifted theoretic daemon. Like the best artists, Paterson evinces a left-lobe–right-lobe androgyny: so to speak.

how his inspiration to do Rilke was partly due to his wish to have a portable Raine in his repertoire.) In this fabulous poem, a saint in a cell bereft of candles has his left arm light up from within to read by. It is a metaphor in the historical anecdote being used as a metaphor for a passed peer and friend. Indeed, being a metaphor of/about a metaphor, the next poem, 'Funeral Prayer', ends with a similarly reflexive idea. The poem speaking speaks of the passed beloved as "spoken" at the funeral detailed in the poem, speaking. This middle area of the collection, this more serious part of a collection that is at times comedic and close to parodic (of himself as well as others), follows on with a third commemoration, for his father, I presume, titled 'Lacrima'. And the story told, to tally with some of the themes elicited so far, is about how a son fathers a son fathering. It is about how an earlier rebellion against a fatherfigure is retracted as that son himself enters the mantel of fatherhood. Paterson here is like the twins addressed in 'Letter to the Twins' . Or, to add spice, he is begotten as such in the book that comes after, and quite a while after, *Landing Light*. From walking in "darkness" (paradoxically), to "following" the "light".

Two passages now of true high-souled, deep-souled brilliance; the first from a love sonnet (making one), called 'Two' (I was reminded of Graves's 'The Thieves');[13] the second from a sonnet titled 'A Scholar':

> Each has drawn so long and drank so deep
> from the other's throat or root, they cannot tell
> tongue from tail or end from origin.
> Sleep would halve them so they will not sleep.

---

13. In particular, the middle stanza: "After, when they disentwine / You from me and yours from mine, / Neither can be certain who / Was that I whose mine was you. / To the act again they go / More completely not to know".

> The light is dying, and the clock has died;
> the page succumbs to the atrocious care
> that disinters the things not wholly there
> by which your solemn field is justified.

This latter, later "dis-interring", ends with a mention of Shakespeare, Paterson's own. And much like some of the begetting business highlighted earlier, there are (inevitably, inescapably, insuperably, irrevocably) many references to Shakespeare in this book of *40 Sonnets*.

In a sonnet of comic brilliance, 'The Fable of The Open Book', after the margin kills off the page, feeling it "time" to make its mark, all that it ends up with is "dark". The rhyme, euphonious, the idea, well, something more interstellar; matter of/for the interstices. Typifying the collection's mix, at times quite heady, of laconic humour and souled insight, the first quatrain of the sonnet 'The Eye' runs:

> The empty mind you finally display
> ten weeks into the yogic agony
> of your silent retreat, you will discover
> in the latter stages of a gin hangover.

Indeed, the six guitar strings in 'The Six' play songs to his beloved but sadly, "because now it's too late … " Significantly, given the central idea, this failing song is written in a music more failing, intentionally off, when compared with the majority of the collection, sweet, but not saccharine. Two more poems, finally, in a more experimental, less conventional format, will allow me a "roundabout", to come full "circle". In 'A Powercut', the bane of being stuck in a lift spurs a litany or inventory of images beginning with the indexical: "this"; nicely, at the turn or volta, the litany is disrupted slightly, preventing the whole poem, or sonnet, from being overdetermined in its rhythm, finishing with a Joycean "this" (the everything of "yes", the no-thing of "the").[14]

And yet "this" is not just a comic tic, or comic tick; it also refers to the poem's poem-ness as well. As though no matter was no light (gone the "land", gone the "light") . Then in the archly-titled '7 Questions About the Journey', a kind of liturgy of voice and answer ends with "Where are we going so light and riderless? / – *Nowhere. Fast*". Telltale paradox, sting in the tail, again.

If the first sonnet, 'Here', ends with the Shakespearean idiom of "Mother, why so far afield?" – in 'Wave' we read of how the poetic persona was:

> … nothing but a fold in her blue gown
> and knew [he] was already in the clear.
> I hit the beach and swept away the town.

Landlocked: and not so. There, here, and back again. Lines in the third sonnet, 'The Air', speak of "air" itself as "breathing"; Paterson is able to be both the"hammer-beat" that says "you are, not I am"; as well as the voice that speaks of itself being printed off "like a telegram", a voice which questions the answer, or better the solution, with:

> What do I say? How can the lonely word
> know who has sent it out, or who has heard?

---

14. "Yes" is the "feminine" ending of Joyce's archetypal day-book, Ulysses; "the" is the end of his archetypal night-book, Finnegan's Wake. I should say that like most sane literate people, at least those who are not or do not (presently) want to become Joyce scholars, I have not read these two works cover to cover, although I have generously sampled in them with sheer delight at the meeting of a spiritual brother. (This footnote, and appending it: are themselves one, or two, Joycean moves …

This (to re-turn) comes just before the turn of the first sonnet, 'Here'.[15]

It echoes and dovetails (with) the"end" of *Rain*, (the sea) so to speak…

After 40 days and 40 nights – so: who has heard? Well, at the least, I have.

15. Another way of stating the purport of my critique is to say that even "here" Paterson is "there", and vice versa. (Indeed, the Antonio Porchia epigraph, already adverted to, which opens *40 Sonnets* – as one did *Rain* – is redolent with the question of "here" and "there".) Subject and object (mind and body; language and sense; expression and truth content) are seamlessly immanent and at one in the universe of Paterson's work – at least when at his best. And this is one definition of a metaphysical poet.

15

Translations "About" Ghassan Zaqtan: On the Powers of Laughter

'the deep brotherhood that leads to no wisdom
the talk that's no longer suitable for high altitude.'
from 'The Canyon'

'The hermeneutic temptation to read these details as symbols and to search
for their hidden meaning should be resisted: they are exposed fragments of
the real which resist meaning. The meaning of their context—the terrible
situation of the Shoah—is too traumatic to be assumed, so this sudden focus
on material details serves the purpose of keeping meaning at a distance.'
Slavoj Zizek, *Less Than Nothing*

In perhaps his most distinguished work, *The World, The Text and the Critic,* Edward Said suggests that Conrad's stooge-like innocent in *The Secret Agent,* Stevie, provides a reading direction for how Conrad, qua artist, viewed the state or being of the writer 'in extremis.' He suggests that Stevie is this kind of icon, by being wrenched between the two poles of an autistic and endless doodling on the page and being blown to smithereens. Said anticipates a view common in Conrad scholarship, that Conrad's 'impressionism' or early modernism highlighted the 'an-archy' of the literary in the modern world; was a writing targeted to display (or impress?) the disintegration, the 'un-writing' of and in a world which, to use Kermode's term, no longer had a 'sense of an ending.' In the introduction to his translations in *Like a Straw Bird It Follows*

Me, and Other Poems, Fady Joudah makes a somewhat similar claim for the Palestinian poet Ghassan Zaqtan. Putting the two together—a synthesizing which is actually at odds with Zaqtan's aesthetic as critiqued below—we might see this logic of disintegration, this, as we will see, 'purposiveness without a purpose' (Kant), as indeed emblematic, par excellence, of exilic status.

That said, Palestine-born Zaqtan now lives in Ramallah. If he is an 'exile' it is, I would argue, because Palestinians aren't at home in their own home. Indeed, and this is something that I will alight on below: the reason they are so harrowed and hounded by a terrorist state, is perhaps because, suffering all the irrationalities and highly skewed rationalities of a wild persecution complex, the Zionist state (and not of course, by any means, all the inhabitants), is itself not quite at home in its own psyche. In his introduction, Joudah reiterates that Zaqtan's presiding mentality or structure of feeling is that of a skeptic, which is to say, a doubting conscience. But doubt, logically, cannot exist if all there is is doubt: it needs must feed on certain certainties. Zaqtan's doubt is the doubt of the scarred and damaged. And one is damaged because one was once whole. What's doubtful about Zionism is that its unhinged identity is as it is, because it is always, always reactionary, in both senses, not integral. Indeed, this panic was recently evidenced by the US government. Intending to tour America with his translator (Joudah), Zaqtan was refused a visa. Which tells us something: poetry might 'make nothing happen' in the UK, say, or in the US by its native denizens, but the case is different with critical instances, like Palestine, like Ireland, like China. In any case, reading Zaqtan (and for the first time), something did happen to this reader. In his poetry as I read it, Zaqtan finds a way of housing what seems to be unendingly nomadic. Perhaps most of all, by *not*totalizing damaged experience: rather by flaunting the wounds: and this both thematically and, often, in his lightsome free verse, which seems to flit, like a bird, a straw bird: a bird harrowed, hollowed.

Indeed, the act of writing, being both Other-sourced and Other-directed, is a way of spending (a kind of *kenosis*) the self or the subject. A way of losing one-self, or at least, using the resources of the authorial self to reach back (expressively rather than discursively) into the 'real' of a pre-configured way of being, a kind of reality before the dire ego's organization. There is, thus, a commonality between what I have suggested (after Joudah) is Zaqtan's Humean or skeptical endeavor and the more licit kind of 'postmodern-ism' teased out in various ways in the discussion which now proceeds. If, say, modernism is a registering, speaking generically, of a new realization of exilic status, of being un-housed in the world as 'absent whole,' *here* we have it, quite literally, compounded, *squared*. In his introduction, Joudah suggests that part of this artistic gambit is achieved by list-making, a disenchanted form of litany, a detailing of the demotic and the quotidian. True. But Zaqtan makes use of other techniques as well: one which I will highlight being the infinite regress, the (implicit) *reductio ad absurdam*, the duplicity that leads to a sense of abyssal dispersal—all of which might be a way of seeing Zaqtan as that kind of 'chameleon' poet with a 'negative capability', a kind of 'impersonality', which Keats made his ideal after Shakespeare. The (somewhat hidden) Palestine behind Zaqtan's liberating verse is, after a manner, a kind of 'Kurtz'; which is to say, a break-down, an analysis, though deeply lyrical, of mentality or ideality into the vivid life of the bare and nude and sensual. After the sort of mindless persecution Palestinians have undergone, it is quite understandable that the 'symbolic' register—where life is *essentially* a 'tragedy' — is deftly replaced by a more existential or pragmatic kind of imminent/

immanent 'building' of day-to-day worth in and for the surviving, the living (see also 'Cavafy's Builders'—a reference perhaps to Cavafy's demotic reworking of classical *mythoi*). Zaqtan, thus, is arch reflector of a people at tipping point:

> some murmur sprang from the walls
> and resembled the air
> as it says to you: Here
> here
> Who's in the city besides us?
> ('Neighboring Sounds')

The indexical (spoken by air!) is a last resort, after discourse no longer avails. And, invoking Cavafy's notorious conceit perhaps, it is the last resort, the extreme of a self *questioning itself;* a self in the process of ending, *at the ending.* The liminality, which is in fact the equivalent of (the impossibility of representing) death is revealed as significantly evident in a different manner later in this article. For Zaqtan, then, as dispersed, 'the birds have bought my journey' ('A Regretful Young Jaheer Man'); as within 'The Canyon' he begins to 'climb', so he seems to write merely 'because the matter requires it;' a world, then, where 'the signifier and the signified get lost' ('Alone and the River before Me'); the poet's 'only profession' in 'This Is My Only Profession,' is at its base exilic, a being left radically stranded and in the cold, untenanted, a thoroughgoing inhabitation, we might discern, *of sickness*: 'This is my only profession / ...and gathering their sleeves from the corner of their seats / like a cold I gather them.' Thus the ill logic of the world for a Palestinian and a professional Palestinian, which is to say, a Palestinian *poet.*

To outline the remainder of this article: I will now proceed to discuss the following constellation of senses to be read out of Zaqtan's verse: one, the effects of duplicity and of doubling, abyssal sense-making or sense-wrenching; two, a postmodern temporal mooring, a weird way of seeing the present from the perspective of future anteriority, a stance highlighted by Jean-Francois Lyotard in his notorious work on the postmodern condition; three, the displayed aporiae of language itself, as against the *auctoritas*of a (safe or housed) 'intentionality'; four, the sense of moral responsibility which Zaqtan evinces by inhabiting the perspective of the Other, rather than sentimentally, facilely and dichotomously opposing victimhood to power; five, under Freud's banner of the 'uncanny' we will see a politics emerge which is virulently opposed to different kinds of borders and borderlines—ambiguity at the last shown to be a boon: as against the opening images of 'light', we finish with the light of a 'light' which is itself lightless. The conclusion will implicitly be that the only way to fight power—as evidenced in Zaqtan's poetry as I read it—is to reduce its effects, however affectively, to absurdity. Bullies are most riled by laughter after all, however deeply embedded and deep in mode that laughter is.

The volume opens with 'The Dead In The Garden'.

Beneath the light
their dust was coming apart
it had rained at night
all night.

Beneath the 'light' the dust that *just is*(or perhaps was) the dead is 'coming apart.' With the poem's ending, we have a subtle double entendre: both the sense of time, night, and the figurative sense of 'darkness,' or the evil, whether moral or natural, of 'death.' We start, then, with death; but not finality or some sort of transcendent sanctioning or guaranteeing. Even the dead, as dust in the light, come apart. A fact of nature is gathered for other purposes, but only as a fact of nature. Or, opening 'Additions To The Past:'

> The letters are in the widow's room
> in the straw basket
> on the bed that is purged from sleep…

Death, early on, fore-grounded again. What exactly *is* 'a bed' 'purged from sleep'? We would, perhaps in Aristotelian mould, normally associate purging with the opposite of sleep, a way of *waking up* to the wounds of the (represented) world. But it is not *us* being purged, which is to say, not human beings. The 'bed' is being purged. As we will see later, in different ways, subject and object are (intentionally) blurred. A way of saying the world, or our wounds, do not quite make sense. And the past, however hurtful, is only compounded ('Additions'), not redeemed by representation: '[p]erhaps because the light / needs to find its way' ('The Song Of The First Patrol'). Whether in time or in place, death means, in effect, that 'the dead / return through the door's opening to steal / the bud vase / the orange sheets / and blankets ('Additions To The Past'). This last ending of the poem, suggests, again, that death is *not* a purging *for us* (the letters have not been opened yet), not a way of totalizing life into sense, but rather an endless dying of the dead, so to speak. Indeed, that last cadence reminds me of the ending of Larkin's 'Home Is So Sad,' which ends, quietly plaintive with the short gesture of a sentence: 'That vase.'

There is perhaps another double entendre in the title of 'Like One Who Waits For Me', in which, much like the (more recent) Heaney of 'The Blackbird Of Glanmore', the poet, though addressing his father, *is also* becoming his father. The poem opens: 'When I remember him standing / under a soft light / like one who waits for me to remember him,' and in this context the future memorializing is done by both father and son (subject and object) at the same time—his father like/ as one who waits for him, and he, 'like' his father, waiting for one who waits for him. Exile, thus, displaced and condensed within the bounds of intimacy. Or, as later, 'Biography In Charcoal' has it:

> Then the sound sculpts me until I disappear
> in order for those who saw to remember me.
> Thus the singer
> and the song
> are alike.

Or, similarly fudging time and place and person, ending (significantly titled) 'The Absentee's Song:'

> you aren't real for us
> to love you as we would
> other girls, leave for twenty years
> so we can love you
> and wait for you,
> and don't grow older in the fog
> lest we die.

It's as if distance, both in time or in place, or as earlier, from person to person, whether alive to alive, alive to dead, or dead to dead—*intransitivity*, in short, however smooth the verse, is the prerequisite of sense or harmony or, just, love. Which is to say, the impossible makes the possible happen; or, in other words, it is only (to refer to Conrad again) at (literally) the end of one's tether that one can begin to tether. In 'The Camp Prostitute'—and we are already alienated by the title characterization—'The intentions of those heading to her houses…. / behind the children / behind the carriage / and the coffin,' are 'pure on their way to intent.' There is arcane laughter in the temporal texture here, as otherwise. The soi-disant 'pure' are being ironised as distinct from the passed 'prostitute.' They are only 'on their way' to 'intent'— the latter being the hallmark of a self. The past is before them, in both a temporal and figurative sense, and won't 'grow older in' that/this 'fog.' The past, to make use of another 'translation', does 'not go gently into that good night.'

Indeed, in 'The Horses' Hymn' we close with:

> The horses that released our kin
> from the garments of smoke
> then tossed their turbans in time
> did not wait for us to say
> The horses
> the horses
> the horses!

The real, or just (most nude, rudest) being, is ruptured from the 'I' that thinks or intends onto the page; poetry, however fine, not literally, but as encoded, becomes in a way the doodling pen. To paraphrase the Lacan of Seminar XX: where the horses are (time's fleet, say), we are not, and where 'the horses(!)' are, the horses aren't (ours!) Life, the wound of life, does not quite add up—and perhaps as shown above by the line-breaks among other formal features, it is only the expressive in *poetry* that can both be a writing of sense and an 'un-writing' of sense (*pace* Joudah's introduction and indeed my own above.) The sense that it is time (the horses) or language ('the horses') which are aporetic, is suggested for me in a stanza in 'A Graphic 1994' which I read, however askance, as an image for language's native dispersal of itself and of its putative bearer (an old poststructuralist motif of course):

> The glass windows let the night flow into the

rooms
where now some other people breathe,
watch the belongings of strangers in silence
and remember their absence.

Maybe the glass windows are representation itself. And representation or poetic expression is thus something which, as shown above, is not only other-sourced and other-directed ('some other people') but also, a bit like Lacan's 'phallus' as 'the signifier of lack,' a re-'sounding' re-presentation of strangers 'in silence' which, to compound it, re-members 'their absence.' This leads me to my penultimate point: the way in which Zaqtan is able to disavow emotional collusion *and thus*(ultimately) political collusion. (This is in fact, the nub of one of Gillian Rose's arguments in her *Mourning Becomes The Law*.) Ending 'Salty Hills,' then:

What shall we do for your sake
when the horn is blown
for our sake?
What shall we do for your sake
when every time we fall asleep
we someone other than you?

The title is redolent with the fate of Lot's wife, someone who 'looked back;' which is to say, someone who reflected. This dialectical maneuver is of the essence. It is of the essence in Rose's late work, for truth, or value to emerge, to eschew bi-polar or dichotomous ways of thinking. One should not—*unlike,* say, the film *Schindler's List* — demonize the other; rather to be faithful to your-self, the victim, one should imagine or re-represent the other in its own 'otherness;' a conflicted Nazi, say; a conflicted Zionist, say. This is meaningful in regard to the above poem because the father

of Arabs is named there, 'Ismail', that 'other' progeny of
Abraham. Indeed, in 'An Enemy Comes Down A Hill' there is
almost tenderness in the description of the foe with

> His caution when he comes down
> like one postponed by a hush,
> and by his not being "us"
> and not "here"
> death begins…

The hale paradox I've intimated is perhaps lived out in the
force-field between the discourse of 'his not being us' and the
near-frontal rhyme of 'hush' with 'us.'

I conclude with what this last reading direction—the
sturdy countenancing of otherness—suggests. It seems to
harness all the senses so far read into Zaqtan's poetry, namely,
doubleness, anticipatory retrospection, disintegration of
selfhood, and moral responsiveness and responsibility.
Famously, in his essay on the 'Uncanny' Freud added to the
usual sense of the blurring of boundaries—between say, real
and unreal, or self and other—the temporal duplicity of déjà-
vu. Speaking literally, the latter is, though not necessarily
cynical, at the least skeptical. It leads to or allows for solipsism.
And it is this sense of solipsism with which I would like to
end. If Zaqtan's titling and imagery at times uses the voracious
image of 'wolves'—and we know that 'man is a wolf to man,'
special ground for the skeptic no doubt—then he also, at a
deep metaphorical level I'd like to argue, suggests the *pragmaticor
immediate* solipsism of a 'one-state' solution. As Edward Said
often argued, it is 'utopian' from a power-politics perspective:
however it is the sole solution which has and might have
objective validity or longevity. And perhaps it is only poetry,
as language which is 'about' language, in a sense, which

can—*impossibly*—re-represent such health-giving tunnel-vision.

So, opening and ending the (archly) titled 'A Picture Of The House In Beit Jala':

> He has no return to shut that window,
> it isn't entirely clear
> whether this is what he must do,
> things are no longer clear
> since he lost them,
> and it seems a hole somewhere within him
> has opened up….
> he aimlessly walks
> and the day's small
> purposes are no longer clear.

Or, just two pages later, in 'As If She Were He', a gender-bending which mimics the minuet of narrative and lyric throughout the book, '…he could not discern her face, who kept / remembering him and sending a hazy confession of sins he almost / recognized….' Re-cognised is apt. It suggests the temporal dimension, as well as a spatial and a public/private, subject/object aspect of blurring. Indeed, remembering his mother in 'Where She Used To Stand' he closes with: 'She was telling him of the chill in her room / when she died –' and we have impossible temporality *realized* in verse, a fuzzy utopia which is of the essence. The dying fall of the whole book, the death of a poem titled, 'Everything As It Was' runs:

> and the gentle light through the back window
> remains in its same old place
> Only the jasmine continued its climb, its eyes
> on the ceiling.

Throughout the first third of the book at the least, for all the paradox I've elicited, 'light' sprawls all over the place. So 'as it was,' it is here at the death, a death which is 'the same old place,' *rather than*some symbolic tragedian's transcending transcendent. And yet, what German Idealism—literally the cusp between Kant and Hegel—would call a 'concrete universal' or a 'purposiveness without a purpose' ends this powerfully evocative book of Zaqtan translations. The above, final image is thoroughly, thoroughl*y concrete.*But as if to laugh at his own fore-gone an-archy, as if to laugh at the enemy that is himself—for Zaqtan and/or us, there are perhaps deeper intents.

PART 3

Lasting Occasions…

16

Only Plenitude at the Void: On Christian Wiman

'To love is to feel your death
given to you like a sentence,
to meet the judge's eyes
as if there were a judge,
as if he had eyes,
and love.'
('Gone For The Day, She Is The Day')

Christian Wiman's spiritual meditation, *My Bright Abyss,* is in my view, on a par with another outstanding spiritual autobiography from just over a century earlier, *Orthodoxy,* by G. K. Chesterton. Indeed, in the 'Preface' of perhaps the most penetrating book written about Chesterton, Hugh Kenner's *Paradox in Chesterton,* Marshall McLuhan avers that Chesterton possessed a 'metaphysical intuition of being.' And I'd say the same about Wiman. Part of the 'metaphysical' aspect of Wiman's gambits in this superlative collection, *every riven thing*, shows up in how integrated the formal craftsmanship is with the sentiments expressed thereby. Wiman is both like Eliot's 'metaphysical poets' in this sense, anything but dissociated, as well as in a very pronounced way echoic of Eliot himself. Part of the 'metaphysical'

The first poem in the collection, 'Dust Devil,' starts us in Wiman's childhood, 'in a time when time stopped.' The devilishness of the toy 'top' detailed in the poem is a complement to the toying of both child and adult author, recollecting – but more than this, as we'll see, the devilry of Fate or God toying with him. In this thin-versed poem, Wiman speaks of his 'art' in paradoxes, as 'flourishing / vanishing,' or as artifact of both, 'cohesion / illusion.' And this tallies with his (already mentioned) superbly poised spiritual meditation, where he follows in the footsteps of the likes of Bonhoeffer and Weil, and the Jurgen Moltmann of *The Crucified God*. Whether we call it 'affliction,' 'the void,' or what have you, these Christian thinkers were eminently modernist in seeing God, not as necessity, but as 'contingency.' The essence of Christ's mission resided for them in his penultimate words, about having been forsaken. These thinkers – Wiman in their train – locate God, plenitude or infinity, precisely in His absconding and voiding. God is the god of reality, thus: which means that the essence of mortal life is what happens to you, shorn of your own egotistical intentionality or wishes or projections. If God is the Real, then there's nothing romantic about God.

The next feature that struck me about this collection was how often Wiman thematized poetry itself. By this I don't mean the idea expressed in 'This Mind Of Dying,' in which the prayer runs, 'My God my grief forgive my grief tamed in language / to a fear that I can bear;' or, later, in 'Late Fragment' the implicit redemption of a painful memory by way of sweet musicality:

> My father was a boatbuilder.
> Prow of a man, his world a sea to cleave.
> I learned a dangerous patience,
> to navigate night, live on nothing, leave.

No. What I mean is that poetry in essence is the alienation of selfhood into language; in this sense, poetry finds its apogee in the lack of self-regard, which latter tends towards unwitting self-occlusion. We see this effective 'othering,' for instance, in the arced use of a 'tree,' 'the unyielding one,' in 'After The Diagnosis,' or, later, in the telling list:

> All stories stop: once more you're lost
> in something I can merely see:
> steam spiriting out of black coffee,
> the scorched pores of toast, a bowl
> of apple butter like edible soil…

Or, then, opening the closing poem of the first section, 'A Good Landscape For Grief,'

> A good landscape for grief
> has no hill higher than a furrow,
> a few gouty cacti,
> perhaps a withered tree or two
> if only to remind you
> of what's missing.

For all his speculative boldness, Wiman's descriptive flair evinces both a highly refined (and playful) ear and a truly seeing eye: both, immanently. Highly idiosyncratic, effortlessly fresh, as well as deeply accessible and engaging, we read of how – speaking of an adult neighbor from his childhood – he '…loved the eyesore opulence / of his five partial cars, the wonder-cluttered porch / with its oilspill plumage…' ('Five Houses Down').

Homonyms and puns loom large across the collection. In 'The Mole' we open with 'After love / discovers it…' Which is to say: after something eminently new. Embracing both 'moles' – cancerous blemish and animal-metaphor – we read how 'he breaks

into a wide
smile, as if joy
were the animal
in him, blind,
scrabbling, earth-
covered creature
tunneling
up from God…

Paradox and punning again: here towards the end of the second installment of 'Not Altogether Alone,'

When there is nothing left to curse
you can curse nothing
but when there is nothing left to love
the heart eats inward and inward its own need
for release…

Nuanced laughter in the face of tragedy, again, in the fifth installment of the latter,

To live amid the jackal looks of unlove,
all the relatives circling eerily warily the scent
of their own blood…

And in 'Voice Of One Head,' a poem which tells tales from 9/11, we read of how, 'It seemed there was not one of us / not one of us….'

There are echoes of other devotional poets throughout the collection. Donne's sonnet, praying to a 'three-personed-God,' is evoked when we read at the end of 'Small Prayer In A Hard Wind,' 'shatter me God into my thousand sounds.' By turns, Wiman is synesthetic, as when in 'And I Said To My Soul, Be Loud,' he speaks (a tad mock-heroically) of how he's '…the sound the sun would make / if the sun could make a sound.' Re-visiting the theme of constituting the sacred from radical contingency, perhaps there's something of Eliot's 'etherized' patient closing the following (later in the last-mentioned poem):

> For I am come a whirlwind of wasted things
> and I will ride this tantrum back to God
> until my fixed self, my fluorescent self
> my grief-nibbling, unbewildered, wall-to-wall self
> withers in me like a salted slug.

The eponymous poem, 'every riven thing,' uses difference in repetition across a highly taut, but nonetheless effortlessly fluent form. Wiman thematizes how existence ('thing') is only itself or only becomes itself as 'riven.' 'To believe is to believe you have been torn / from the abyss, yet stand waveringly on its rim,' ('One Time'); '…I say God and mean more / than the bright abyss that opens in that word,' (from the second installment of the same).

Singing in 'I Sing Insomnia,' we read at the last of how the poet is:

> awake my little while
> alive without a why

The chiseling of his craft away from maudlin elegy marks, in my view, the authority of Wiman's spiritual endeavors. This soulful maturity is articulated in the penultimate stanza of the collection's eponymous poem,

> God goes belonging to every riven thing.
> He's made the things that bring him near,
> made the mind that makes him go.
> A part of what man knows,
> apart from what man knows…

That final instance of word-play sums it up: the fertile antinomy of a god abandoned by god; a god – thus abandoned– who can therefore be God, for us, riven as we are, inside our mortal coil, by privation, natural and moral.

17

Mud and Holy Water: A Question of Ends: On Paul Muldoon

Coming to anything late in the day has an allure all its own.
'Los Dissidentes'

Paul Muldoon's Oxford Lectures, *The End of the Poem*, is one of the most brilliant books on poetry I have ever read. What I found so thrilling about it was the way both formal analysis of chosen poems and the elicited historical/ biographical contexts fitted so neatly and with such aplomb in Muldoon's discourses. Indeed, so neat was the hanging-together of the critical, authorial insight across the 15 lectures that it became clear, at a sort of depth-grammar level, that Muldoon's dilations were just simply "objectively" the truth of the matter behind and within and through the poems. Having started with that observation, I have chosen to read Muldoon's latest collection through the lens – one, no doubt, of potentially many, many more – of different and eliding senses of "ending". Let me start with the "end" or purpose of the title itself.

Like Auden's iconic poem 'Musée des Beaux Arts', and more pressingly, as we shall see, like Joyce's even more iconic *Ulysses*, Muldoon's title holds within itself a fertile antinomy, between anchoring mythos and waylaid contingency. Auden's 'Museum' is both redolent of commemorating value and the stuffiness of doing such in such a (self-)destructive century. Joyce's epic is anchored in an objective myth, but also indicates radical contingency: that day in Dublin being, in a very purposive manner, *equivalent* of any or all other days, here or there, then or now. A thousand things worth knowing is both suggestive of the idea of mere "general knowledge" – "dirty data" as the end-poem of the collection dubs it – and holds also a metonymic or almost-Biblical load as well. Both the mess of (as we shall see) a post-modern world over-flooded with dis-integrated knowledge, "mud", and, as we shall also see, the serendipitous use made of, made out of, such dispersal, the "holy water" as it were (this juxtaposition taken from 'Pelt'). One more bit of "cunning" while we are at it: there are 35 poems in this collection, 35 being the traditional age of one's "climacteric", the age when one archetypally realizes one's ends or ending, one's most integral projects as well as one's mortality. Indeed, the first poem in the collection, 'Cuthbert And The Otters', a fascinatingly-woven elegy for Seamus Heaney, is made from seven-line stanzas; which is to say, an odd number, and a number between the eight and six of the romance form (sonnet's) octet and sestet – that latter conjunction making up the paginated units of the last poem in the collection ('Dirty Data').

In that first poem there is, again, (playful) anchoring in Heaney's work and legacy, such as his seminal *Beowulf* translation, and other poems, with much boyish syllabic play and reference to etymology. And that latter invocation of words' associative life and operative roots is both an instance of order and organization (the unity of words from roots) as well as a cue for profane litanies. Significantly, starting this opening elegy, the word "Notwithstanding" suggests, as throughout the collection, the subordination of consequential or univocal narrative, to a more paratactic sensibility making radical use of juxtaposition, of images, of arguments, of narratives. These juxtapositions are, like all analogies, both instances of erring from a rigid over-determination and at the same time indicative of that unity that allows for distinct counter-position. Take, as an early example, the"ending" of 'Dromedaries and Dung Beetles' . After telling the story of an ancestor at Gallipoli, Muldoon ends by wending down to his own father, and then (semi-parodically) to his own relation to that determining lineage:

> "It's only a blink … " my father used to say. "Only a blink."
> I myself seem to have developed the gumption
> to stride manfully out of a Neo-Napoleonic
> latrine and play my part in the march on Casablanca
> during the North African campaign.

Both unity and recursive debunking. Both gravitas and bathos. Both war and death and mortality, and "playing" a "part". Indeed, this opening quotation of his father is, whether intentionally or not, very suggestive of the "end" poem in Heaney's District and Circle, 'The Blackbird of Glanmore', in which Heaney effects a similar ploy (although without bathos) of detailing his father's mortality becoming his own.

As I say, juxtaposition or parataxis typifies the aesthetic in this collection, such as the idea that "Irish monasticism may well derive from Egypt" ('Cuthbert And The Otters') or such as the:

> […] Five wise virgins
> are no more likely than five foolish to trim a fish-oil lamp to illumine
> the process of Benedictine nuns spinning and weaving yarns

Otherwise put, paradoxes inform this collection: the idea of ends elicits antinomian senses: of a meta-narrative, in which "we" are all united, an objective humanism, and the idea that each is equal to each, not in the sense of possessing the light of reason but (more post-modern) because each is just as random as the other.

Staying for the moment with the opening elegy, there is a sense, via the use of almost nonsense verse, or a kind of magical realism here and there, that after the"death of the author" so to speak, coherence or harmonious and univocal order become a nonsense, just as much as Muldoon finds the death of his friend and peer nonsense. I was reminded in this respect of the sonnet 'The Kaleidoscope', from Douglas Dunn's *Elegies*, in which the death of the loved one produces (the conceit of) plurality. And again, staying with this opening elegy, we read lines like "We use a guideline when we dibble / cauliflower plants so things won't go awry" and then "Let's not confuse candelabras with chandeliers", and the antinomies abound. Order as a way of staving off overwhelming emotion, potentially indefinite word association and slippage named by one of its most astute practitioners. However, at the last, "We know neither the day nor the hour of our summons". Both randomness, chaotic chance, then, and, via the grammar of"we" and "our", the common or unified fate of "all" of us facing such. In a similar manner there are instances of ekphrasis ('Pip and Magwitch' or 'Camille Pissaro: *Apple Picking at Eragny-sur-Epte*') which make punning use of kinds of ending.

Ending the first of the above, we read of "this hard-line neighbor" and:

> his cigar twirling in its unopened sarcophagus
> like an Egyptian mummy, one dismissive of the
> chance it will ever come into its inheritance

Not only the magical juxtaposition of simile, but that "one" is a (subliminal) pun, with neighbouring senses: it both refers to the preceding "mummy" (cigar) and perhaps to the "one" of "Pip", "dismissive" perhaps of what might have been a, or his, happy "ending".

Lists and litanies (such as in 'Dodgems' or, doubly so, given the list-like title,'Barrage Balloons, Buck Alec, Bird Flu, and You') typify the non-consequential aesthetic of the collection. Similarly, there is recursive, almost abstract (in one sense) play, using dovetailing:

> The bee does its level best to become a horse.
> As for the horse,
> just look at the barbed arrow it draws from the rose,
> the faint rose lifting from its underlip.
> The rose, meanwhile,
> [...]

And this in a poem already recursive in its titling and theme: 'Frederico Garcia Lorca: "Death"'. Other post-modern (or mortem) effects are, for instance, the invoking of "Selfies" or the self-conscious invoking and use of other historical poets, such as Whitman or Dickinson. And in 'Recalculating' we have another late-coming pun, perhaps: "Re" "Calculating", which is to say (*Ulysses* again) regarding cunningness; but also the idea of re-visiting a verb, doing something (yet) again: and this becomes emphatic when we look at a sample verse, ratiocinative in the extreme, in so far as it is not so much reliant on discursive or paraphrasable content, but rather, like algebra, on the relations between counters:

> Arthritis is to psoriasis as Portugal to Brazil.
> Brazil is to wood as war club is to war.

War is to wealth as performance is to appraisal.
Appraisal is to destiny as urn is to ear.

Something here of Beckett's (Irish) humour. Indeed, speaking of recursions, one poem in the collection is titled 'Paul Muldoon: "Pompeii"' – a kind of hot selfie.

Throughout the collection, this play of play and gravitas is continually instantiated by a kind of magical realism, much in the manner of, say, D. Nurkse (e.g. in *Voices Over Water*). When we read, for example, of "Alexander and Cleopatra / and several of their collaborators / tucking into a paella" ('Saffron'), we have to be sure a "post-modern" effect. And yet, by being so overt and scurrilous, this ironizing becomes a serious comment on the contemporary situation (and ends, in at least two senses) of art (poetic or otherwise) and configured meaningfulness.

As a closing parallel, in Jean Anouilh's Antigone (that tale of siblings), the use and mention, within an ancient Greek setting, of a character writing on a "postcard" or smoking a "cigarette" is both an irony speaking to the self-reflexive derivativeness of the story or mythos (the "supplementarity" to use Derrida's term), as well as being a sign that such tales (and especially in his instance, regarding Vichy France) have (or will always have) the status of universal redolence. Which is to say, in the end, even if there are a thousand waylaid things to know, they are (Biblically or not) "worth" knowing.

18

Avant La Lettre: Browning's 'Sludge' and Ford's *The Good Soldier*: A Poetic Reading

'His work has the mystery which belongs to the complex; his life the much greater mystery which belongs to the simple.'
G. K. Chesterton, *Robert Browning*

'In short, a hit proves much, a miss proves more.'
Robert Browning, 'Mr Sludge, "The Medium"', 368

As a Ford scholar, I have found it strange that in all Ford's writings there is no specific and extensive treatment of Robert Browning. He is mentioned here and there with other 'Great Victorians'. Strange because Browning was ahead of his time, his 'Mr Sludge, "The Medium"' having, precipitately, precociously, much in common with Ford's The Good Soldier, or similarly, Strachey's Eminent Victorians. This brief article aims in the main to pinpoint a few features of Browning's great prolonged monologue, with specific reference to aspects of Ford's The Good Soldier, and via the latter, in conclusion, to the Great War – if only with metaphoric reach. After summaries, I begin by picking out some features of Ford's seminal novel, and then move onto addressing Browning's dramatic poem.

Of course, Ford's magnum opus, Parade's End most overtly deals with the Great War, as well as its specter and aftermath, in gritty detail, cubistically visceral. However there are features of Ford's other (earlier) major novel (The Good Soldier) that indicate a link with the Great War. Firstly, he wrote it in 1914, before and (supplementary) after the War's onset. There is still a debate about whether the recurring date in the novel (one of many patterns in the only-seeming seamlessness and flux of the narration) 'August 4 ', was a coincidence, or whether Ford (after the onset of war) posthumously inserted this pivotal date. There are four features of the novel I'd like to register for heuristic purposes below. But first: two brief working synopses of both Ford's work and Browning's – the comparison between which comprising the (almost syllogistic) purport of this piece.

Ford's 1915 novel is a tale told by a cuckold named 'Dowell' – and the limpidity of the prose and the (self-reflexivity of the) telling is highlighted by this narrator when he says, early on, that he will imagine telling his tale to a sympathetic listener by a hearthside. (This oral-tale- telling element, nominally at least, similar to a 'monologue'). The story, not told with anything like chronological order, is about how Dowell came to marry Florence (a minx), and how the two of them (East Coast Americans) met another typically English upper class couple, 'good people,' Ashburnham (the 'good' soldier) and Leonora, at a spa in Nauheim, to which both couples retire for a portion of every year. Nauheim is a spa for convalescents. Having 'a heart', which both Ashburnham and Florence are 'supposed' to have, is the Edwardian idiom for heart-illness, but also, like the notion of 'goodness', is an equivocation (given this story) playing on the idea of passion. From the two couples, both Florence and Ashburnham turn out (but never lucidly relayed) to have had affairs with others, and with each other. To cut a long story short, Florence – on realizing that Ashburnham doesn't love her, loving another (as we'll see), and that her covert history as a minx has been found out – commits suicide. Ashburnham, in turn, on finding a true love, not just, as before, products of his egocentricity, kills himself as well, because the one woman he (truly, and finally) loves is a ward under his and Leonora's care. Having killed himself, this ward (previously sent away, due to the amorous danger), 'Nancy', goes mad. In the end Nancy ends up with Dowell (but yet again, in an eminently unconsummated cohabitation) and Leonora remarries a regular bourgeois. Not only is the tale in the telling, Dowell's highly opaque, if smooth, telling veiling how much he knows or doesn't know, and if and when, as well as veiling how much he is or is not lying to himself – but there is a kind of moral in the last part, an implicit critique of Victorian or Edwardian rigorism. Dowell comes to the realization that those with 'hearts', i.e. those most passionate and idiosyncratic, the un-herd-like, are almost inevitably sacrificed to the machine of society – as has happened. The two survivors ending up being the two (supposedly) straitlaced bourgeois, those most 'passive' in the story about (others with real) 'passion'. So Dowell writes early on in his plaintive address to the reader (now in the wake of the tragi-comic, muddy affairs), overtly perplexed, but also revealingly (of his self-deceit):

> 'At what, then, does it all work out? Is the whole thing a folly and a mockery? Am I no better than a eunuch or is the proper man – the man with the right to existence – a raging stallion forever neighing after his neighbour's womankind?'

Browning's 'Mr Sludge, "The Medium"', is a long dramatic monologue enacted by a highly characteristic conman, a supposed spirit-seer, a type that boomed in the Victorian period. From the first line, we enter in medias res: the background clearly being that Mr Sludge is a fraud and has been caught after many years of successful hoodwinking. His monologue (as we'll see) is like Dowell's, 'shifty', both in a literal sense (zigzagging across the topography of the text as it were) and in a figurative sense, Sludge being so desperate as to offer a profane litany of many different excuses, justifications, rationalizations, now caught. However the pertinent fact is that both his character and what he represents (for Browning's purposes) are revealed to be radically self-contradictory. He is a tragi-comic figure, who is both guilty and innocent in a way. Browning's modernism is revealed by the equivocal nature of his character and what he represents. Though on the face of things a villain, the reader comes to love him: a bit like Milton's 'Satan' in Paradise Lost. And the tale is also in the telling.

Having summed up the works, for my purposes, I begin with some fruitful comparisons.

Firstly, and this is a cliché, both works make use of 'unreliable narrators.' Except, they are differently deployed, and this difference is significant for what I suggest below. In many ways, the far more overt, open and self-immolating registering of the con in Browning's poem renders that narrator far more honest or 'good' than the fictional 'author' of 'the good' soldier. Secondly, there is a similarity in rhetoric deployed by both shifty narrators. As only one instance, early on, as throughout, Dowell uses (telltale) hyperbolic metaphors in order to imbue (or hoodwink?) the reader with a sense of the impending gravitas of his (saddest) story.

> 'You may ask why I write. And yet my reasons are quite many. For it is not unusual in human beings who have witnessed the sack of a city or the falling to pieces of a people to desire to set down what they have witnessed for the benefit of unknown heirs or

of generations intimately remote; or, if you please,
just to get the sight out of their heads.'

This is one of many examples of Dowell's 'protesting too much'; Sludge too offers different kinds of self-justification; however Dowell's seemingly seamless telling (i.e. prima facie, non-shifty) is far more sly than the hyperbole of Sludge. As we shall see, though both stories shift back and forth, Sludge's monologue is shifty in a far more overt way, almost changing personality with changing rationalizations – thus making him far more reliable at a meta- fictional level.

A second feature that the two works have in common (again, something picked up later) is the fact that both narrators elicit an osmotic effect: which is to say they are not sufficiently individuated. In his shaky telling Dowell seems (still) attached, both to all the characters he 'makes you see,' and through them, his blinding and binding attachment to the (un-mastered) past, his 'horror' as it were, revealed as something preventing him from penning a more straight reminiscence, which would entail sufficient distance. Indeed, the main way in which Dowell is guilty is by being both character in and narrator of the 'saddest story', but never being able to distinguish between these roles. Quite unlike Sludge, who knows very well when he's being disingenuous, as do we. Sludge is far more loveable.

Finally, the most pivotal scene (tying the main illicit love-affair with the just as illicit affair of modernity more generally) is the 'Marburg scene' where the (treacherous) 'minuet' of characters, the two eliding couples view the displayed relic of Luther's protest as part of a tour or day-out from the spa at Nauheim. This recognition of the (Luther's) 'letter' so to speak, plays a symbolic role, signifying modernity's disenchantment (i.e. via the onset of Protestantism), in which the sense of selfhood is dispersed via the dispersal of any sense of authority. (Ford's modernist credentials in other words.) 'Authority' being polymorphous-ly poignant thus, for obvious reasons. For Luther in effect highlighted mediation (like a medium): both critically and affirmatively. (Which is to say, he was against the middle man, the kind of mediation enacted by authorities like priests and the body of the church more generally; as well as valuing above all else the individual's experience of Gospel truth and/or God, each according to his own lights – each his own (or a) medium in that sense.) But to return to the Marburg scene: by itself and in its connection with the whole novel, it is suggestive of the doomed attempt of the Enlightenment (witness WWI) – just as much as the more imminent doom in the affairs of the 'heart.' The war of the sexes was a parallel thus to that other looming internecine warfare. And just as Sludge's rhapsody is impassioned, the sense of 'passion' is duplicitous in Ford's novel; both evocative of lust, and the conundrum of passivity as against integral (good) action. Indeed, (partly) tying these together, I only recently realized that in The Good Soldier, Dowell meets Florence at a 'Browning Tea.'

All these aspects can be discerned as part also of the sludge and mire, avant la lettre, in Browning's dramatic work. Indeed, just as we might see Dowell, on a recursive reading at least, as involved in a kind of novel-wide 'panic', so there is muddy sliding, a kind of Panlogism in Sludge's narrative. He shifts throughout, at times between modes, tones, attitudes, at others in the (already-known) doomed contents of his hydra-headed special pleading.

As I see it there are at least five different, mutually eliding, gambits which Sludge essays. And some are part of Browning's powerful and insightful characterization, and others, in addition to this, show a subtext Sludge enacts on behalf of his creator. Indeed, a 'medium', he seems at times to be a 'reflector' in more than the narratological, or theosophist, sense. At times, indeed throughout, he reflects a newly emergent sense of modernity in the mid- Victorian period. This being a descriptive thought-piece, I am not so much concerned with the formal features of Browning's verse here; merely in mapping certain prominent patterns. Onto the mud and melee, then, of Sludge's polymorphous rationalizations – and, shifty in this, in no special order...

First, there is the argument from fiction, topical in terms of the changes in literary aesthetics emerging in Browning's period. Sludge in effect justifies his long con by comparing himself to a fiction writer or romancer, a poet, or indeed an actor, thereby registering the late- romantic sense that reality and fiction are not as dichotomously opposed as all that. For instance:

> '... Well, they paid for it,
> And not prodigiously; the price 'o the play,
> Not counting certain pleasant interludes,
> Was scarce a vulgar play's worth. When you buy
> The actor's talent, do you dare propose
> For his soul beside!
> (645-650)

The second reason he gives is if you like the argument from poverty, with the addendum of an argument from human weakness in the face of the temptations of comfort put into relief by that original poverty. As an instance:

> 'I lied, sir, — there! I got up from my gorge
> On offal in the gutter, and preferred
> Your canvas-backs...'
> (263-265)

Third, changing tack, a sign of desperation, he appeals to the desperation of those he faces. He shifts the blame, making, in modern fashion, the reader so to speak the author of the crime. The gullibility of his clients carrying the burden of moral guilt. A dubious argument. So:

> 'If such as came for wool, sir, went home shorn,
> Where is the wrong I did them? 'Twas their choice;
> They tried the adventure, ran the risk, tossed up
> And lost, as some one's sure to do in games…'
> (630-633)

Fourth, adverting to (the 19 century) notions of continuous or if you like Whiggish 'progress' – again, then, confusing or muddying the difference between speaker and listener – his argument is that his duplicitous practice snowballed; that once started there was (he seems to be saying) a certain justifiable boldness and hilaritas in being and continuing to be resolute in that practice:

> 'I think myself the more religious man. Religion's
> all or nothing; it's no mere smile
> O' contentment, sigh of aspiration, sir –
> No quality o' the finelier-tempered clay
> Like its whiteness or its lightness; rather, stuff O'
> the very stuff, life of life, and self of self….'
> (1005-1010)

Then, as ever checkering between abjectness and a kind of desperate anger born of fear at having been caught (quite a straightforward psychology) he not only shifts the blame, but completely changes tack by saying that the whole experience wasn't in actual fact so much better than his youthful poverty; that he (the conman) has been treated with ire, and so on and on:

'Don't talk of gratitude to me! For what?
For being treated as a showman's ape,
Encouraged to be wicked and make sport,
Fret or sulk, grin or whimper, any mood
So long as the ape be in it and no man...'
(599-603)

These are just some of the different ways Sludge, now a convicted charlatan, attempts to justify the unjustifiable, meanwhile being, as I say, shifty in tone or attitude, ranging from fawning and abject, to boyish and playful, to desperately a-feared and desperately angry.

To return to Ford: witness the following passage:

'For, if for me we were four people with the same tastes, with same desires, acting – or, no, not acting – sitting here and there unanimously, isn't that the truth? If for nine years I have possessed a goodly apple that is rotten at the core and discover its rottenness only in nine years and six months less four days, isn't it true to say that for nine years I possessed a goodly apple?'

Just so, the Great War crept up on a deluded Europe. With Ford here, we've the evoking of an epistemological problem. Ford was a skeptic, which is to say someone who found the problem of solipsism both exemplary and troubling. The idea being that just as one can't know what's at the bottom of the other's 'heart', so even within oneself, perhaps only what's immanently perceived and thus believed is what's true, as opposed to some independent or objective notion of truth. So that one's truth might be what a more commonsensical notion of truth would dub untrue or false (or indeed, fictional). In Browning this sentiment, alluded to by his unreliable narrator, has a slightly more affirmative effect. Because both he and we know it is an excuse. Sludge is in this sense more of a humanist, his obvious guilt being a cipher of unity with the reader and with his (fictional) listeners. Dowell's stance is far more nefarious (and complicit with evil) for its whale-large claiming of innocence.

As mentioned, the date August 4 is a pattern recurring in Ford's novel, much like the three deaths which end three of the parts of the novel. And it is death, symbolically considered or not, that ties up Ford, Browning – both seminal respectively – with the seminal event of the Great War.

The completion of the syllogism, then – this being a poet's poetic critique.

It is well documented that the huge and, more significantly, absurd incidence of death – doubly absurd, because for the first time the violence was as if out of the hands of the men who'd made the machines – whisked away the erstwhile guarantor of meaningful life. Writers like Ford or Sassoon often relayed this radical visceral unease by speaking of the War as an experience of the loss of control over one's life or soul – such a loss of comprehension being a prime trigger for panic. Significant also, this war was the first 'Total War', where previously guarded distinctions between public and private, army and civilians were blurred. Thus, the panic that ensued during and after is cognate, in my view, as a kind a metaphoric avatar, with the shifty logic of pan-ic in the gambits of both ('authors'), narrators. When one is no longer in control of one's destiny (the latter, a pivotal word for Ford) one is equally unable to pen that same reality in a straight or straightforward manner. There as it were a feud raging in one-self, leading to a (conflictive) lack of being at-one with oneself. Hence (with symbolic congruence) the two duplicitous narratives. Both ('authors'), narrators are out of control. For panic is like a little death. In classical Freudian mold such anxiety, narrativised / dramatised or not, is in its essence a harbinger of death.

What, then, I am suggesting is that the features discussed – Browning unto Ford unto the equally conflicted pan-ic of the experience of war – show that Ford's first major novel, as a telling parallel to Browning, is just as much a registering of the Great War, even if not biographically intended or even chronologically able to do so. Long after his own war-trauma, Ford wrote that a new 'form' was needed for the world after the war, as opposed to that before. In a letter to a correspondent in 1931 (after the completion of Parade's End), then:

> 'The world before the war is one thing and must
> be written about in one manner ... the after- war
> world is quite another and calls for quite different
> treatment.'

What I'm insinuating (and it will have to remain a poet's dodgy insinuation) is that in the symbolic and formal as well as substantive ways Browning foreshadows Ford, Ford himself foreshadowed himself. He was a kind of seer, after all.

Part, then, of the goodness of the (made) mediums was to reflect the awful sense of crisis, privately and publicly; and not only on behalf of their creators, not only for their readers, but also by being icons and indices of the swiftly, dangerously changing times. Both creators, authors, if not both narrator-characters, were like operative breaths ('spirits') blown upon and through the matter, the brittle letter.

19

On Fiona Sampson's *In Search of Mary Shelley: The Girl Who Wrote Frankenstein*

Frankenstein, whose bicentenary falls in the present year, was published at first anonymously. Perhaps, then, a biography of its true author, Mary Shelley, speaks louder to the significance of this bicentennial anniversary than any commemoration of the novel itself. And part of what makes Fiona Sampson's 2018, *In Search of Mary Shelley* (Profile Books) such an astoundingly compelling read is that the attitude and voice that guide the reader–through what is very much a work of archaeology, a speculative but still highly definite reconstruction of a life–are so aptly *searching*, inquisitive. Even if in her 'Introduction' Sampson seems to disparage the notion of (fictionalising) 'reconstruction' as the way to go, warning us, readers, that we'll be able to go straight to the source (using sources, as she does, with real dexterity) –I would still venture that for all its realism, Sampson's biography leaves the reader with the same colourful, brilliant imaginative impression more typically associated with poetry or drama.

Tallying with much of her oeuvre to date –whether as editor of eminent poetry organs, such as *Poetry Review* and, now, Routledge's *POEM* (as well as of a slim edition of Percy Bysshe Shelley's poetry, published by Faber in 2011), or as poet and critic –Sampson is effortlessly empathic in her approach to Mary Shelley's life. She wants, as always, to understand from the inside, without ever losing focus on her subject's gripping biographical trajectory. Indeed, part of what makes this biography so unique, is that it out-romanticises in some ways 'Romanticism.' Which is to say, looking, searching for the inner-truths of her subject, Sampson's biography does not stay unduly riveted on the romantic movement, on which there is of course much extant fare; her approach is more centered on the individuality of Mary Shelley, both as intellectual and creative artist and as a woman in the early nineteenth century.

Much like the Mary Shelley whose *Frankenstein* was part of a modernising 'turn to the subject,'emphasising the meanings of motives and intentions more than the scaffolding of dramatic plot or events, Sampson inhabits the personae of her tale, and her empathy, like Mary Shelley's for her own characters, becomes ours, seamlessly. Indeed, one of the most telling literary devices, however implicitly deployed, in this at times highly filmic biography involves the signal dovetailing of alternating focalisation of public events and of personal ones–whether Sampson is going from historical, political or cultural contexts (such as the rise of the Gothic, or the Napoleonic wars) to personal journal entries or letter citations; or, simply moving from the topography of a home, the play of light in a room, say, to the topography of the mind of one of her found characters. For instance, that the chiaroscuro of the Godwin (Shelley's father's) home might have subliminal reach into Mary's Gothic masterpiece, is indeed a fresh insight for a biographer to broach. Like the *Frankenstein* of her biographical subject, Sampson's tale moves between frames, meant both serially and structurally. And this deft movement is a manumission, allowing us *into*, or perhaps better, *through*lives, especially Mary Shelley's–in what is a rigorous attempt to eschew teleologically-closed narrative.

As in much of her critical work (such as *Beyond the Lyric*, Chatto & Windus, 2012, a detailed reconnaissance of the different 'schools'as it were on the contemporary British poetry scene; or *Lyric Cousins*, Edinburgh University Press, 2018, a highly sophisticated and searching foray into the ways in which musical form can inform and illuminate the understanding of poetry), Sampson's search in this work is phrased with rigorous inquisitiveness, sometimes using different kinds of imaginative counterfactuals to tease out the possibilities of what the past 'in question'truly may have contained. For instance, in the chapter, 'Becoming a Couple', which traces the textured formation of Mary and Percy Shelley's young coupling, Sampson offers a passage investigating, almost counterfactually, the episode in which Percy Shelley seems to have encouraged Mary to sleep with one of his friends, Thomas Jefferson Hogg. One would have thought, it might just be down to Percy Shelley's fulfilling his notorious views about 'free love.' However, Sampson suggests a range of at least nine options, factual or psychological, to parse this episode in their young coupling.

Another technique which dominates throughout–and much like the at times novelistic narrative in her recent work of place-writing, *Limestone Country* (Little Toller Books, 2017), in which four different places of travel and experience (and four different seasons) are dramatized by their sharing a sedimentary community, all being based on bowl-shaped limestone –is the use of a very vivifying grammar of the 'historic present.' Reading this moving biography, packed as it is with the kind of blade-like *insights*that became a model of 'intellectual beauty'so to speak at the time in question, is often like watching a powerfully-conceived documentary on television. The past of Mary Shelley is deftly made with and into our own present. We walk the historic path in question, as though contemporaries of the Shelleys'and their often troubled entourages. One small instance of us travelling inside Mary's footsteps, comes in the chapter in which Mary sojourns with Percy and Byron and others, at the 'Villa Diodati'. At the time of the famous scene in which a friendly competition to write a ghost story ended up with Mary Shelley's *Frankenstein* no less, Sampson reads Mary's journal entries about the landscape there, and how 'anthropomorphic' she is in her descriptions of it. 'This unhomely sense of a wild landscape that is somehow sentient and observes the human who has strayed into its grip will reappear in *Frankenstein*.'

Sampson's 'search'is a kind of teasing inquiry into who Mary Shelley was, but more pressingly into how she became who she was, and this among a matrix of others. Sampson is meticulous in placing Shelley in a wider literary and political circle of friends, family, and acquaintances. It's not just her absent (intellectual) mother and namesake Mary Wollstonecraft, say, who, in a perhaps staple biographical gambit, is seen to be Oedipally relevant to many of the patterns in Mary Shelley's later life, but also the wide array of other personae, from her father, the great political philosopher, William Godwin, and her young and fateful lover Percy Bysshe Shelley, to Byron and siblings and half-siblings, and so on. The ground of all these relationships may have been well-covered before, but it's Sampson's querulous empathy that makes her account so much more compelling to the reader in the present day.

It's significant, of course, that Sampson is a highly distinguished, experienced poet in her own right; this seems to allow for a mass of insight which a biographer who wasn't engaged in a primal way with literary creation, might have missed. For example, the affair of the anonymous publication of *Frankenstein,* then Mary's vindication is dealt with –contrasting Mary with her 'lady'writer contemporary Jane Austen, and her Victorian successor Mary Anne Evans (who had to use the male penname, George Eliot) –in a highly empathic way, from woman writer to woman writer.

Literary criticism is also a very telling facet of this work of intriguing reconstruction; often Sampson will look at tonalities and attitudes in letter and journal entries and read from them potential stances in many of the formative relationships that made 'the girl who wrote *Frankenstein*.' Indeed, in the final chapter, an 1839 portrait of Mary Shelley, by Richard Rothwell, is used as a final, closing literary device, in a way which typifies the biting but ever-generous intelligence of this biography. The look on Mary's face is searched by Sampson, both ratifying the biography that has gone before and propelling the reader to its close.

The portrait is used in an ekphrastic manner, to do many things at once. First it allows for a 'time-shift'to a later time in this closing chapter, but at the same time also provides cues for the backstory that is then filled-in. This typifies the resolute freshness of the biographer's narratorial skill. And it wouldn't be too far from the mark to say that the way the portrait is read by Sampson and her reader, is also a description in a wider focus or frame, of what is being done in this (searching) work more globally. The suggestion for instance of causticness in her portrayed smile, say, or the suggestion that she's on the verge of saying something, but also that she may be in the wake of stopping herself from saying something telling, are put to good use in Sampson's reading of Rothwell's own pictorial description. The nuances of the portrait discussed, and the nuances with which it is discussed, end as a master-metaphor for what this book is: a searching portrait, the happy paraphernalia of brushstrokes doing their tell-tale business.

If *In Search of Mary Shelley* often comes off as a powerful, riveting documentary, it is also much like a mystery story, filled with puzzles that provide Sampson with opportunities to explore possible readings. Sampson has animated her subject as the latter did 'Frankenstein'(and *Frankenstein*) but happily with not such a Gothic or occult result. That said, the history of the Gothic and not only in the British Isles is one of the most intriguing contexts outlaid by Sampson. Indeed, given of course the opening caveat, that the book is duly, brilliantly researched, there are a large amount of liminal, if well-informed, wanderings in this book, native perhaps to highly imaginative, creative mentalities –whether Shelley's or Sampson's. Opening the chapter on the 'Villa Diodati', for instance, Sampson swerves with real freshness between inside views and outer ones. If the 'first scenes of Mary's life are brightly illuminated,'spending her childhood in 'a house lit by large, modern windows;'and if by the time she's 'eighteen', having moved, 'a chiaroscuro seems to enclose her,'Sampson nonetheless tries overtly to 'visualize' her growing subject, paralleling the murkiness of her new outer surroundings with the murkiness of 'cross-currents' in a period of both much 'domestic upheaval' but a period as well of 'wide reading, continued self-education, further pregnancy and the birth of her second child, William.' Tellingly though, as though to add yet another 'frame', the movement between outer murkiness and inner, outer light and inner, is mirrored meta-fictionally by Sampson's noting how her (illuminating) biographer's role is also made 'murky' by certain lost 'journals' of this time. This liminal cross-current of insight between frames typifies the biography as a whole. For all this fertile errancy though, the results of Sampson's limpid search are unfailingly felt to be concrete, definite, authoritative.

20

On Svetlana Lavochkina's *Zap*

And neither can be certain who
Was that I whose mine was you.
Robert Graves, 'The Thieves'

Shortlisted for the Tibor & Jones Pageturner Prize in 2015, Svetlana Lavochkina's debut novel, *Zap* (short, tart diminutive for the Ukrainian city, 'Zaporozhye') is a kaleidoscopic and enchantingly scurrilous *tour de force*. Emphatically, shamelessly literary, the experience of reading this debut novel can be compared to getting uproariously drunk, laughing your head off, and then sleeping the joyous inebriation off by dreaming of getting uproariously drunk and laughing your head off. The literariness of this novel is not just due to the dense, brilliant palette evinced by the sensual style (which, though flamboyant, is still rigorously precise); and it's not just due to the litany of literary names that people and precipitate the novel's plotting (from Pushkin, Chekhov, Dostoevsky, Tolstoy, to Dickens and Hemingway and Nabokov, among many others). No, beyond all this salutary fare, the novel is literary most of all because of the cohering and poignant way the voice and the style of the prose prove as fittingly heady (and funny) as the infectiousness of the relations and interrelations of the tale's bombastic cast of characters, zipping and zapping between Russia and Ukraine.

I won't comprehensively précis the plot, because it would be both highly difficult — given how dense the rigmarole of thrilling happenings are — and also traitorous to the incumbent delight of future readers.

In brief outline, the tale is set between Zap, Odessa and Moscow (apart from some letters from America, from a central character who absconds there). The book opens cinematically, in Ukraine in 1821; we have Pushkin taking a swim in the Dnieper, having had a famed turquoise ring, betokened from an equally famed paramour, stolen and buried by some louts. This talisman, this memento, is of course central to the novel's plot and its rounding-off in the end, primarily by the way in which its fate is followed by and follows the fate of the protagonists. The tale then moves to the mid 1970s, to be moved again into the eighties and into the Perestroika period at the finale. Matching this strategic dating, much of the most significant action is set on dovetailing New Years' Eves, a choice that highlights the exemplary intentions of what is a highly, highly idiosyncratic tale. New Years' Eves are literal turning-points which, perhaps, indicate more symbolic ones.

Pushkin shadows, as much as he foreshadows, the tale throughout – via quotations of his verse at strategic points, via ridiculous or serious claims of ancestry from some of the late twentieth-century Soviet cast, and via his legendary dip in the 'Dnieper', a river that rivers, too, throughout *Zap*. There is a sense that not only do we never step 'in the same river twice', but that we do in fact step in the same river more than twice. And this seeming contradiction is dramatized by how the reflexive weave of characters has a river-like economy; like water, every particle ends up being (connected to) every other, and like water, flowing, each has his or her own fate in what is still an eminently congealing plot.

But the Russian Pushkin, father-figure of the novel, is matched by the American Hemingway, studied to the point of plotted delusion by one of the central characters, 'Alka' (a 'PhD in English Philology'). Moreover, though this novel starts with the iconic Pushkin, it ends with the youngest character, a mere child throughout most of the tale, 'Sonka', having moved to America. The last line, part of a belated and valedictory letter, ends on the note that she, 'Sonka' has now forgotten all her 'Russian.' As another apposite instance of canny thematic reflexivity, 'Hugh Winter', the father (and grandfather) of one and some of the characters, both built the 'Dnieper Dam,' and then, later, the 'Hoover Dam.' Compounding these thematic clues, the three major women characters ('Alka,' 'Rita' and 'Svetka'), are 'painted' as *'trois déesses sovietiques'* ('Three Soviet Goddesses') in a triptych by another character, an artist. The artistry (not to mention the storied fate of that art) in the tale, thus, seems like a metonym for that without, framing it.

Sex is not only one of the funniest, most fateful, and redolent themes of the story, but may well be a metaphor (as in the epigraph, made-use of heuristically above) for how coital and serpentine the relationships that forge the plot turn out to be – a skein of enchanting vertigos, a moving scaly map of ardor and lust, a fanfare of humors and happenings. A curt way of putting it is to say that the texture of this tale is like a fertile marriage, say, of Henry Miller and Mikhail Bulgakov. There is Miller's crab-like an-archic movement from scenic array to scenic array, garnished by the thrilling and honest obscenities which disclose living characters – but all contained in near-serial order, and with the light touch of a Dickens or Molière (the last of whom was I believe, tellingly, one of Bulgakov's major loves and subjects.) There is madness within the tale, and the prose jingles to the pipes of pan; but this rousing carousel of character and fateful event is always felt to be under the controlled hand of a light and masterful touch. The reader gets to know the cast, as they intermingle within and across chapters, as they do 'Zap,' which is not only a place, a setting, but becomes by the end a kind of eponymous mythos.

The artistry of this book is infectious. What is suggested to the intelligent reader is how one might multiply connections and interconnections, indefinitely. And though in one sense, the novel comes full circle, with Pushkin at the start and 'Pushkin' at (or at least very near) the end; in another, the asymmetry of Russian iconicity and its anglicized disappearance at the end, indicates more of a spiraling off, than the closure of a circle. This duplicitous imaginative reading direction is similar in my view to the way that reading Nabokov's synesthetic prose can prod and spur the desperate urge *to write* in his writerly readers. *Similar*, in that the (role of the) 'imagination' is perhaps one of the novel's most neatly-beveled themes; whether we look for closure or its elision, both are proffered here. And this imaginative byway may be another way that the book is highly 'literary,' in the best sense.

And all this, might I say, thankfully, without 'gimmicks'. While the book may have a (very) faint whiff of sparkling, freewheeling post-modernity about it – there is nothing disintegratory or chaotic about the tale or the way it is shaped. Indeed, by using the word 'enchanting' in this brief account of my reading of *Zap*, I hope to indicate the soulful and magical nature of this book. Its spells and its rhapsodies emit from a fertile and constructive imagination, and not from either, a too-cerebral self-defeating self-consciousness, nor from a fanciful hodge-podge.

I will end this brief reader-ly reaction by quoting the 'spell' cast in 1821 by Pushkin's minions, as they bury the treasured ring – a passage not only reprised towards the end of the novel when the spiral circles, but also indicative of the scurrilous and inventive talent of this debut novelist:

"Who finds this is a pig's snout, mare's arse, slaughterhouse cur, unchristened brow, grandson of the Serpent, and the crick in my dick… The devil shits, and you eat. You touch this treasure and your balls be bust and thy mother be screwed. For this kiss my Cossack arse."

Now that's my kind of curse!

21

Dancing About Rodin: On Patricia McCarthy's *Rodin's Shadow*

'I start to work in dawns: hiding-places
re-opened in the winded breath of statues.'
From 'Exercises for Two Hands'

'Oh waltz and waltz through me
who should have been your bride.'
From 'The Waltz'

In his first work (I believe), *The Romantic Image*, the late Sir Frank Kermode spent the central chapters dilating on Yeats' image of a 'dancer' wholly spent in the 'dance;' Kermode suggests that this was emblematic of the symbolic turn into modernism. Much the same phenomenon as that aphoristically elicited in the 'Princess Lizard' section of Theodor Adorno's *Minima Moralia*, the beloved image is imagined or fantasized as without individuation or depth of her own – that projected lacuna allowing for the constitutional need of the lover to 'stage' a 'rescue'; the idea being that a symbolically-precocious loving gaze, that of a deeply imaginative man, needs such a tabula rasa upon which to bestow his erstwhile surfeit of ego. Patricia McCarthy's Debussy speaks, thus: 'Despite your claim // to dislike music, you gave me the naked flesh / of ultimate sound to compose

289

into courtship // in the small hours...' ('The Sweetened Fiddles'). Or, later:

> a new ballgown from her crêped skin, then
> dance in it alone: slow, slow, quick, quick, slow,
> so slow she would stop moving, desired forever,
> the dance of love a stasis in death's strong arms.
> ('She hears of Rodin's death')

Rodin's Shadow, an exceptional work of vivifying ventriloquism, is the answer to this complex. The once-silent women now speak in turn. And all the voices in this collection, either talking or talked about, whether former lovers, spouses, colleagues, students, revolve around the eponymous Rodin like planets round a sun. The theme of 'dance' will be central to this review.

The first way in which I'd like to tease out this sense of dance, is by suggesting that in the title's conceit of a *singular* 'shadow', we have the very expressivistic idealism and holism (rooted in romanticism) of dance. All participants, refractions and participations, vocally emerge from out of the impact of *one* man. There is a centre (of gravity) to all movement(s). Dance, as I like to think about it, and as I will show as implicit in different ways below to *Rodin's Shadow*, is, like the idea of 'Incarnation,' a seamless mediation of mind and body, spirit and letter, act and patterned story. Dance is both a virtuoso individual act, and, in a sense, more sacramental, a way of sharing one's physical discretion with others. Whether it's Camille Claudel, Gwen John, Rose Beuret, Claude Debussy, Clara Westhoff, Auguste Rodin, or Rainer Maria Rilke – there is, necessarily, the suggestion of a meta-narrative. What this means is that, like, for example, Rilke's 'transcendentalism', alluded to in the collection, all aspects of spiritual or meaningful reality have one source and one end. That, to put it bluntly, we're all in it together.

So, as in, say, the title poem, the speaking voice says to Rodin that 'weights hang from your aura,' so all the lovers and participants in the latter's life are also, *as configured and woven here*, part of *each other's* life. Good examples of this holism are, 'Cet homme couvert de femmes', where, Rodin's life-long partner, Rose Beuret, picks apart her husband's paramours; or, more direct, 'Cats' Chorus', where the speaking voice is the 'we' of two of Rodin's lovers, Gwen John and Camille Claudel. What *we re*pained shadows become, in re-collection, one 'Shadow.'

The Prologue to the collection, which invokes the stitching/unstitching work of the loyal Penelope, is actually both a comment on art and artistry in general and a preparation for the art pursuant, and of the combination of both in the personae and themes. For all its expressive revelations, Art, like the epic Penelope, is (to invoke Kermode again) also 'the genesis of secrecy.' Which is to say, being essentially meaningful, art is not part of a zero-sum discovery: the hermeneutic circle entails that each revelation of the artist is also a way of hiding or concealing another aspect. Camille describes her 'unborn children', for example, in a cognate way, as 'layer by layer unwrapping the void, their gift.' In a sense this endless quid pro quo, is of the essence to the art of sculpture. One chips away, *and* one reveals a presence. In a way, poetry too is a sculpting or chipping (and a revealing at the same time) of the self. Indeed, as Glyn Maxwell most recently argues in his *On Poetry*, the very artifact of the 'line-break' is the essential difference between prose and poetry: which in a way is of a piece with sculpting (but on the page.) Sculpture as poetry, then: read, for instance, Camille Claudel ending 'Camille Alone:'

> I chip away at myself, paring skin down to bone,
> dried rose petals and drunken laughs on my breath.
> I order myself to be marble, flint, uncaring stone.

Or, much later, Clara Westhoff to Rainer Maria Rilke in the first installment of elegies to Rilke, 'Word-Bells' (perhaps the highlight of the whole collection):

> There you waited for secrets of statues, for streets to descant

> to you a syntax wherein you would lose and find
> yourself…

If sculpture is the master-metaphor for the native and charged ambivalence of artistic creativity, dance, as I say, is also another symbol for the way in which there is, to use Hayden White's phrase, a 'content of the form;' or, in other words, a seamlessness between expression and discourse. Rodin himself says ('The Rodin Sculptures') that his achievement has been to make his objects of desire and art 'exist with me in every context.' Dance is useful in this respect, regarding sculpture, because it suggests the tautness of a parable, where, in Walter Benjamin's terms, 'truth content' and 'expression' are immanent to each other, a seamless unity: where in other words, sense is not zero-sum, and limited to one place or time, but, almost mathematically, ranging. Indeed the idea of movement or spirit within the rigidity of a body, dance, like sculpture, is suggested in 'Hotel Room':

> I changed in and out of onyx
> and jade, letting him claim me as a trophy
> beneath all my skins as he liquefied me.

Or, later on, similarly suggestive of artistic expression as opposed to frigid discourse, in 'The Louvred Shutter':

I shall whisper an acknowledgement
like a breeze through the grille

but offer no word, wary of stirring
that maze of levels and layers
which spirals without path,
post, exit or explanation…

Indeed, like dance, the opening and closing movements of the collection persistently put to signal use bodily images, of skin or cells or blood say, for meaningful responses of love and emotion. Like a sculpture, the women, most often, expressing how they've introjected or internalized the 'sun' around which they revolve, aim to show movement, motive torsion and, simply put, depth, by way of a stringent and tweaked 'surface.' It is, like an 'Incarnation', a form of 'embodiment,' or a showing of the essential facets of 'personhood' or spirit, via the appearing body in the world and in time. ('The Rodin Sculptures'): 'I have inserted my hand / between the stone and its unfingered interior.'

One way, again, in which dance provides a presiding metaphor for both the creative in general and for McCarthy here, is the way, like T.S. Eliot's 'Metaphysicals', the poet is able to, literally, think *in and by poetry*, rather than something more crassly dualistic: rather than, as against dancing, slipping on a banana skin! Good instances of this labile embodiment then: ('Rodin's Shadow') 'Do you require me to cast your shadow // in nights consisting only of that shadow?' Or a little farther on, Camille Claudel opening in 'Letters Unsent:'

In the record heat meant to be ours,
I have been seen as a woman flying
out of a window with a red umbrella
to set fires to forests which cannot

burn out…

And again in 'Cleansing' the jilted lover makes use of the physical act of ablution, literally washing off her touch and scent, as a vehicle for a deeply emotive tenor. Whether it's in the opening of the collection, or, later, the deployment of the conceit of a 'Danse Macabre' ('Occupation'), or the end of the collection, in the last installment of 'Camille on her Deathbed in the Asylum':

> Show me, my women, as I give you the best attire
> for allaying the anxiety of being alone:
> the dance performing while performed. In stone.

Throughout, man and woman, subject and object, act and value, form and content, surface and depth, mind and body, *dance,* chiseling the air.

Another instantiation of 'rhythm', of timing, or pacing, is the interpolation of both bold first-person speech and third-person remembrance. For there are both in this collection. And this sense of structural 'texture' is also lived out, in another version as it were, in the way, say, three of Rodin's planets and beloveds, while all sincere, offer complementary and contrasting tonalities or attitudes. We have the mentally unhinged genius of Camille Claudel, redolent with melancholy possessiveness and jealousy, the calm and resigned, semi-literate spouse, Rose Beuret, and the sparkling innocence of Gwen John. The checkering of voices, and of points of view, is itself a kind of dance, a kind of baroque building of layers in a palimpsest that mediates Rodin, his reflectors, his refractions.

Essential to 'romance' is a pattern, based according to Northrop Frye, on Biblical scripture, but its secular variant, of descent followed by ascent. Witness, then, in 'Lace Letters':

to have, in the choppy wake of qualms,
more than only my writing looping itself
into lace on the page's dead calm.

Indeed, just as Camille can talk of her 'Stations of her cross,' so, to invoke another kind of dance, all the heart-wrenching pain expressed in this collection, all these negatives, are in fact the condition of 'ascent' or (following Geoffrey Hill) 'at-one-ment'; Heaney's term is 'redress'. The fourth section of this twelve-sectioned (apostolic number!) collection, is titled 'Shed Wings,' and this image crops up within this section in 'Exercises for Two Hands':

> Lining up rickety props of scaffolding
> from abandoned studios, I balance
>
> on shed wings, convincing myself
> that severance is inseparable from meeting.

Or in 'The Gossamer':

> Instead of those girls from bygone parts,
> I will be the gossamer webbing our two hearts.

Just as all the flames revolve as affected effects of one central flame, so the centripetal unities of poesis *are constituted by* the frittering felt in and by time past, and the privation, the lack, the prodigal spur to the person. We best bear witness to, and are refractions, motive shadows, of the sun: *having been burnt*. After deploying the image of a wrecked ship:

> …I know a momentous sea-change has happened:
> pebbles wrapped in weed flung against rocks

like dice painted by waves not in our favour.
('Sea Change')

The dance, typical collection-wide, is one between the literal and the figurative, body and mind; the dance *is body as mind.*

22

The Headiness, The Heaviness of
Womanhood: On Zoe Brigley

'I train to the trellis what once was wrecked,
and await the springtime of candling plants.'
'Walls Have Ears'

This superb collection opens on a heady, dizzying note,
which is at the same time atoned by the formal choices made.
Out of the shifting and sly juxtaposition of subjects and
pronouns in 'My Last Rochester' – 'She, her, you, him –'
we are faced with experience in medias res, what Sir Frank
Kermode called a 'middleness,' and what one of the founders
of modernism, Ford Madox Ford, called an 'affair.' The
(disenchanting) last line of this opening poem reads 'It was
never you that she wanted,' thereby suggesting what this
poem, as a whole, effects, namely a corrective to an hackneyed
and male portrayal of femininity. As opposed to the idea of
some kind of 'empty signifier', where a woman is what
whatever bad infinity is desired of her, we have in this last
sentence a tonic; not to mention the assertiveness of lines in
the blunt indicative like, 'She's writing after so long, sensible
or not. / She's not asking for anything, not ever.' Another
rewriting of masculine, skewed views of femininity, is offered
by the formal pattern, which is by turns synchronic/
contrapuntal and diachronic, of the first and third verses, and
the second and fourth verses, corresponding – leading to the

pursuant development of the last two verses. When Brigley
writes, 'you both made your way to the hotel in silence…'
what is evoked is not only intimacy, but also her ability to
stand outside of herself, to *not be* a victim of her experience,
but its shaper, both within and without the poetic space.

After this heady opening, the dramatization of texture,
the lit contrariety and drama of womanhood, is immediately
laid before us. In 'Behind the Looking Glass,' Brigley begins
with, 'She tries not to remember the things he did to her,'
and then half way through the poem, like a kind of Proustian
memoire involontaire, she double-crosses herself with:

> '… Certain things do come back to her.
> How on the way home from the pub, her legs
> collapsed beneath her. How she was so light
> that he carried her home, not for love's sake,
> but to turn her over and over in his hands.'

Or on the next page, in 'The Bell Confessing,' a victory, a
'conquest' which *is not* quite a victory or conquest (as opposed
to that masculine repression subverted in the second part of
the collection), is adverted to. As against the 'nest of pigeons /
…murmuring never-told secrets:'

> 'I recall my own riddles: the unspoken truth
> of you and I, our silent closeness that is for me
> a sweet, blank victory…'

Being a riddle to herself, using, perhaps, the outer world as a
peripatetic foil for the tension of her with her-self, is lived out
in the last two lines of the last poem of the opening section
of the collection ('The Adventuress'): 'Beneath my dress is a
ladder of desire, / that I climb tonight and each night after
that.' It's a bit like prayer, say: in that any serious theologian

will tell you that, the relation being incommensurate, the only sensible way to understand prayer is to say that God prays 'through' you, or that contrition and forgiveness are mutually immanent, two sides of the same coin. Brigley's persona frames her desire as a tension of self with it-self, and the (vertiginous) layers of the latter's symbolization.

Much later in the collection, echoing Nabokov's famous opening couplet to *Pale Fire* ('I was the shadow of the waxwing slain / By the false azure in the windowpane…') Brigley bodies forth the drama of womanhood as follows: 'Dressed in finch's gold, I look to the window / but it reflects back only the darkening garden: / the honey of all my appetites wrecked.' Indeed this juxtaposition of 'wreck' and 'garden' (what we *might* view as subjective and objective views on same person or state) is, as earlier with 'sea' and 'journey' and 'nunn–ish' images, another formal choice of Brigley's. Iconic images such as these are made to dovetail, from one poem to the next, strategically, suggesting the unity of executive authority throughout the collection, as opposed to some skewed view of femininity as distention or dispersal. (Indeed, there are continuous and overt references to the Bronte's in this opening section – which is to say, icons of female *auctoritas*.) A couple of examples of this 'dovetailing', this simultaneous continuity and discontinuity, will put into relief another thematic and formal motif.

At the end of 'Passage,' Brigley's persona compares herself, someone who's visibly gained by risk and experience, to a nun, 'those women who are never to sail out of harbor.' On the next page, the (sub)title rings out: '*The Nun in the Pear Tree Bower*.' Or, later, from the end of 'Pennsylvania Winter,' to the opening of 'All of which are American dreams,'

'Something is growing, blossoming with frost in every cell:

the snow drifts up to the window now and is still
fattening.'

'American dreams are ill-fitting shoes that fatten
your heel to a blister…'

Again, the paradox and double-coded-ness of snow 'fattening'
and the self-lacerating 'dreams' which fatten 'your heel to
a blister.' Again, that is, disenchantment.   But, as in the
epigraph quote to this review, that first citation above
highlights a formal story being told by such reflexive
positioning of images. Could the 'snow' which 'fattens', that
fertile chill, be a metaphor for the way poetry transfigures
sense experience into 'meta-physical' insight? At the end of
'The Mandrake Baby,' at the *death* of the poem, Brigley writes:
'My baby still waxes onscreen, lunar and golden, / a tiny
moon in my womb too barren to be born.' One is tempted
to think of Donne's 'Death, thou shalt die!' Which is to say
the formal election of beginnings and endings thematize the
poetic act of story-telling or configuration in general: or, to
invoke Kermode again, the 'sense of an ending.' Indeed, a
lover and cohort of the Anaïs Nin whose quoted words open
the collection, Henry Miller, begins his groundbreaking work,
The Tropic of Cancer by rhapsodizing over the *death* of a sickly-
genteel culture. To begin something, something must have
ended.
      The ineffability of creation, whether of life or of poetry, is
lived out in the penultimate and ultimate stanzas of the poem,
'Daughter.' Suggestions of the furtiveness and uncanniness of
creativity, as in Ted Hughes's 'The Thought-Fox,' are stirred
when we read:

'Something black is crossing the hillside now:
a dark orb on the white wing of a butterfly,

a beaded owl eye nesting in creamy feathers,
a black beetle hunting on the face of the clock.'

This silent litany, or litany of silence, is mirrored in the dying fall: 'She's inside me somewhere / in a place I can't reach, like seabeds where no sound has been.' This is the motto of a poet as well as a potential mother. And suggestive too of what Lacan dubbed 'feminine *jouissance*' as opposed to 'phallic *jouissance*.' The former relates to the latter as larynx to empirical word, as *condition* of all presence without *being* any extant presence it-self. So, to the 'sea' (ancient motif of the feminine), the unseen depths compound ('bed'); un-reachable, 'no sound' is thus the echolalia beyond and beyond her (here) re-sounding-ness and resonance. Daughter is more woman than woman and Mother. *And that very abyssal relation* or connective intimates the vertigo, whether happy or sad, of the feminine to her-self – thankfully in her own eyes.

The second section of the collection, eponymously titled, 'Conquest,' aims in different ways to ironise and subvert the gung-ho and acquisitive/aggressive masculine. The last four lines of both (same-length) stanzas of the piece 'Atlas-eating,' run as follows:

'… The maps of harbours,
with their sea snakes and turtles, are nothing
compared to creatures gathered onshore:
the squat, warted toad of the colony.'

'Out of the alchemy of colony cells,
white and tubercular grow the New World men.
Parasitic, they swell from soil to burst:
And shriek like mandrakes torn out of the earth.'

Another dualism is suggested here. Much like the (modernist) argument of Adorno and Horkheimer's *Dialectic of Enlightenment*, we have a critique here of repression: the outwards repression, 'conquest' of native lands is both mirror and product of the (puritanical/ rootless) repression of the 'nature' or 'natural' (matrix) side of the self. One thinks, in this context of Eliot's notion of 'dissociation of sensibility.'

And so, as opposed to ('Arches') 'the *Mayflower* men / [who] build their settlement: a rancid poultice that infects the land,' we have ('All of which are American dreams') the 'dream, like you and me, of one slow, inevitable touch.' Perhaps that 'inevitable touch' is the touch of God. For the final poem of this second section, 'The Blue Rose' gives us a list, a Babel of different languages' words for 'rose,' and in the next verse, again, a list and Babel of (imaginary or not) names of kinds of rose. The 'blue rose of forgetfulness,' in this poem dedicated to Brigley's passed paternal grandfather, is like, to repeat, the absence that is requisite and that in-forms what's present in the world, things like this redolent collection.

In the last of the three sections, romantically titled, 'The Lady and The Unicorn', we have, again, images of disenchantment amidst the more expected spells of fantasy. The sequence of poems in this closing section were written after Brigely's visit to the Parisian Musée de Cluny, and the six tapestries on display there: five to represent the senses and the sixth and last one titled, '*A mon seul désir*'. One assumes that that which is beyond (meta) the fives senses, that which is desired after the satiation of all physical desire, is God, or, we might say, as opposed to different refractions of concrete loves, a final 'participation' of Love . (This is an ancient idealist motif, appearing in Plato's *Symposium*, and revivified in the twentieth-century in Ford's *The Good Soldier,* Greene's *The End of The Affair* and Durrell's *The Alexandria Quartet.*)

And so: the minuet of disenchantment and fantasy, as in,

say, the counterpointing of ('The face in the Mirror'): 'The spell of his eye breaks when his ego flowers / to nothing, so he is only a man in the garden;' with ('Full Moon, Full Bloom'), 'All night, he is a flaming victory flag, a lit window / in the dark, where nothing can disturb the sweetness / of my long-ago dreams, the desire of my budding years.' Perhaps that final image is a return to the opening heady gambits of the collection, and, more minutely, a return to or reconfiguration of a father figure out of a lover (God?) (I find Brigley far more tender (and clearly less troubled) than Plath, say; yet in no way less intelligent, incisive or intense: merely more understanding of the surrounding world. As author, she has and deploys more pardons.)

And yet, then again, as if to extend the heavy drama of womanhood, on the next page we read, quite conclusively, of 'how women have always been outed, / broken, dissected, grafted, transplanted,' all of which results in [her] 'crumbling orchard walls' ('Don't Touch' – fate, then, of a female Adonis.) She leaves us, thus, alive, wiser, but un-tenanted (the last poem of the collection is titled, 'Home From Home'.

23

The Virtue of Not Being Able to Totalize: On D. Nurkse's *Voices Over Water*

'…and he wished in secret
there was another man strong as he on our island,
so he might kill instead of simply dying.'
'The Island Gospel'

To start slantwise, and to justify later, the guiding spirit over this memorable volume of plosive poetry is, for my purposes, Mikhail Bulgakov. As I read Nurkse's work, its major tenor for me is that of a magical realism. Just as Bulgakov's limited hero in *The Master and Margarita* only achieves 'peace' rather than 'light' at the conclusion of his magisterial novel – *as index of his limitedness* – so for me the major pattern to emerge from this volume is, if you like, the impossibility of totalization, or of experience going neatly into one valence or another. In a way, what I intend to suggest below is what Theodor Adorno once criticized Walter Benjamin for, in his work on Baudelaire, namely an un-mediated or we might say un-processed combination of 'magic' and 'positivism.' This, for me, is of the essence of Nurkse's effects: namely a deadpan demotic, a ruthless colloquialism which shapes a kind of (exilic) experience that points – but *intransitively* – beyond the plain of immanence.

To complicate this picture, and to add texture to it, let me begin with the beginning *and* ending of the volume – which contrapuntal parallelism may well suggest that at a higher level of abstraction, the content of what I tease out below, is contradicted; which, if I too am thinking poetically in my interpreting, both proves my point, and I guess, refutes it – *which, again, is the point.* (I am *not* trying to be funny….)

In the opening poem, 'The Nursery,' we read: 'and each day when it was light / only in my mind, I played one game since I was born / and another I had never played before…' And then, closing the volume, the only thing left from the old-world Estonia from which the main couple (whose voices or personae predominate the telling of pre-exilic, exilic and post-exilic experience) have emigrated to Canada, 'is a locket / showing the infant Mozart playing silence / on a tiny clavicord, behind cracked glass.'

Opening and closing, then, images of infancy. So in this sense there is a kind of closure. And yet look at *what* is being told in the simple, direct idiom: not only is the 'light' solipsistic, rather than what allows for perceptual objectivity, but the games being played are *both* one having been played *since birth* (realistically-speaking, impossible) *and* one never played before. Which is to say, the solipsism of the child leaks into the ill-logic of what's *trying to be* represented; and this is, I think anyway, the point. It's the charged tension between a pat or deadpan voice and a content that is immanently imploding. The positivism of stuff, like a childhood game, pitted, intransitively, against the magic of metaphor – the two, as we will continue to see in farther examples, creating a kind of irreducible or un-resolvable force-field, which may well denote the essence of poetry, or a kind of thinking that is 'poetic.'

And so, at the close of the volume we end on the note of

unfathomable play or creativity, with Mozart playing 'silence' on a musical instrument, in a locket, behind 'cracked glass.' *Right at the last*, on the cusp of closure and the reader's exit, vertigo *enters*. It's a bit like a medieval litany in this respect: it intends by its multiplication of devolving levels of sense, like a Russian doll, to hint at an infinite regress or the ineffable. Indeed in the first partition of the book, while the heroine is still pre-exilic, we read in 'Island Music', of the young girl skipping and thinking she was 'listening to the whistling rope / and to laughter and my breath, but I was hearing / a force unknowable as my body....' The body, *par excellence,* is in and of time and space, the most measurable part of us. And, as Levi-Strauss once argued, 'music' is the purest art-form in that it is beyond time and space; it somehow taps into a Real which is before (and perhaps beyond) cognition. So again, the un-knowability of what is, strictly speaking, the most knowable part of us – *that paradox there* – becomes a metaphor for the way poetry (music) transcends dichotomous conception, does not go neatly into a clear and distinct idea. The real positivity of the body is discretely pitted against the magic or sur-reality of music.

Another way in which the effects of Nurkse's poetry evince irreducibility is temporal. The three sections of the book are pre-exilic, in Estonia, the coming into exile in Canada, and the vestiges of the main couple's life at the end – the latter, in a way, looping back to the beginning, but in a spiraling, indefinite way, rather than a totalizing, circular way. What I want to suggest is that the 'logic' of temporality, the senses of 'before' and 'after', 'then' and 'now' (or vice versa), and the senses of continuity and discontinuity, are *just as much* constellated as equivocal. The point I think is that exile is an experience of such irreducible torsion that it is sublime, obscene. In the third section, the heroine, recounting her effort at song (music again), writes: '…then I open my mouth / and the voice comes out and it is monstrous: / part squawk, part labor moan, more imperious / than my own forgotten bitterness, floating / like a huge ghost between me and my neighbors.' The sense of ineffability (to continue the note on the sort of metaphysical wit I've labored so far) is evidenced for example, here, as what Derrida called 'the logic of the supplement.' So: 'they fastened the word Unlucky to me / before I had a chance to suffer;' or slightly later, again in the first section: 'At twilight a huge man stood in the road with an axe / and when he saw us he whimpered in terror and plunged into the undergrowth / though we were just two peasants, a child, and a deaf horse.' Verily, Alice in Wonderland stuff. Indeed in 'The Occupation' livestock are reported as having been lined up and shot for having broken 'an unannounced noon curfew.' Not only is it non-human animals, then, not only is the curfew 'at noon', but it is also 'unannounced.' Without being funny, the devolving, abyssal logic almost intends that the animals are right to be executed!

Now in exile, the husband writes (in 'Plains'), 'In this country there's a thousand miles / between one milestone and the next….' Or, similarly, in 'The Market Holds', 'our children / cry from dreams not hunger.' Or, near the end in 'Writing Home' the heroine writes 'herself' a letter, is scrupulous enough to blot it, but is so 'tired' that after blowing on her 'cold' (!) tea she intimates that 'it may take a lifetime for the news to arrive.' And this is of the essence: is 'writing', that work of objectifying in an Other-sourced and Other-directed medium *itself* a kind of exile of self from same self? And in this way, is there another abyssal element to the sense-making? That is, writing within and without, exile within and without, *ad infinitum*? In the first two citations above exile is seen as discrete from home. In the last, exile is compounded. The overall picture, as redolent throughout the collection, is the simultaneity, if you like, of identity (or coherent/cohering experience) and non-identity (experience which is, essentially, *poetic* – which is to say radically ambivalent – *against itself*.)

Which leads me to my final way of cashing out this (radically) paradoxical sense-making. The force-field, as it were, is also one of simultaneous, antinomian necessity and contingency: which might be viewed, again, as the fertile tension of a deceptively simple and colloquial idiom shaping a content which bursts the bounds of that very facility. So, early on, in 'Civil War,' 'the women had divorced their husbands / to marry their children.' Or, ending 'In Sickness', 'the distance between my hand and the night glass is greater than the journey / from my tiny country to this unmade bed.' Or in 'Cold Brahms', we end on the concluding note of the heroine saying that she 'might live / as long as I had to.' Which is to say, the subjunctive and the pluperfect, the counterfactual and the over-determined verily brawl through and past the end of the empirical black markers on the page. And whether it's 'war', 'sickness' or 'coldness', what is being expressed by these aporiae is an exilic experience, an *untenanted* refuge for the homeless, which is mirrored by the (perhaps) nomadic vocation of the (or any?) poet.

24

The Ways of Empathy: On Fiona Sampson's *The Catch*

'The acting out of articulation is dance. Dance is the pure profile of freedom, for spatiotemporal beings like ourselves…. In dancing we make angles, strange ones, surprising and unfamiliar (to others and to ourselves); we show by doing how far our freedom reaches; sometimes we create new joints altogether…. And all this newly found freedom must be supported by solid muscles….

…. freedom is… a connective… A variety of behavioral structures are appropriated wholesale, and what I am is the particular capacity that belongs to this being… of combining them in certain patterns and not others, of reaching from one to the other along certain specific paths. And my growth, the deepening and expanding of my liberation, consists of appropriating new structures and creating new paths….

…. to be really playful and creative, one must let automatisms take over, and just intervene at key times to redirect them ever so slightly, to have them cross each other's path…. This of course takes a lot of trust….'
Ermanno Bencivenga, *Dancing Souls*[1]

'…being complicit…'
'Collateral'

A long-time reader and admirer of the work of this eminent poet, Fiona Sampson, I was somewhat caught by surprise on reading this latest collection, *The Catch*. While

---

1. Ermanno Bencivenga, Dancing Souls, Oxford: Lexington Books, 2003, p. 99-101.

previously an extremely sophisticated poet, there was always the sense, perhaps, that the woman herself was not quite revealed, was slightly hidden, behind the glorious limpidity of image and theme, technique and reference that have always been redolent in her poetry. To put it in a nutshell, to grasp the kernel of the matter, the first impression any reader will get on reading and going-through this collection, will be of a woman who's come into her own; a woman who – either overtly, as poet on the page, or implicitly as person behind or beneath the new effects and the tint and tone of the (same) sensibility – is just more *answerable*, and primarily to her-self and those parts of her-self she loves: flora, fauna, persons, memories, and so on…

This response-and-responsiveness, for all of us, let alone that particular tuning-fork known for a poet, involves trust in certain ways – trust of oneself, and trust of the world in which that self is beveled, of which it is a part. So when I invoke the concept of 'empathy' as the beeline of this article, I am not lagging into some trite notion of femininity; in fact – *though not*thematically or in terms of attitude and feeling – technically or stylistically, Sampson's footsteps in this collection are the most strident they've ever been; the path she walks down, her avenue, is perceptibly more adamantine.

There are many senses of 'empathy', taken poetically, which I hope to show are evinced by this collection: from syntactical, grammatical, verbal, conceptual, experiential, temporal, spatial, and of course holding all these together, the birth of a new style. The epigraph from 'Sir William Cornwallis', which involves the eponymous idea of a 'catch,' suggests the simultaneity of ending and beginning, or, the 'brightness / between the trees' ('The Catch' – last words of the collection.) However, one way it seems to me of eliciting this dominant homonymous structure, is to think of Sampson's aesthetic here, her revealing and answerable sensibility, as a form of 'continuous discontinuity' (a phrase coined, or at least signally-used, I believe, by Theodor Adorno). In fact, the interplay, the mutual-immanence of pattern and structure with the unraveling or river-ing of new experience in new forms of representation, is actually a mirror for how empathy works, built as it is on trust.[2] You needs must allow a certain distance of respect, be it with the outer world, or with one-self, in order to truly be 'complicit' with either, or both.[3]

> all day the wind soughs below you
> in the trees and in your mind's ear
> sound of distance and of home
> making its promise that the breath
> you hear is your own.
> ('Bora')[4]

So… The catch is: that between beginning and ending. In the first poem 'Wake' we open by waking 'again.' So: both *a new* wake *at the start*, given that a wake is a funereal valediction; and opening, as well, simultaneously, the death of the previous waking as we awake again. This sounds convoluted, but opening as it does, it foreshadows much such self-looping senses peppered across the collection; a dance between givens, repeated across lines, rhythmically, and tweaking those givens in (implicitly) vertiginous ways.

Moving on: after waking (again) to first light, we learn of a 'dark' 'that won't give up the night / where roots go down'

---

2. See 'At The River,' which ends: 'is someone there / watching the water / move and stay move and stay?'

3. Sampson is a known aficionado of T.S. Eliot. Indeed, the idea expressed above is *a form of* the central idea expressed in 'Tradition and The Individual Talent.'

4. See, as another brilliant instance, the poem 'Bear Dancing', which opens, 'What is bear and what / is the dancing man / inside the bear skin….'

(two mo(u)rnings, then), and yet how here we've 'another,' 'feet fall feet lift / nothing to it.' The literal walking steps and the poetic feet are so one – that 'nothing' is some-thing. Poem and poetic tale, like wake and wake, border on both sides a movement which encompasses by implication or by indication so much more than the mere twelve lines which open the collection. One way of putting this latter point is to say that there is both a knowing music within and between the lines of this collection, as well as a more global implication of music's more infinite terrain.

There is much syllabic play in this collection, much acute music, but it is not quite 'playful.' The music is essential to the sentiments expressed. There is no sense of technical prowess covering (and thus slackening) the 'solemnity' of these 'creatures great and small' coming 'into the light,' 'all of them strangers / all of them naked as the white / moths that skitter...' ('The Border').[5] In fact, the above or the beyond, and the below or the beneath, find places throughout this collection of mutual-trust, mutual-empathy. We've already seen in the opening poem how the night sky goes down into the earth like 'roots.' In this second, border poem, which ends on 'the brink of dream' creatures across 'your bright path' are

> knowing themselves seen
> in the headlights
> but not by whom staring through you
> as if starstruck

The poet, too, we learn, arriving 'once again at / astonishment.'

Indeed, in that last poem, the small things of the world

---

5. I'd like to note that the 'skitter' here is a typical boon of Sampson's poetic mind. Throughout much of her oeuvre she makes use of very idiosyncratic (yet engaging / telling) verbs; it is one of her most gifted gifts to us.

are given dignity, as 'emissaries.' Much like as in 'At Bleddfa', the 'dogs / wander like clouds', 'familiars // of the kitchen / as of the wet and sunny grass.' Not only do dogs do a very humane business here, wandering, like clouds above, but they 'settle things / into place....' You see, as we learn towards the end of this poem the poetic persona holds and beholds enough trust to admit fear of newness, enough trust, thus, to admit it in, and let it out, there becoming here, here becoming there. So, closing this third poem:

> I was afraid
> and not afraid
> of the how the day hung
> above the still house
> how in my mind
> there was nothing
> but a stilled sky.

And then, here's some music, a toying across the structured lines, both within (between) the poem, 'Neighbors', and across to other moments in this at times contrapuntal collection; this, as it were, catching collection. *And again*, to boot, hale amphibolies between above and below, and between now and then....

> ...the voices
> of my neighbours
> at the paddock gate
> arrive clear and baffled
> by grass
> as they sounded all my life
> singular
> and clear
> voices in the great room

> of outdoor voices
> that will guide me
> when I'm old as when
> in early memory
> they arrived
> while I was lost…

To put it tartly, the world of time and the world of space not only neighbor each other here, but permit neighbourings within each other's own realms. To be, Sampson seems to indicate, is to be 'complicit.' At the end of this piece, the 'pansies', the 'lion faces / black and gold / these were new / as I was new.' Indeed, '…sometimes / small things reveal to you / how you're alive and how you live…' ('Daily Bread').

There is very little punctuation in this collection. It results in both continuity and discontinuity, simultaneously: the music of ending beginnings and the beginning of endings. In a simple sense, when the reader is confronted by lines like, 'Sometimes it's just the daily bread / of thought just the visible / being itself,' ('Daily Bread'), he or she can read senses in homonymous ways (I won't elaborate). In other words, while literally or empirically continuous, the lack of punctuating marks spurs the reader to make distinctions, even liminal and blurring ones. As one title has it, we are 'Visitors' in this collection, both new guests (visiting) and made to feel at-home, well-hosted.

And yet, Sampson having a known past career-path in music, I do want to make one more emphatic point about the (empathic) music of this collection. We read, again in 'Daily Bread', of the coffee's 'blur of steam like a breath

> and the word lying below it
> waiting to be spoken you can't

quite make it out what is it
humming all day out of hearing…

Or later, to reprise the same theme (of a kind of reprisal), in
'Noli Me Tangere' we find ourselves:

wanting to touch
something that's shifting
out of sight
even as you
recognize it
if you do…

Or closing this latter, then, with 'what is moving', which is

there already
passing so close
it could almost
touch them
as it goes.

These lines about transcendence, going-beyond the empirical,
typify music and its naughtiest lovechild, poetry. In everyday
experience we use what Hegel called 'speculative concepts,'
imaginary constructs to story and shape our daily
lives. Concepts like the 'unconscious' or like 'society', which
are empirically unverifiable, being metaphors – go beyond,
like music, or that staggering of line-music that is poetry, not
by positing some transcendent being or way of being: but go
'beyond' the literal, empirical, atomistic, by being *thoroughly
through*the latter; being 'complicit.' Indeed 'Daily Bread', with
all it implies of sacred liturgy, is directly associated with 'just
the visible' 'a cup of coffee.' Or, in 'Stucco' a 'bright patch
of wall' speaks with its 'light on the yellow wall' a voice
'speaking to you quite distinctly.' Sampson, as I say, seems

less to be trying to master her surrounding universe in this collection, and seems more to seam and be complicit with it, more negatively capable, as it were.

> rolled by an imperative
> deeper than sleep
> he rolls over like a wave
> that turns itself over
> sleepily within the sea's deep

Here, in 'Drowned Man,' the syllables enact the conceit. Music, after all, has no inside or outside. Indeed, 'his dreams swim among hers where / she hears his breathing far…' And then to end, at the beginning of day, we read how she drags him up 'out of deep tides crossing / their legs once more and morning lies / motionless to the horizon.' The use of line-endings (or their lack) is essential to this music. The use of the catch: as it were. For there are many peripatetic senses, evidently, which overlap or dovetail in that last quotation, and this polymorphous effect i s y et t he e ffect of a qu ite strident artistic intentionality. The morning for these lovers 'lies' in both senses, both senses' legs entwined.

There is music, within/without in 'Rite' as well. Like Bishop's pun at the end of 'One Art', between 'writing disaster' and 'righting disaster' – here's the oneness of a humane condition, conditioned by beginning and ending:

> from here it's too far
> to see too cold
> too long ago
> our forefathers
> and mothers
> making their way
> as if towards

us as if
towards some other
destination.

Again, the homonymous effect of 'us as if' being placed on
the same line is exemplary of the whole collection, making
there and here the same, making them and us the same; music;
'being complicit.' Indeed when the 'end is air' ('Dante's Cave')
it's no wonder that (in 'Visitors') 'the smells of sleep / still
clinging to us /

half awake
we saw ourselves as they had dreamt us
walking between them
as they walked between us.

And then, again typifying this continuity of discontinuity, we
end 'Street Music' with another touch of ambivalent music:

so the lamplight from the street
breaks
so all the shining things
tremble and break.

Which is to say two logics, or two grammars for the two 'so's'
– complicit in how they break from each other (in order to
share in each other.) For, as in 'The Song Of Those Who Are
To Come,' we are always ending with a kind of beginning, so
to speak:

we bless you
our parents wandering
the valley as if you

have just arrived as if
you understand nothing.
The reader, caught again.

Still, though, allowed to wander / to wonder. Indeed, that kind of musical avenue (radically-empathic)[6]I've scented so far as the dominant scent of this collection is close to *named*in 'Arcades.'[7]

the way arcades go
linking and pouring linked
and poured their speech is one
continual discourse
raising hands to gesture
speaking on and on
in the shade under
the cypress trees they do not
know the morning or the evening
when it comes
they only know this speaking
that rises and falls
in them like song.

6. Note that the second, far shorter section of the collection is titled, 'A Path Between The Trees.' Perhaps: the trees of life and that more moribund tree of 'knowledge.'

7. Indeed, semi-eponymously here, see 'Leap' which is about (logically, topographically) such 'leaps.'

25

Macabre Energies: On Svetlana Lavochkina's *Dam Duchess*

Ukrainian writer Svetlana Lavochkina's brilliant second published novel, *Dam Duchess* follows swiftly on from her first, *Zap* (2017). The manuscript of this short, taut and zipping tale set in 'Zap' again (short diminutive for Soviet city of the Ukrainian republic, Zaporozhye) was runner-up in the 2013 Paris Literary Prize, much as *Zap* was shortlisted for the Tibor & Jones Pageturner Prize in 2015. *Dam Duchess*, far shorter than its predecessor, is however just as much a coup de force, and quite literally.

The one feature of the writing here which makes the novel tick and exhilarates the reader, is its unfailing and pitch-perfect energy. From the prose style in which the tale is written, managing to be both strident, bold and shorn of all ornamentation or redundancy, and yet still highly and colourfully poetic at the same time, to the plotting which connects and reconnects the small but sprawling array of equally colourful characters, to the deft building of world-space, with all the details of a bygone Soviet era rendered more than just real, rather hyper-real – this short foray, reimagining a smidgeon of the early Soviet era, is a page-turner that will satisfy at the same the high-literary purists in one fell swoop. Lavochkina, again, is able to be both a writer for the average educated reader who wants to be riveted and entertained and an experimentalist whose toying with craftsmanship is seamlessly, instinctually executed. Having now read both novels I don't hesitate to say that the talent behind such writing seems to be both inborn and studied, eminently idiosyncratic and of real communal concern.

Across twenty-seven short chapters the tale unravels. I will not spoil the joy for the future reader by literally demarcating the plot, but only indicate here and there the way to my mind the writing succeeds, flourishes and with true aplomb. The novel starts with the sentence: 'Iosif Vis, Viscerionovich Stalin fancied hydropower.' That verb, playful and ironic, sets the tone for this macabre, blackly-comic story. After Mechanic Haim Katz is summoned, the 'Great Helmsman' sets him the task of superintending the building of the Dnieper Dam in Zaporozhye. We learn in the third paragraph that: 'Of all the Bolsheviks, this Katz had made the most incendiary contribution to putting an end to the old way of things.' And starting on this note is apposite to the (revolving) way the novel is paced. Part of what makes a successfully riveting narrative is this play between ending and beginning. Each chapter takes the story forward, but also unfailingly synchronises all the weird and wonderful happenings as part of one small unfolding world.

Haim Katz's wife, we learn in an early backstory, head of Propaganda for the duration of the Zap Dam project, is a certain former aristocrat named Darya, the eponymous 'Dam Duchess.' Just as the action revolves around said limited heroine, Duchess of the honing of river-power for Soviet energy-projects, so Lavochkina is the mistress of her narrative rhythm, also releasing floods of energy from the way she controls its pacing. *Dam Duchess* would seem like an overall metaphorical conceit, whether intended or not. And to the technician's eye what is so apparently successful is the way story and backstory intermingle and meld, world-building detail and plot-racing apace.

Here are three instances. In the first, and after the present action has opened dramatically, we learn in deft insertions of backstory both and at the same time of Katz and of the unified Soviet world-space rendered in this taut, sprung tale:

> Katz had been quickly shown that gunpowder was much safer to handle than ten thousand proletarians gathered in one place, a volatile compilation from all over the huge ex-Russian Empire: peasants who ran away from forced collectivization and mandatory confiscation of crops; runaway felons seeking disguise in the crowd; soldiers of defeated Civil War armies, ruined merchants, petty nobility. Russians, Ukrainians, Poles, Mongols, Armenians, Finns, Tatars, Tajiks cross-breed in the dam nations' crucible, creating gene mosaics hitherto unseen.

This kind of passage typifies the synergetic way a historical picture is drafted, which is a tableau at the same time highly pertinent to the literal happenings of the unique plot underway. In a similarly revealing manner, when the Dam Duchess (selling her sexual favours across the novel to all those who quite neatly take a 'fancy') has a certain Aaron Garlic put to work to produce for her a dress for a small but pivotal mini-ball scene towards the end, we read:

> Aaron hauls the sacks further into his den. Disguised under a couple of blankets is a tailor's dream. Aaron sniffs the silk, the taffeta, the wool, and bursts into tears.

Guard of hoes, robes, blankets, sheets, burlap saps, simple medicine, Aaron misses his vocation so much: he used to be the best tailor in Zaporozhye. All the nobility had their clothes sewn by him. He was the famous specialist for crinoline. Whether the Marshal, his wife or mistresses, or the Town Mayor, or the merchants' wives – only Aaron Garlic was trusted to do the best job.

Even when dealing with subplots like that of the Romani gypsy camp on the outskirts of the Dam city project, the same technique of interweaving then and now, here and there, is at-work; and again, it simultaneously builds a picture of a world-space and details necessities for the current skein of events. The Romani man who will steal the Levi jeans, hanging on a clothesline, of Hugh Winter, the Dam-building American specialist hauled in by Stalin to oversee the Dnieper Dam, is introduced again before we zoom out to a brief and salutary wider focalization:

> The Roma only have the clothes they wear – remaining naked when they wash it. The necklaces of 20-dollar American coins that once tinkled on their women's necks dissolved, coin by coin, along the errant lines of the camp's Europe-long itinerary. The golden Austrian ducats sewed up to their blouses and shawls were all long ago ripped out by the militia squads – swapped for freedom. Men's chests house wind and snow, their leg hairs peep through the thin tatters of what were once called pants.

Another analogy which seams–up for the objective critical eye the inside and the outside of this tale, is the way that very world-building of the author's, her configuring and making, her forging of the story is mirrored by the equally imaginative way in which many of these put-upon characters in the comically-rendered restrictive environment of the Stalinist Soviet Union, also make-do. Whether with serious or scurrilous intents, here are just two small examples. In the first, Aaron Garlic, another colourful character (detailed already) on-set and at-play around the construction of the Dnieper Dam, does his best to make a doll for Darya's daughter, Mania, showing how now and then intermingle:

> The dam stock clerk Aaron Garlic spent the evening combing the severed dark brown tresses, gleaning pearls after tiny pearls of dead louse eggs from each hair. He washed the redeemed locks in a bowl with industrial soap, poured a generous amount of hydrogen peroxide from the dam infirmary…. In a quarter of an hour, Aaron conjured up some bleached fleece, lifeless tow. He rinsed the locks in a zinc bucket… and poured a splash of sunflower oil into the bowl. He put the tresses onto a gray linen pillowcase. In the morning, he yielded a dry, long and pristine mane fit for a princess.

'Yield' indeed. Or later, with more rambunctiousness, Darya pays for the special supply of pre-proletarian music for her anachronistic ball-party which is also pivotal to how the tale ends:

> For each item of real music, Darya paid Armaïs a special sex service he had pre-ordered. Backwards meringue for the Strauss, straddle split galore for the Strauss, the price of each further record unutterable without a shudder. The stunts were so difficult to

perform against the throbbing background of sickness.

Just as in *Zap* – part of the same fictional world, that is to say – the near-mythic figure of Pushkin makes a pitting, repeated appearance like a leitmotif. Other literary figures who people the tale are Hemingway and Dickens, for example. Darya says at one point, like a puppet for that other Duchess, Lavochkina, honing the energies of her own river of plot and character:

> "It's English," Darya said. "When reading Mr. Dickens back then, before all this happened, I thought he had laid the squalor too thick on the page. Now I wish I could kiss every sad passage in this book, so endearingly clean and cozy it looks to me now."

Writing with more than native-flair in what is not her native tongue, English, Lavochkina breathes thrilling and macabre life into a small portion of a perhaps now-forgotten historical period. Indeed, a minor character, Rosa, one of many paramours put to use by Hugh Winter, including the Dam Duchess herself, is seen to describe in free indirect style the sight of a gramophone record playing with real impressionist verve, making, but without intrusiveness, character and author reflexive mirrors of each other:

With its diamond sting, a golden wasp meticulously licked lovely music off a stiff black pancake, always jumping up with a satiated burp before it touched the bright marmalade topping in the middle. Mr Winter had many black singing pancakes in his varnished cupboard, each sitting in a paper jacket with a round slot in the middle, to display the different sort of marmalade on each.

Later, Nikolai and Petro, two almost choric characters

(also from *Zap*) of supposed Cossack descent, will peer-in at the fateful old-world-miming ball held by the Dam Duchess and her cohorts and compare the same gramophone record at-play, in bawdy dialogue, as 'the tit of a negress!' Throughout, thus, the characterisation is richly-effected; each token in the chess game of this little clockwork tale both coloured in unique hues and of a piece with the same hyper-real and macabre imaginary, commanding the lit, woken palette.

For any reader of literary fiction who wishes for a long afternoon of stylistic sparkle and a gilded element of old-world charm, bold and effortlessly colourful, *Dam Duchess* will startle and rivet as much as it will undoubtedly impress.

26

On Geoffrey Hill

As far as we know, human beings are unique in the animal kingdom, in so far as they write and are capable of writing poetry. And poetry, here, may stand in for all symbolic use of language, language which transcends the function of mere communication. How did we get this capacity? And, more significantly, why did we get this capacity? Even if we are merely the last in a slow gradating line from other animals, wherefore this gift? For surely there is something radically different, at-odds with the behaviors of other animals, in telling stories. Yes, it would seem likely, plausible, that story-telling evolved from the needs of communication. But when we look at a signal for mating, or for feeding say, we can break it down into its parts, and put it back together again, keeping the same communicative efficiency. When we use language in symbolic ways however, as in poetry, there is something expressed quite beyond the atomic breakdown of the words or sounds or signs that indicate these added-up survival needs. When we read a great poem, it is surely more than its mechanical breakdown – because it means; which is to say, it is more than, it is beyond, the perfectly-parsed definitions of all its separate words: totted and added up. So: wherefore – or why – this prodigal capacity?

Perhaps it was God? Which is to say, a gift lit in us from within – dubbed tellingly in the Western tradition: a Word, a Logos, or a Ratio – from a transcendent Person or Mind? Whether this is the truth of the matter or not (and none will ever know), the idea of a radically qualitative break, rather than an infinitely infinitesimal gradation; the idea of humanity being special, marked-out, in this sense, is of a piece with the religious notion of God's creation being *ex nihilo*; and this model is in my view the most apt pattern upon which to model our own, mortal, poetic creation. To elicit the meat of this view, along with its attendant complexity, I'd like to discuss and interpret and dilate from the first poem in Geoffrey Hill's first collection, *For The Unfallen*, titled, 'Genesis.'

The declarative poetic voice, a man, is both before and after Man. There are five sections to the poem, representing within them six days of creation. The poet is thus one behind creation – *both in both senses.* The poet is also, presumably, writing from the perspective of the day of rest, one day beyond the content; *as well as* day by day, section by section. Thus the poetic act and/or the creative act are like foreplay after foreplay, to put it tartly: Hill's poem enacts the paradox discussed above in an embedded way.

The first word of the first line is 'Against' ('the burly air I strode') and the first word of the second line is 'Crying' ('the miracles of God.') Two double entendres then: or irony as well as gravitas. The poetic voice is set into relief by and sets into relief 'God'; and the miracles of creation are both cried/lauded by the voice and miracles which are of a nature to cry/weep.

The difference between a 'Logos' and what George Steiner in *Real Presences* calls 'the epi-logue' is implicit in what I've said above and what comes below: which is to say, the difference between being an originating Person and being a latecomer or artifact of that very origin; the difference between a language that references a given world, already objectively 'out there,' and a language that creates reality as it's expressed. The poet is in a sense the 'God' of the poem and (set off) 'Against' Him.

> 'And first I brought the sea to bear
> Upon the dead weight of the land;
> And waves flourished at my prayer,
> The rivers spawned their sand.'

These are the third to sixth lines of this first section. The sea is like the spirit breathed into the letter, the 'dead weight.' If the waves flourish at the poet's 'prayer' though, he clearly isn't the Creator but dependent on such. Similarly, just as spirit is breathed into dead letter, so, 'the river spawned its sand;' namely, the solid comes after the fluid. Again, a force-field in which Creator and creature are fudged, or made ambivalent. '[S]pawned' is both realistic, given the grainy nature of sand, and loaded with Satanic intents. In a similar manner, for all their visceral vitality and vibrancy as penned, 'the tough pig-headed salmon' towards the end of this first section, strive, 'To reach the steady hills above.' Which is to say realism and surrealism, gravitas and irony, creature and Creator beyond the bounds of the senses or the possible are one and many.

In the second section the poet stands and sees the violence of the 'osprey' 'with triggered claw' laying 'the living sinew bare' on the 'shore.' The poet is both witness of creation and penning that very act of witnessing. He is both first person and third person. Below, the 'hawk's' 'deliberate stoop' and its being 'Forever bent upon the kill,' is another description of visceral violence which is ratified by the assonance and consonance, the ruddiness and density of the language. But more than this, this animal violence is perhaps a metaphor for the torsion lived and evinced in poetic creativity, that plucking from the infinite dark both within oneself and within language. Creation is both *ex nihilo* – the poet's unique perspective in space and time, say – and work upon something that came before, and that comes after, namely, language. Self and Other imply each other, like life and death.

So when we read in the third section of the 'ashes of the sea' we are reminded of the hermeneutic interpenetration of life and death, or the two trees which might be signified by what the poet calls, 'the unwithering tree,' that of knowledge and that of life. Indeed the beginning of the next, fourth section, enacts this antinomy by talking of the rising 'phoenix' (a pre-Christian redemption in contrast to the later-invoked Christ) as 'burning' 'cold as frost.' This bird is 'lost' and 'pointless' we learn, so that on the 'fifth day' the poet returns to more mundane reality, 'To flesh and blood and the blood's pain.' This: just before the final section which introduces the more humane or inhumane redemption of Christ and the Christian tradition. But even here, there is paradox: 'the blood's pain.' What could this mean but, again, the pain of the flesh, *as well as* the pain of pain, a bit like the thought of thought, which is one definition of God, Logos; thus, here, again, the alternating of the poet as before and after God and himself.

In the fifth section the poetic voice 'rides' 'about the works of God,' and we are faced with another double entendre: the poet is all 'about' the works of God, lauding them, marveling and also topographically going around them: he both names them and reflects upon them. And though men are made free by Christ's 'blood', and though no 'bloodless myth will hold' – both of which justify the content and the expression of the poet – despite this 'weight' we, that is, those discussed by the poet and the poet himself, by turns, are 'bones that cannot bear the light.' In other words we are epi-logues to a thorough Logos. We don't follow in His footsteps, so walk in darkness I suppose. And yet, we *certainly have* followed the stepping feet of the poet.

When in the last section Hill writes, 'By blood we live, the hot, the cold, / To ravage and redeem the world...' he expresses again the paradox of eternity and temporal existence, life and death. Or, if you like, just as in the implicit contrast between the mythic 'phoenix' and 'Christ,' the contrast between Manicheanism and the more properly Christian view. One suggests that matter preexisted creation, the other suggests that creation was the work of something out of nothing. Similarly, the poet is as original as the language allows him.

In a way, this poem invokes the basic question of metaphysics: 'Why is there not nothing?' When we ask it in language, as a (mortal) sentence, we commit a pragmatic contradiction: just to put 'why' or indeed 'w' is already to assume some thing. We cannot practically get behind the positivity of our own existence; we are inexorably 'thrown' in(to) this world, to use Heidegger's phrase; and yet, if, just if there is the possibility of the meaningful thought *separate from* the material sentence (different in different languages after all), then meta-physics, or the reality of the world out there, is possible and salvaged. There is a spirit behind, through the letter.

If we just had physics, we'd be as clueless or story-less as the rest of the animal kingdom. If you like, the ability to question with a 'Why?', just as the ability to posit (though not access demonstrably) our own nothingness, sunders us from the rest of the material earth with as much of an absolute break as the very idea of creation out of nothing. For 'Why?' means an incipient story: the possibility of *poesis*: con-figuration; 'Why?' means the forthcoming constructions of the imagination; 'Why?' makes us symbolic, not merely literal beings. The rest of the animal kingdom doesn't tell stories, write poetry; as far as we know, they only communicate, functionally. And the paradox elicited so far is parsed here by the question: is this difference between us merely contingent, or is it essential? Are we the poetic creature par excellence, because we were made to be such, authors authored? Or, and at the same time, will we find out in five hundred or five thousand years an Odyssey spoken by the dolphins? This is the humane question posed and considered by Hill's poem, if implicitly.

And yet: can we 'bear' the light? Again, as throughout, the idea of 'weight' is paradoxically redolent: gravity in a physical sense throughout speaking to metaphysical gravity. At the last, unlike God, we are not able to wholly embody both: first person and third person perspectives at the same time – the given facts or data of the world, and their meanings for us. Our meaning-fueled mortality means that we are essentially dissociated (thus, *pace* Eliot, essentially 'metaphysical'). It is our living in the rupture between the two – what is and what it means – that is the source of our drama and creativity.

God, on the other hand, and to put it in an iconic way, 'Is that He Is' – a tautology, with no dramatic or poetic tension; the 'tide's pull' (surreally) mentioned in the poem is how the poet as human animal needs must 'strive' towards (and is also emergent from, surely) silence.

27

Still Points and Turning Worlds: On Fiona Sampson's *Come Down* (Corsair, 2020)

'Snow falls and fills a valley
and under its white roof
a sleeper dreams snow is falling
secretly for her alone
on and on in darkness
it falls like something speaking
noiselessly into silence'
('Noumenon')

A very established presence on the UK and the internationalist literary scenes, Fiona Sampson is a deeply versatile poet and writer. Most recently she has achieved much acclaim for a biography of Mary Shelley (*In Search of Mary Shelley,* Profile Books, 2018), and she has a second literary biography, of Elizabeth Barrett Browning due to be published in 2021. Among other writerly roles, she is a critic, theorist, translator, and of course is well-known in her editorial capacities, most notably perhaps for her tenure as *Poetry Review* editor from 2005 to 2012. But it is as a poet, her primary métier, through which perhaps she has funneled the flourishing scope of her generic range over a decades-long literary career.

Her latest collection, *Come Down* follows on from, catches onto, her previous of 2016, *The Catch,* in so far as it marks the fuller onset of a new departure in her poetic career. From her first major book-length work of poetry, a verse novel or long, interlocking sequence, *The Distance Between Us* (Seren, 2005), through her Carcanet collections of 2007 and 2010, *Common Prayer* and *Rough Music,* to her 2013 collection, *Coleshill,* Sampson seemed at times haunted by her experience of self and world. For all the nuance, depth, range, intelligence and presiding self-awareness as an undoubtedly major poet, it was perhaps only by the time she writes *The Catch* that we see her coming down, as it were, most fully into her own. The overriding aesthetic of the latter and her latest collection, *Come Down,* changes dramatically from her previous poetry. While ostensibly very much the same poet, sensual and metaphysical, sure-footed but also deeply inquisitive and searching, her last two collections bear marks of a fine-tuned structure of feeling finding a way into her deepest individuality, but one which is also eminently readable. In *Come Down,* Sampson to my mind embodies the paradox of a radically idiosyncratic poet who can yet speak to everyman or woman, as in Wordsworth's famed desideratum.

✳

In much of her writing, on writers such as Percy Bysshe Shelley, Amir Or, say, or recently on Tsvetanka Elenkova, Sampson has always championed notions of freedom and of freedom of movement. Indeed, closing her 2007 collection of essays, *On Listening* (Salt), she concludes with some reflections on 'ephemerality' as the hallmark of the literary, one to be embraced, acknowledged, and as recognized as such, immanently redressed. She seems in different places in her writing to almost possess a contemplative's sense of joy in naming mutability and the fleetingness of things, and thus being in a way in a contemplative's position to find still points of realization in admitting the inexorable turning of the worlds of self and other. And it seems to me that this notion of celebrating flux but also of finding a certain deeper tranquility in that celebration marks most resolutely the major tenor of *Come Down.*

It is a book among other things that finds a kind of refuge for a sometime homelessness. Indeed, the book is dedicated 'for my families', and the shorter second partition of the book, a long delving sequence, titled 'Come Down', is dedicated to Sampson's 'immigrant ancestors', referring to her genealogical origins in Australia. And the digging done there (with a conscious nod to Heaney's iconic poem at the inception of his homecoming into his own voice) is both about the 'earth' in parts of that aboriginal land, and of course a kind of poetic earthing, a re-connection to the matrix as it were of Sampson's ultimate reaches and roots.

All Sampson's cleverness and brilliance are here in plain sight in this collection, from the brainy sequencing and structuration of the collection as a whole, with much dovetailing, juxtaposing and counterpointing, to poems titled with highbrow references such as, 'Noumenon', 'Phenomenon' or 'Langue' and 'Parole.' There are references too to Sampson's other writerly concerns, to Mary Shelley and 'Frankenstein's Golem' or 'The Modern Prometheus' or 'The Nature of the Gothic', or to mythic registers ('Mother as Eurydice', 'Line, Manticore' or 'Juno's Dream') which touch on previous Sampson-terrain (notably in her 2010, *Rough Music*). However, the theme I wish to spend most of the rest of this review on is her concern with freedoms of movement and the sort of inner peace, so redolently emanating from the sheen of this collection, Sampson seems to find in recognizing such.

The poems in *Come Down* are far from free verse, however, for all their lability and limpidity and for all their concern, as I've already indicated, with freedoms of movement or movements of freedom. Many of them seem to have emerged formed, formed in one sustained act of concentration on, attention, attunement to, self or world, or self and world. There is an immense sense of discipline quite apparent in these poems. It's no accident, I'd say, not only that Sampson was a successful musician before entering into her literary career, but that some of her deepest concerns also are with musical and poetic form (notably, her Bloodaxe lectures delivered at Newcastle University in 2010 and then published in 2011, *Music Lessons*, or indeed, her more recent monograph, *Lyric Cousins,* EUP, 2016). Indeed, at one point in *Music Lessons* Sampson speaks of a certain Socratic dialectic of 'approach' and 'standstill', which I think typifies some of the searching music of *Come Down*. Part of Sampson's Socratic manner of doing literary business finds expression in the way she always eschews the dominative gambit of seeming to have a dogmatic purpose in mind in her observations of self and world. Her poetry here is closely questioning while still trying to approach the truest, stillest nature of the things that concern her. And, like music, speaking very broadly, it is self-generative of its forms, a free music that seems to *choose* its own delimitations, by the end.

Thus, Sampson's music in this collection of unpunctuated poems aims to capture the living breath of her life-worlds; those of her intellectual itinerary as married to personal concerns, and those of her more plain-souled living and experience. Systole and diastole, so to speak, this collection often enough attempts to locate and express the ways movements freely into form and life itself just happen, and/ or how in their movements they might come to move us, as they have moved her. She wants to capture, with an almost mystic attitude at times, not only the movements of things, in here and out there, but also the movements of how those things are or become what they are, in their becoming. This approaching towards (and of) the essence of mutable things, things in her own life and times and things in others, involves the poet breathing life into what are replete already with life, and many different living breaths.

So, opening 'March Lapwings', Sampson writes of wingbeats in a way:

> Now everything
> begins to move
> and everything stays
> where it is

Or then, on the page opposite, still early on in this highly aerated collection, we open 'Frankenstein's Golem' with:

> Who is this
> moving swiftly
> through darkness
> in a landscape
> not yet given
> form by daylight

The inquisitive mode suits not only the uncertainties, the negative capabilities as it were, of the chosen theme, but serves, as throughout this collection, the many ways Sampson wishes to 'illuminate' how the givens of self and world are 'given / form by daylight.' The poet's lines seem to wish to limn the light inside and out, and in the opening of the mythologically titled, 'Line, Manticore', the first of six parts reads:

> I
>
> The line that is a creature
> scratched in stone is
> also a line of light
> lipping along the mineral

edge of itself
light shining from stone
like flame from flint the lion
man shines and burns
in the holy stone
and blurred along the cut's
meniscus like tears
that absorb and spread
brightness its mineral
grain comes to light

Half human, half lion, the 'Manticore' is a version of the Sphinx, and Sampson, it is quite evident in parts of this sequence, wishes to ask ultimate riddles of herself as much as of what she sees. Striking too, in this collection as elsewhere (vitally in Sampson's writing), is that blurring 'along the cut's / meniscus like tears'. The enjambed movements and the invoking of being 'moved', typify Sampson's metaphysical imagination. She wants to capture not only the way things inside and out emerge, uncannily, but also how in emerging they are always redolent with a blurring of boundaries, a certain oceanic osmosis, the way, say, the wavy movement of a sea cannot quite distinguish one movement from the next, one wave from its successor or predecessor, and so on. This is, in a manner of speaking to find still points in what are undeniably turning worlds.

Thus, 'Wild Equinox', a sequence of nine parts opens with:

I
These days are still
cold the line of feeling
working its way thinly

up so we might touch
a pulse almost to life
or make the heart inside
an egg an echo or
hear ants underfoot
raising their secret cities

As in her *The Catch,* Sampson catches onto the openness of being, the way up there and down here, meld into each other with living fertility. Indeed, in the opening prefatory poem, '*Come Down*' 'sky' is continuously 'stepping' upwards out of the river in question there; and the final poem of the collection is titled '*Surfacing*.' Moved, and moving us, Sampson wishes always to observe and then express the movements of the self's music and that of the world's as they intermingle among each other. And then, in the second part of 'Wild Equinox', we read, moving from the above notes of intimate declaration to her staple Socratic searching mood and mode:

II
Could we build
slow
slow from these

splinters
these frayed grains
strangely consorting
nails wire
tarpaulin
that seem to fit
is this the way

> frail   shaking
> at our touch
> a barn begins?

Touched, as much as touching, again Sampson is searching perhaps *the* metaphysical problematic, the problem of 'emergence', how things come down into being what they are, how things leave off being what they are, becoming the next thing, or something else. And note how she does all this, while still being attendant to the immediate vicinities of her mundane worlds, a 'barn' in this case. Indeed, this note of or on becoming applies most resolutely to the moved movements in this collection about Sampson's searching for belonging. 'Boat Lane' is a sequence written about her adoptive father, and as previously mentioned, the eponymous second partition of the book, 'Come Down', is a long and delving, searching-out of origins. It ends:

> figures pass you moving
> through the orchard
> as a breeze stirs
> breathing seems
> to fill the leaves and look
>
> the old ones
> keep passing through us
> saying world is wide we
> must come down
> together into its valley

World is wide, indeed. The moving and the movements of and in this note of acceptance are also an urgent injunction for all of us to 'come down' into making a better world, inside as out. I couldn't think of a gesture of humane solidarity more in blessed keeping with our own world's contemporary climate, riven as we are by the present worldwide crisis.

Epilogue: The Charlatan

A glass of scotch asks not for love, only to be drunk, be it sipped or be it gulped; and by hook or by crook it will have its chief, or at least, presiding desire sated. A glass of scotch, you might say, is, thus, a very fortunate member of the human race – most of us if not all so rarely satisfied with our landed lot. Indeed, to put a fine-tuned point on it, a glass of scotch like this, so sated and accounted for, beds among the rocks it nonetheless makes its own, turning these icy stones into honeyed, honeyed waters. But to start with that is merely to start with the curtain call, or, if it's preferred, given the odd delicate temper among my readers, is to start with a late, desperate cue from the wings. That now said, a matter of belated urgency quelled, quaffed, I hope to start now, if again, with a brief discussion or disquisition on the subject of a certain, hairbrained charlatanry. There is nothing perhaps so false, sham-like, so much a pitiful foil diverting the traffic of licit thought, as what I believe is termed (jargon-now-shorn) a 'faux-European.' A phony, of course, what the local Arabic idiom of recent, close vicinity dubs with much good neighborliness, '*Fannas*', I will try the trial of trying to make sense of this term, matt or abyssal as it may turn out to be. The first thing apposite, I'd have thought, to state in clear and distinct, strangely periodic prose, is that I am a British citizen, or, to solve now, preemptively, the school of pedants champing at the bit, a British subject. The recent hoopla, hullaballoo, or brouhaha surrounding the debates, the actants and the issues of 'Brexit' may have only muddied the archetypal waters I'd hoped to surf, or glide across, as part of this ineffable gambit of parsing a term. So, as of some in-wending date, (which is to my feeble mind – one that failed and fails to follow the humdrumness of current events – a wedding date with the devil) I presume I will cease, a British subject, from being a European member. For parsimony, then, to make the soi-disant theorem I here attempt to elaborate more elegant, let us assume that that devilment of a date has arrived and landed and rendered me non-European. Fine. This eventuality, in the event or not, would not, I don't think anyway, render me a 'faux-European;' only a non-one. Thus, as we begin to untie the various due philological knots, the term at hand and in question, must mean to intend something more forceful than a mere external negation. It must, I'm now of the mind to think, intend in all its intension, a true-boned internal negation, a man, or woman, or child, who is not only non-European, but is somehow using Europe or the European as a screen to shore up some gap or hole in the national identity they may erstwhile hold. To be a 'faux-European' must mean to ape Europe in the blood-rills, while having, shall we say, Timbuktu pulsing down the avenues of one's veins and arteries. Fine. I believe we might just be getting somewhere, marking ground – meaning: something more than a mere pleonasm with what has been said above. We must, in short, be making incisions, which is a grand thing to do. My next estimation, one rung above a guess, is that a 'faux-European' might be a man or woman or child who reads a text, originally penned in some European tongue foreign to Anglo-Saxon, but reads it in translation, knowing only Anglo-Saxon. Even here, though, there seems to be a small knotted difficulty. You see, if a text, let's *Alice in Wonderland*, is originally written and published in the original high German, and yet, there does pertain in the extant universe of matter, in whatever hypothetical corner or nook or cranny, an English version, then I'm still unsure how the non-high-German-reading chap or dame or kid would be committing a falsehood. I will try now the trial of making this point clearer, freeing it of dregs or pellets, and, perhaps, siring it with a newer pellucidity. First, is the obvious point, I hope, that if there is an English translation, it was not commissioned to become so, and thus to be marketed so, in whatever backwoods bookshop, for the reason of the rabbit hole. My most native assumption in this scenario, call it if you wish a conservative intuition, is that such an English translation of, say, *Alice in Wonderland*, was published in order to be read – and even if not to be read, which is quite logically possible, to be purchased, in order for the publisher who'd effected the daft commission in the first place, to at least recoup some of the overlaid cash-money spent. Now, imagine you are the seven-year child in question and – having strayed from your parents among the milling crowds of Leicester Square and found yourself, briefly-orphaned along the Charing Cross Road – you decide to enter one of the many secondhand bookshops that hawk their wares there. After, shall we say, a good twenty minutes of deep and detailed perusing, you alight on the high German original of *Alice in Wonderland.* Naturally, you are delighted with the cover-image most of all, not being a scholar, as yet at least (but this may well change in a decade or so, should the possible world decree it in the actual), of high German, and you approach the counter, a foot above your chest in height and quietly enquire if there might be, present and to hand, or in the possible world of down the road, perhaps, an Anglo-Saxon translation of the plaintive tome in your hands? Now, imagine you are the luckiest, flukiest seven-year-old in town, and the shopkeeper (who, by the bye, has just returned from a matinee performance of some opera of Mozart's) announces to the second rung on the ladder of your delight, that yes, he does indeed possess the book in question traitored into English. He now reaches back behind him to a shelf closeted to the rest of the world and brings the precious gem forth. The seven-year-old, by all the fluky fates, has a twenty-quid note in his pocket, and decides to purchase the book. Later that evening, having rejoined his parents (the how-so of this issue, being a point nugatory to the plot of my niggly task at hand here) – the child decides to read the book. And now, having done the goodly bit of the goodly analytical philosopher, the heurism opens itself out to the original question: in reading the work of high German but in the Anglo-Saxon translation, has he now, all seven-years of him, his tissue, bone, fat, nerves, cells, and microbes to boot – has he now, in the alchemies of the European academy subtly transmogrified into what I believe is called, 'a faux-European'? Needless to say, I have put this question to dozens of colleagues in the philological domain(s), at over a dozen conferences over the last five years, years spent puzzled by this conundrum, and have come to no resolute solution. That being so, I then prayed to the good God, having spent a small while translating the prayer I wrote out myself in my own hand, in Anglo-Saxon, into high German, on the off-chance (and who knows?) that God prefers to discuss such matters in that high-toned idiom; I prayed and prayed, asking God to do what He then, thankfully, did indeed do (proving by the bye, that prayer in high German is a good wagering gambit for the supplicant). He proceeded, under the supervision of two arch-angels, specialists in this field of divine intervention, to dig up, recompose and reinvigorate Friedrich Nietzsche and then Tolkien (author of *The Lord of the Rings*). On waking, reborn, the two gentlemen – one suffering still, and perhaps strangely, with the syphilis that turned him a crazy man unto his death, the other, smoking the same pipe he'd perished beneath the day of his own passing – the two gentlemen, one resolutely gentle, sure, the other, a bit more of the maverick, were, after short bylines, assiduous to help me in my deep-bound philological endeavor. My assumption, unannounced of course, was that any work these veterans of the study at hand might work at beat tussling, and without joints or flesh or even skin, with the earth's mites and grubs and lice, and so on. And I think I was right in this assumption. Alas, the honorary gentlemen were of no concluding aid. Nietzsche averred that the seven-year-old was full within his British rights to read the high German in translation. Tolkien, however, not the most modernist of men, believed that the child inside the heurism in question might well possess the right which Nietzsche judged his due, valid possession, but only if the child also read the text, and first of all, in Latin. I found the sparring of the two expert opinions of not much progressive hope in the end. And so, I suppose I must find this landing light: that to be a 'faux-European' means perhaps to be a citizen (or subject, perhaps) of a continental European nation and to read the books written and published in your own-most native idiom (German, say, French), but only and exclusively in the Anglo-Saxon translation. Just so, good men, women, children, patriots all of them, have died ignominious deaths.

Acknowledgements

The author would like to thank the editors of the following magazines, journals and edited volumes, where most of the essays and articles comprising this work, or earlier versions of such, have appeared previously: (T&F) *POEM*; (T&F) *Prose Studies*; (T&F) *Life Writing*; *The Chesterton Review*; *Nexus: The Journal of the International Henry Miller Society*; *Spear's Magazine; Agenda & Agenda Online*; *The Oxford Culture Review*; *The Wolf*; *Poetry Ireland Review; Envoi*; Ford Madox Ford's The Good Soldier: *Centenary Essays* (ed. Max Saunders & Sara Haslam); (EUP) *Victoriographies; The International Ford Madox Ford Conference* (Montpellier, France, 2017); *Sciences of the Mind 1850-1950* (Kent, UK, 2018).

About the Author

Omar Sabbagh is a widely published poet, writer and critic. His first collection and his fourth collection, are, respectively: *My Only Ever Oedipal Complaint* and *To The Middle of Love* (Cinnamon Press, 2010/17). His fifth collection of poetry, *But It Was An Important Failure,* was published with Cinnamon Press at the start of 2020. His Beirut novella, *Via Negativa: A Parable of Exile*, was published with Liquorice Fish Books in March 2016. He has published as well much short fiction, some of it prize-winning. His Dubai novella, *Minutes from the Miracle City*, was published with Fairlight Books in 2019. A book-length study of the work of Fiona Sampson, *Reading Fiona Sampson*, was published with Anthem Press in 2020. He holds a BA in PPE from Oxford; three MA's, all from the University of London, in English Literature, Creative and Life Writing and Philosophy; and a PhD in English Literature from KCL. He was Visiting Assistant Professor of English and Creative Writing at the American University of Beirut (AUB), from 2011-2013. He now teaches at the American University in Dubai (AUD), where he is Associate Professor of English.

About the Publisher

Whisk(e)y Tit is committed to restoring degradation and degeneracy to the literary arts. We work with authors who are unwilling to sacrifice intellectual rigor, unrelenting playfulness, and visual beauty in our literary pursuits, often leading to texts that would otherwise be abandoned in today's largely homogenized literary landscape. In a world governed by idiocy, our commitment to these principles is an act of civil service and civil disobedience alike.